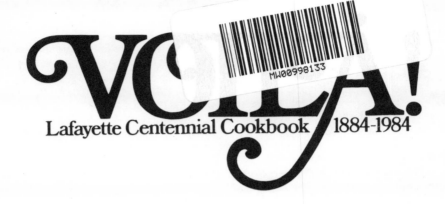

VOILA!

Lafayette Centennial Cookbook 1884-1984

by
Jean K Durkee

celebrating the

1884-1984

LAFAYETTE
CENTENNIAL

CENT ANS DEPUIS VERMILIONVILLE ™

Lafayette Louisiana U.S.A.

THE FLAG OF ACADIANA

r. Thomas Arceneaux, a descendant of the real Louis Pierre Arceneaux, was inspired by his ancestral history to design a flag for Acadiana, the 22 parish area in southern Louisiana.

Three fleurs de lis, silver on a blue field, represent the French origin of the Acadians.

A gold tower on a red field represents Spain, the nation controlling Louisiana when the Acadians first migrated to Louisiana.

A gold star on a white field symbolizes both the patroness of the Acadians, Our Lady of the Assumption, and the participation of the Acadians in the American Revolution.

The flag symbolizes the hard-working people of the region who take a deep pride in themselves, their heritage and their way of life.

Additional copies may be obtained by sending $11.95 plus $2.00 for shipping to address below. Louisiana residents add applicable tax.

VOILÀ! LAFAYETTE CENTENNIAL COOKBOOK 1884-1984
P.O. Box 30121
LAFAYETTE, LA 70503-0121

| First printing | November 1983 | 10,000 copies |
| Second printing | January 1984 | 30,000 copies |

Library of Congress Catalog Card Number 83-91087
International Standard Book Number 0-9605362-2-1

Author
Jean K Durkee

Cover Artist
Jean Angelle

Illustrations and Design
Randy Herpin

Cookbook Title
Anne Meleton

Printed in the United States
by S. C. Toof & Company

FOREWORD

Ten national flags have flown over Louisiana since 1541 and each governing nation has left its mark. Two of its banners have been Spanish—1541 and 1769, two have been French—1682 and 1803, and two have been flags of The United States of America—1803 and 1862 to the present. The other four flags were British—1763, West Florida Lone Star—1810, Independent Louisiana—1861 and the Confederate Flag—1861.

The Attakapas Indians originally inhabited the Attakapas Prairie which we now know as part of Lafayette Parish. The first French colonists arrived in 1714 and through the years were followed by German, Acadian, Spanish, West Indian, African, Italian, British and Americans.

Jean Mouton, an exiled Acadian, settled in the Attakapas country in the 1760s and became a successful cotton planter. By 1821 Mouton was able to donate five and a half acres to the Catholic Church for the Cathedral of St. John. A small settlement, Vermilionville, with the Cathedral as its heart was established by him. A north-south grid of streets and lots were designated with each street named for U.S. Presidents, except in front of the church, which was called St. John Street.

The State Legislature created the Parish of Lafayette, January 17, 1823, named after General Lafayette of France who was visiting the United States at the time.

Later, in 1824, Jean Mouton donated land, and a small frame building, to be used as the Parish court house for the new Parish of Lafayette. It was not until March 11, 1836, that the village of Vermilionville became officially incorporated by an act of the State Legislature. The name was changed to Lafayette by an amended charter on May 5, 1884, a fact which we celebrate in this Centennial year 1984.

LAFAYETTE CENTENNIAL COMMISSION

Rhonda Lastrapes, Honorary Chairman
E. Glynn Abel, Coordinator

Judith M. Hebert, Co-Chairman
Marilyn Tarpy, Co - Chairman

One hundred years ago, on May 5, 1884, Vermilionville took the name that it had always wanted—Lafayette. And the town has more than lived up to its name. This community, its accomplishments and its residents, have a great deal of which to be proud. Lafayette has a heritage and a quality of life that other communities would love to possess including a full range of social and cultural opportunities. Lafayette's educational facilities are considered among the finest in the South, and we are in the vanguard of petroleum technology. Our priorities are well-placed and our opportunities to excel are abundant.

True, there is much to be done and many goals yet to be achieved. Importantly, Lafayette citizens are not shrinking from these challenges, but rather rising up to find new innovative ways that will boldly take us into the future.

Joseph W. Berey

ACKNOWLEDGEMENTS

Author Jean K Durkee

Associate Editor, Historical Orpha Valentine

Associate Editor, Composition Yvonne Morse

Cover Artist Jean Angelle

Section Artist & Illustrations Randy Herpin

Historical Research

Mathe Allain	Leona Guirard	Eleanor Straub
Lucille Arceneaux	Mary Katherine LaFleur	Jacob Valentine
Jim Bradshaw	Marguerite Lyle	Orpha Valentine
Fred Daspit	L. C. Melchior	Eleanor Yount

Index Editor Deanna Dupuis

Recipe Coordinator Jeanne Millet

Recipe Testers assisting Jean Durkee

Dukie Abel	Elizabeth Ford	Sue Ann Mills
Sue Alves	Lucile Freeman	Sally Moores
Pat Andrus	Barbara Gerami	Yvonne Morse*
Shirley Anderson	Martha Green*	Betty Palmintier
Laila Asmar	Susan Guilbeau	JoAnn Patterson
Betty Bares	Virginia Hagelin	Wilma Piccione
Lurnice Begnaud	Rosemary Ham	Mamie Lee Pickett
Judy Berey	Mary Elizabeth Hamilton	Barbara Pooler*
Verlie Boudreaux	Hascal Hardy	Jean Quellhorst
Kathryn Breaux	Dot Harris	Carolyn Richard
Diana Broussard	Janet Hiatt*	Flo Rickey
Katherine Broussard	Lil Hoffpauir	Peggy Rogers
Pearl Bush	Linda Hollier	Marguerite Rosser
Olympe Butcher	Betty Hollingsworth	Candy Rougeou
Carolyn Camardelle	Verlie House	Nancy Rougeou
Ginger Capps	Rose Ingram	Ruth Rougeou
Alice Carlin	Lucille Jones	Donna Rylee
Evelyn Chiasson	Lucy Kellner	Willie Schutz
Cloeann Clement	Dorothy Lampshire	Frances Scranton
Marjorie Cloninger	Claudette LeBlanc	Helen Simon
Lucille Copeland	Ann LeJeune*	Becky Smith
Louise Cordell	Peggy Lee*	Joanna Smith
Beverly Crain	Jean Leland	Sharon Stewart
Cindy Crain	Jolene Levermann	Alma Stuller
Mabel Crain	Elaine Malin	Orpha Valentine*
Virginia Davidson	Betty Manuel*	Kathy Van Wie
Mary Dennis	Anne Meleton	Louise Webre
Maude Escudier	Nell Miller	Lessie Wynne
Joy Fincke	Jeanne Millet*	Frances Zink

Typists

Yvonne Morse	Alyce Tatum*	Orpha Valentine

*Also proofreaders

Bonjour mes amis, bienvenue à la bonne cuisine de Lafayette,

Compiling **VOILÀ! The Lafayette Centennial Cookbook 1884-1984** was like preparing a gourmet meal: careful planning, combining the right ingredients and serving it in an appealing way. Over 800 recipes were received from the best cooks in Lafayette and the surrounding areas. Some recipes submitted were from grandmother's mother who had more chores than time and were the essence of brevity. Some recipes were jotted down scantily, only to seed the cook's memory, which would shame today's computers. A note on one recipe included the comment "French cooks don't measure!"

From these entries, eighty-eight ladies from Chez Amis Women's Club, Chapter Y-P.E.O., Preceptor Alpha Chapter Beta Sigma Phi, the Centennial Commission and many friends helped me test and taste the recipes, of which 417 were selected for this book. Each tested recipe has been edited to insure accuracy. Many of the recipes have microwave directions or shortcuts. Also, microwave hints and old-time remedies may be found in the last section.

Enjoy these recipes, "Receipts," from the past 100 years...some old...some new, but mostly recipes passed from generation to generation, changed only by new cooking methods and ever available fresh, frozen, canned or dried food from today's super market. Many of the recipes have withstood the test of time and taste. Try cooking "Tomato Ketchup"...starting with 30 tomatoes and finally, 3 hours later, filling only 3 jars with a flavor that cannot be bought anywhere. Smile if you will, but with a warm heart, remembering that our ways, too, may bring a smile to those to come... 100 years from now.

Jean K Durkee

INTRODUCTION

"First, you make a roux," is a standard opener for a South Louisiana recipe. Is there anything more French than a **roux**? A Cajun **roux**, however, flour and oil lovingly browned over a slow fire, is a far cry from a French **roux** of butter and flour, **roux blond** or **roux brun**, depending upon cooking time. The principle is the same, but the execution and the ingredients differ. The rich, spicy Louisiana crawfish bisque with stuffed "heads" and fluffy rice hardly resembles the delicate, subtle cream soup the French call **bisque d'écrevisses**.

Louisiana cuisine in general, and Cajun cuisine in particular, had to adapt a French heritage to a frontier environment. Dairy products were scarce, hence a **roux** made with oil and a **bisque** without cream. Wheat did not grow on the eastern prairies, hence corn bread. Until the twentieth century, beef meat was, travelers accounts all agree, tough and fibrous, hence the French **grillade**, broiled meat, became that South Louisiana stand-by, steak cubes swimming in a rich brown gravy heaped on rice. Chickens were not eaten until past laying time, thus the ubiquity of chicken gumbo. Is there, except for **coq-au-vin de Bourgogne** or a Cajun **fricassée**, a better way of tenderizing a tough old hen?

Lafayette cuisine began, thriftily utilizing what could be grown, raised, fished or hunted nearby, resourcefully adapting traditional French **recettes**. Eclectically, it borrowed from other ethnic groups, okra and cush cush from the Africans; **filé** from the Indians; bell peppers and tomatoes from the Spaniards, blending all the elements to produce something original and tasty.

It should be noted, however, that much of what is considered "traditional" Lafayette cuisine in 1984 did not exist in 1884. See how many of the recipes in this book call for finely chopped onions, bell peppers, green onions and celery, inextricably bound with the South Louisiana culinary tradition, so we think. But in fact, celery until the 1930's was a luxury item, used sparingly, a rib or two purchased thriftily to flavor a vegetable soup, not a basic seasoning to be used in a free-handed manner. That luscious crustacean the crawfish, now a spring staple in restaurants and homes, was consumed by few families, usually boiled. Some households, those with New Orleans connections, made bisque. Crawfish pie, crawfish étouffée, fried crawfish, not to mention crawfish Thermidor or crawfish **au gratin** were unknown until some twenty-five, thirty years ago.

Travelers' accounts made it quite clear that in the nineteenth century, Cajun fare coincided with the standard diet of poor Southerners: cornbread and molasses, salt meat and beans, turnips and mustard greens in season, the monotony occasionally broken by fruits, game or fish. Only coastal dwellers ate seafood, and rice did not become a daily staple until the end of the 19th century when Germans and Midwesterners introduced its large-scale cultivation in the prairies. Gumbo, both as **gombo fevi** and **filé gombo** appeared early, as did the **boudin, chaudin, paté de tête**, sausage, salt pork produced by butchering a hog, and the **tarte à la bouillie** which graced festive occasions. But in general, South Louisiana diet lacked variety until improved transportation and preservation made a diversity of produce and meats available and until the growth of the oil industry made people affluent enough to buy what they did not grow or raise themselves. South Louisiana cooks developed new recipes from old basics and created a tradition.

Over the last hundred years both Lafayette cuisine and Cajun music cheerfully borrowed from every culture encountered, creating unique tastes and sounds. Now, previously unknown vegetables, tofu, snow peas, bean sprouts and jicama, and newer foreign culinary traditions have challenged Lafayette cooks to create still more gastronomic delights. Anyone interested in a dinner date for May 5, 2084?

Mathe Allain, USL Department of Foreign Languages
Associate, Center for Louisiana Studies

TABLE of CONTENTS

VOILÀ!

Lafayette Centennial Cookbook -1884-1984

the
1880s & 90s

n the early 1800 s the abundance and quality of the wines served was said to be the only major difference between the table offerings of the various Louisiana plantations. When Vermilionville became Lafayette, May 5, 1884, that statement was still used to describe the cuisine of this area. It is certainly a credit to her excellent cuisine, her ease and joy of life and living that those who sample her offerings are less satisfied with what they knew before or had elsewhere.

Although the population of Lafayette did increase from 866 in 1800 to 2,106 in 1890, outside influences had little effect on the French speaking residents of south Louisiana. Lafayette had already begun what she has historically been noted, the absorption of other nationalities and making them her own.

It was during these burgeoning decades of the 1880s and 1890s that our nation was led by four presidents: Chester A. Arthur, Grover Cleveland, Benjamin Harrison and William McKinley.

By May 1880 regular train traffic was rolling into Vermilionville. The first engine to enter the town was The Sabine. The railroad served as a link with the world. It brought not only new people, but new ideas to south Louisiana.

Despite outside influence staples remained the simple garden and farm products of the area: corn, squash, Irish and sweet potatoes, tomatoes, melons, beans (white, red, blackeyed, lima or butter) all cooked with salt pork, and served as a thick soup or even thicker with rice. These represent but a few of the products available to the average citizen. Suffice it to say that Louisiana has always been a gardener's paradise, summer and winter.

Most kitchens could boast of a cast iron stove. Every home had at least one large black iron pot. Consider some of the aromas which were common then: green coffee beans being parched black over a low fire; pork sausage smoked over sugar cane; roux or gumbo simmering over a warm winter fire; fresh baked bread; blackberry pie or gingerbread.

Our ancestors accepted all of these delights as commonplace necessities, to be served in infinite variety with the abundant fresh seafood, wild fowl and game, with the pork, beef or fowl raised locally. Whether it was necessity, willingness to experiment, or an adventurous palate, more exotic animals such as raccoon, opossum, nutria, alligator and rattlesnake also found their way to some local dining tables. Remember, it has been said that a Cajun will cook and eat anything that will not eat him first.

Fred Daspit
Professor of Art
University of Southwestern Louisiana

9

Food Preservation

Bread

MAWMAW'S FIG PRESERVES

4 quarts fresh figs
1/2 gallon boiling water
4 tablespoons baking soda
2 pints sugar
2 pints water
8 (1-pint) jars, lids and tops

Rinse figs and cut off thick part of skin. Pour boiling water with soda over figs in 6-quart pot. Let sit 15 minutes. Drain. Pour cool water over figs. Drain. In a 6-quart pot combine sugar and water. Cook 10 minutes. Drop drained figs into sugar syrup one at a time. Cook fast 5-10 minutes. Lower heat, cover, cook 2½ hours. Let sit overnight to plump up. Heat next morning. Ladle into 8 hot sterilized pint jars. Seal. Process 5 minutes in hot water bath. *From the recipe files of my mother-in-law, Mrs. F. M. Hamilton.*

Mary Elizabeth Hamilton (Mrs. Herbert A.)

LINDA'S FIG JAM

3 cups fresh figs, mashed or
      ground
2 cups sugar
2 (3-oz.) packages any flavor
      Jello
1/2 cup water
1/2 slice lemon
5 (1/2-pint) jars

Mix figs, sugar, Jello, water and lemon together in large pot. Cook on high heat until mixture comes to a rolling boil. Cook on medium heat 20 minutes or until thick, stirring occasionally. Pour into 5 hot sterilized jars and seal.

Linda Hebert Hollier (Mrs. Lloyd, Jr.)

FIG JAM à la MICROWAVE

3 cups fresh figs, pureed
1 (3-oz.) package lemon flavored
      gelatin
1 (3-oz.) package apricot flavored
      gelatin
2½ cups sugar
5 (1/2-pint) jars

Puree figs in food processor. Combine with gelatin and sugar in 4-quart glass casserole. Stir well. Cover and microwave on **HIGH (100%) 10 MINUTES** until boiling, stirring at 5 minute intervals. Continue to microwave on **HIGH (100%) 3 MINUTES.** Pour into 5 hot sterilized jars and seal immediately.

Tout de Suite à la Microwave II
by Jean K Durkee

CAPONATA

3 large eggplants, peeled and
    cubed
Salt and red pepper
1/4 cup olive oil
1/4 cup corn oil
3 large onions, chopped
6 ribs celery, sliced thin
10 cloves garlic, sliced
3 large tomatoes, peeled and
    coarsely chopped
1 (4¾-oz.) bottle pimiento
    stuffed green olives, drained
    and sliced large
1 (3¼-oz.) bottle capers,
    drained
2-3 teaspoons salt
1/2 teaspoon black pepper
1/4 teaspoon red pepper
6 (1-pint) jars with lids and rings

In a large covered Dutch oven wilt eggplant in olive and corn oil, salt and pepper to taste. Add onion, celery, garlic, tomato, olives, capers, salt and pepper. Bring to boil. Cover. Cook on low heat 1 hour, stirring occasionally. Check seasoning for taste. Vegetables should retain their identity. Serve hot as vegetable or cold with crackers and beer.

To process: Fill 6 hot (1-pint) sterilized jars with Caponata (eggplant mixture). Tighten sterilized lids. Immerse in boiling water bath and process 30 minutes. Water should remain around jars during processing.

Yield: 6 pints

Betty Baquet Bares (Mrs. Allen)

TOMATO KETCHUP

30-35 (6-7 lbs.) very ripe
    tomatoes
1 quart white vinegar
1 cup brown sugar
2 large onions, thinly sliced
1 tablespoon dry mustard
1 tablespoon black pepper
5 teaspoons salt
1 teaspoon mace
1 teaspoon allspice
1/2 teaspoon whole cloves
1/2 teaspoon cayenne pepper

Wash, quarter and cook tomatoes in a large covered pot over medium heat. Press with potato masher once or twice to release juice while cooking. When tender, pass through presser. Measure 1 gallon of juice and add vinegar, sugar, onion, mustard, black pepper, salt, mace, allspice, cloves and cayenne. Cook to desired consistency, about 3 hours. Stir occasionally. Strain. Pour into 4 (8-oz.) hot jars. Seal. *From the recipe files of Virgie Ewell Heard Wallis (Mrs. Hugh).*

Yield: 24-30 ounces

Virginia Wallis Hagelin (Mrs. John A.)

SEVEN MINUTE MICROWAVE DILLS

1 quart (2-3 in.) whole cucumbers
    or 1/4-inch unwaxed
    cucumber slices
1 clove garlic, peeled
1/2 teaspoon dried dill weed or
    1 head fresh dill
1/8 teaspoon turmeric
1 hot pepper, optional
1 1/2 cups water
1/2 cup cider vinegar
2 tablespoons salt, uniodized

Fill sterile 1-quart canning jar with washed and dried cucumbers, garlic, dill weed, turmeric and hot pepper, if desired. In a 4-cup Pyrex measuring cup combine water, vinegar and salt. Microwave on **HIGH (100%) 4 MINUTES** until boiling. Pour liquid over cucumbers until covered. Add additional water if necessary. Cover jar loosely with plastic wrap. Microwave on **HIGH (100%) 3 MINUTES**. Cap, leaving plastic wrap in place. Cool and eat! Store in refrigerator for maximum crispness. Will keep 1 year.

Yield: 1 quart

Mary D. Skarda (Mrs. Steve)

ICEBERG MIRLITON PICKLES

6 to 8 pounds mirlitons (after
    peeling and cutting)
2 cups pickling lime
2 gallons water
Ice and water

Syrup:
2 quarts vinegar
2 quarts sugar
1 tablespoon salt
1 (1 1/4-oz.) box mixed pickling
    spice

Cut peeled mirlitons into 1-1 1/2-inch cubes. Place in large porcelain or enamel container (not aluminum) with pickling lime and iced water. Soak 24 hours, stirring occasionally. Remove and wash each piece well under running water. Return to container. Soak 4-6 hours covered in ice and water. Drain. Mix syrup and pour over mirlitons. Leave overnight or 8-10 hours. Add pickling spice in cloth bag or cheesecloth. Bring to boil and simmer for 1/2 hour, stirring occasionally. Fill jars with pickles; add syrup. Seal and put in hot water bath.

Yield: 8 pints

Paul A. Barefield

How to keep preserves: Apply the white of an egg, with a brush, to a single thickness of white tissue paper, with which cover the jars, lapping over an inch or two. It will require no tying, as it will become, when dry, inconceivably tight and strong, and impervious to the air.

SPANISH OLIVE OIL PICKLES

2 pounds cucumbers, (after
    peeled and sliced)
2 medium purple onions, sliced
3 large bell peppers, sliced
Large handful of salt
1 cup iced water
1 quart white vinegar
2 cups sugar
1 tablespoon celery seed
1 tablespoon mustard seed
1 1/2 tablespoons grated
    horseradish
1/2 tablespoon turmeric
3 tablespoons olive oil

Mix cucumbers, onions, bell peppers and salt in large pot. Let set overnight or at least 8 hours. Drain. Add iced water, slosh around and drain well. Mix vinegar, sugar, celery seed, mustard seed, horseradish and turmeric in large pot. Bring to boil. Add cucumbers, onions and peppers. Boil hard 5 minutes. When mixture has cooled, add olive oil. Place in 6 hot sterile jars. Seal. Either refrigerate or put in hot water bath 45 minutes to seal.

Yield: 6 pints

Paul A. Barefield

BREAD & BUTTER PICKLES

14 medium cucumbers
6 white onions
1/2 cup salt
1 tablespoon alum
3 cups sugar
1 tablespoon mustard seed
1 tablespoon celery seed
2 tablespoons turmeric
1 teaspoon ginger
1 quart white vinegar

Slice cucumbers and onions. Soak in water to cover. Add salt and alum. Soak 3 hours. Drain. Mix sugar, seeds, turmeric, ginger and vinegar. Bring to a boil in 3-quart pot. Put in pickles and boil 3 minutes. Place in hot sterile jars. Seal.

Yield: 6 pints

From the recipe files of Mrs. F.M. Hamilton

REFRIGERATOR "ICE BOX" PICKLES

8 cups thinly sliced unpeeled
    cucumbers
4 cups thinly sliced onion
4 cups vinegar
3 cups sugar
1 1/2 teaspoons mustard seed
1 1/2 teaspoons celery seed
1 1/4 teaspoons turmeric
1/2 cup salt

Slice cucumbers and onions. Place in sterile jars. Mix vinegar, sugar, mustard seed, celery seed, turmeric and salt together in large mixing bowl. Pour over cucumbers and onions in jars. Cover and refrigerate. Keep at least 5 days before using.

Yield: 6 pints

Rosemary Ham (Mrs. Harold H.)

14

FLAMINGO RELISH

24 red sweet peppers
15 large onions
Boiling water
1 quart cider vinegar
1 tablespoon salt
2 cups sugar
6 (8-oz.) jars

Remove seeds from peppers and peel onions. Grind together in food chopper. Mix well. Cover with boiling water and let stand 5 minutes. Drain and squeeze dry. Add vinegar, salt and sugar. Boil 20 minutes. Seal hot in hot sterile jars. Excellent to serve with lettuce salad.

Yield: 4-6 (8-oz.) jars

From the recipe files of Mrs. F. M. Hamilton

SHREDDED SQUASH RELISH

4 pounds yellow summer squash,
    shredded
6 medium onions, shredded
1 cup shredded red bell pepper
1/4 cup salt
4 trays (or equivalent) of ice
    cubes
3 cups cider vinegar
3 cups sugar
1½ teaspoons mustard seed
1½ teaspoons celery seed
1 teaspoon turmeric
6-8 (1-pint) jars with lids and rings

Alternate squash, onions and bell pepper as you shred them in your food chopper. Place in large 4-quart crock. Cover with 1/4 cup salt. Lay ice cubes directly on top of squash and salt. Let sit 3 hours. After 3 hours, rinse mixture 4 times with cold water. Heat vinegar, sugar, mustard seed, celery seed and turmeric. Add squash mixture. Bring to full boil. Immediately fill hot sterile jars and seal. Place in water bath and boil 5 minutes. Remove jars and allow to cool.

Yield: 6-8 pints

Cloeann McDowell Clement (Mrs. John P. III)

PICKLED OKRA

2 pounds small fresh okra
5 garlic cloves, peeled
5 hot pepper pods
1 quart white vinegar
6 tablespoons salt
1 tablespoon celery seed or
    mustard seed
1/2 cup water

Wash okra. Pack in 5 hot sterilized pint jars. Put 1 clove garlic and 1 pepper in each jar. In a 2-quart saucepan bring to boil vinegar, salt, seed and water. Pour over okra and seal jars. Process 10 minutes in a boiling water bath. Let stand 6-8 weeks before opening.

Yield: 5 pints

Barbara Haynes (Mrs. Johnny)

Bonnie H. Buratt (Mrs. Leycester)
omits hot pepper and water and adds 2 tablespoons liquid crab boil.

FRENCH MARKET DOUGHNUTS

1 package active dry yeast
1½ cups warm water (105°)
1/2 cup sugar
1 teaspoon salt
2 eggs
1 cup undiluted evaporated milk
7 cups all-purpose flour
1/4 cup soft shortening
Oil for frying
Confectioners powdered sugar

In large bowl, sprinkle yeast over water; stir to dissolve. Add sugar, salt, eggs and milk. Blend with beater. Add 4 cups of the flour; beat smooth. Add shortening; beat in remaining flour. Cover with plastic wrap and chill overnight. Roll out on floured board to 1/8" thickness. Cut into 2½" squares. Deep fry at 360° 2-3 minutes until lightly browned on each side. Drain on paper towels and sprinkle heavily with powdered sugar. Serve hot with café au lait. Note: This dough can be kept for up to a week in refrigerator and actually improves with age; just punch down when it rises. Dough can also be frozen; simply thaw, cut and roll, or shape doughnuts before freezing. *Tastes like the original!*

Yield: 5 dozen

Marguerite Richard Lyle (Mrs. Michael)

CREAM PUFFS

1 cup boiling water
1/2 cup butter or margarine
1/4 teaspoon salt
1 cup sifted all-purpose flour
4 eggs
Whipped cream for filling
Powdered sugar for sprinkling

Bring water to boil in a medium saucepan. Add butter and salt. Stir until melted. Add flour all at once. Stir briskly until a ball forms. Remove from heat. Cool. Add 1 egg at a time, beating after each addition until smooth. Drop by tablespoon onto greased cookie sheet. Bake in **preheated 450° oven 15 minutes.** Reduce temperature to **325°** and continue to bake **20 minutes.** Cool and fill with custard or whipped cream. Sprinkle top with powdered sugar. *Puffs could be filled with a shrimp or crawfish mixture.*

Yield: 24 servings

Lillie Nellie Clark (Mrs. J.O., Jr.)

16

COUSH-COUSH

3 cups yellow cornmeal
1½ teaspoons salt
1 tablespoon sugar
1 cup water
1/4 cup oil

Mix cornmeal, salt and sugar in bowl. Moisten with water. Stir well. Heat oil, in 5-quart Dutch oven, over medium heat until hot. Sprinkle a teaspoon of cornmeal mixture into oil, if it sizzles, add remaining mixture. Cook 20 minutes, stirring often, until dry and a golden color. Serve hot or cold with butter, milk or syrup.

Yield: 3 servings

Ella Latiolais (Mrs. Pierre)

KUSH KUSH, AN OLD LOUISIANA DISH

Take two teacups of Aunt Jemima's cornmeal, and scald with 1½ cups of boiling water. Add 1 teaspoon of salt. When cool, add 3 teaspoons full of baking powder, 3 eggs beaten together.

Now put on the fire a thick iron skillet and put in it a good teaspoon full of lard, just enough to keep it from sticking. When the skillet is very hot, pour in the mixture.

Cover the pot tightly and let it cook for 5 minutes, then uncover and scrape from the bottom before it forms a crust.

Now cover the pot tightly again and lower your burner or fire, and cook for 10 minutes more.

Now take up and serve hot, on a hot dish, to be eaten with butter, or hash, or with sugar and cream. *From my grandmother's, Mrs. John Cameron Nickerson, recipe files.*

Cherie Chappuis Kraft (Mrs. Ralph)

SWEET POTATO BREAD

1/2 cup butter
1/2 cup granulated sugar
3/4 cup brown sugar
2 eggs, beaten
1 cup flour
1 teaspoon baking powder
1 teaspoon cinnamon
1 teaspoon nutmeg
1/8 teaspoon salt
3 cups grated raw sweet potatoes

Cream butter and sugars in large mixing bowl. Blend in eggs. Add flour, baking powder, cinnamon, nutmeg and salt. Fold in grated sweet potatoes. Pour into a well-greased 8-inch black iron skillet. Bake in **preheated 350° oven 1 hour** or until tester comes out clean.

Yield: 6-8 servings

Donna Schexneider (Mrs. Don)

17

BUTTERFLAKE HERB LOAF

2 (1/4-oz.) packages dry yeast
1/4 cup warm water
1/3 cup shortening
1/4 cup sugar
1 tablespoon salt
1 cup scalded milk
2 eggs, unbeaten
4¹/₂-5 cups all-purpose flour
Sesame seeds or poppy seeds
    to sprinkle

*Herb Margarine:
1/2 cup margarine
1/2 teaspoon caraway seed
1/2 teaspoon crushed basil
    leaves
1/2 teaspoon grated onion
1/4 teaspoon oregano
1/8 teaspoon cayenne pepper
1 clove garlic, crushed

Instructions: Soften margarine and mix all ingredients until well-blended.

Soften yeast in warm water. In a large mixing bowl, combine shortening, sugar and salt. Pour hot milk over this and stir until cooled to luke warm. Blend in unbeaten eggs and softened yeast. Gradually add flour to form a stiff dough. Knead on floured surface for 2-3 minutes. Place in a large well-greased bowl and let rise until double in size (1¹/₂-2 hours). See page 19 for Shortcut Rising Method.

Roll out on floured board to 1/8-inch thickness. Cut 14 (5-inch) circles. Spread Herb Margarine* on half of each circle then fold in half.

To form a pull-apart loaf, place each folded circle on large greased cookie sheet, lapping folded circles 1/2-inch with folded sides touching cookie sheet. Form 2 loaves of 7 sections. Spread remaining Herb Margarine over tops of loaves. Sprinkle with sesame or poppy seeds. Let rise in warm place 30 minutes.

Bake in **preheated 350° oven 20-25 minutes** until lightly brown on top. *This is excellent to serve with wild game.*

Yield: 14 servings

Pauline Winn Laland (Mrs. Rick)

HUSH PUPPIES

3/4 cup yellow corn meal
3/4 cup self-rising flour
1/3 cup sugar
1 teaspoon salt
1 teaspoon baking soda
1 egg
1/3 cup milk
1 small onion, chopped

Mix cornmeal, flour, sugar, salt and soda. Beat egg. Add milk then add to dry mixture. Stir in onion. Batter should be stiff. If batter is too dry, add milk or if too liquid, add flour. Drop by small spoonfuls into deep hot oil 370°-380°. Dip spoon in oil each time to ease dropping.

Yield: 32 hush puppies

Bonnie Buratt

ITALIAN CHEESE BREAD

With a shortcut rising method à la microwave

2 (1/4-oz.) packages dry yeast
1 cup margarine, softened
6 large eggs
4½ cups sifted all-purpose flour
1 teaspoon salt
2 teaspoons sugar
1/4 pound Swiss cheese
1/4 pound sharp cheddar cheese
1/2 cup grated Parmesan cheese

Dissolve yeast in 1 cup of warm water. In a large mixing bowl, beat margarine until fluffy. Beat eggs in another bowl until light. Add eggs to margarine, blending well. Stir in dissolved yeast water.

Sift flour, salt and sugar together. Gradually add to egg mixture, continue to beat until satiny.

Cut Swiss and cheddar cheese into 1/4-inch cubes. Stir cubed cheese and Parmesan cheese into mixture. Place dough in a 4-quart greased glass mixing bowl. Cover and let rise until doubled in volume (see Shortcut Rising Method, at bottom, for microwave).

With spoon, gently stir (do not punch). Cover bowl and let rise until doubled, again (see microwave method). Grease a 10-inch tube pan. Gently stir dough down. Pour or drop by spoonfuls into pan. Let rise again until doubled. Bake in a **preheated 400° oven 35-40 minutes.** Use cake tester to test for doneness. Cool 10 minutes out of oven. Lift bread out by tube and cool 20 more minutes. Eat while warm or cool. *This is one of my favorites. The 'ohs and ahs' make up for the time it takes to make it, when the aroma fills your kitchen. Delicious with a cold glass of milk!*

Yield: 1 loaf

Pauline Winn Lalande (Mrs. Rick)

Shortcut Rising Method from **Tout de Suite à la Microwave II**
1. Bring 3½ cups water to boil in a 1-quart glass bowl on **HIGH (100%) 7-8 MINUTES.** Place glass mixing bowl containing dough in microwave on top of bowl of boiling water (make sure both bowls fit in microwave before you begin). Microwave on **WARM (10%) 5 MINUTES or DEFROST 2 MINUTES.**
2. Let dough rise in warm place 20 to 30 minutes until doubled in bulk.
3. With spoon, gently stir (follow recipe instructions).
4. Again, bring 3½ cups water to boil in bowl. Repeat steps 1 and 2.
5. Follow recipe instructions for baking in a tube pan.
Later if you want to warm just one slice of bread, wrap it in wax paper and microwave on **HIGH (100%) 20 SECONDS.**

SCACHATA (SICILIAN PIZZA)

1 (1-lb.) loaf frozen bread or loaf
  of your own bread dough,
  defrosted
2 cups chopped green onion tops
1 (3¾-oz.) can sardines, boned
  and chopped
1/3 cup olive oil
1 cup Italian cheese, grated
  Romano or Parmesan
2 eggs, beaten
1/2 teaspoon oregano
2 tablespoons Italian cheese

Grease a 9½ x 13 x 2-inch pan. Spread dough with fingers or roll out to fit pan. Sprinkle onion and sardines over dough. Drizzle with oil and top with cheese. With pastry brush, brush on beaten eggs. Sprinkle with oregano and more cheese. Cover with cloth and let rise about 30 minutes. Remove cloth and bake in **450° oven 12-15 minutes** or until brown on edges. Cut into squares and serve.

Yield: 4-6 servings

Rose Sinagra Ingram (Mrs. Larry), author
CHESTA E CHIDA — Italian-Sicilian Style Cookbook

This is the way my grandmother made her pizza. Grandma, of course, made her own bread. The dough was never rolled out, she used her hands. She would grate hunks of Romano cheese over the pizza. She did not have a pastry brush, so she used sprigs of mint to spread the eggs. Nothing was ever measured, it was a handful or a pinch of this or that. The oven she used was a clay type outdoor oven. It was always such a treat for her to fix SCACHATA! (pronounced SKA CHA TA)

SVENJUNI (ITALIAN BREAD)

2 (13¾-oz.) boxes hot roll mix
  or enough homemade bread
  dough to make 1 loaf
2 (2-oz.) cans anchovies, sliced
1 pound lean ground meat
1/2 cup Italian seasoned bread
  crumbs
1/2 cup slivered Romano cheese
1/4 cup grated Romano cheese
Oregano for sprinkling
Olive oil for drizzling

Mix dough and let rise according to directions given on box. Place dough into greased pans, 1 (9 x 13-inch) pan and 1 (8 x 8-inch) pan and push out evenly with fingers. Press cheese slivers deeply into dough, 2 inches apart. Place small pieces of anchovies on top of cheese. Place patties of ground meat, the size of quarters, over all.

In small bowl, mix bread crumbs with grated cheese. Sprinkle mixture over top of bread. Then sprinkle oregano. Drizzle olive oil over top of bread. Place damp cloth over top and let rise until double in bulk. Bake in **preheated 350° oven 25-30 minutes** or until golden brown. *This recipe was given to me by my Italian grandmother. Svenjuni is pronounced 'Fin Junie.'*

Yield: 10 servings

Bonnie Robin (Mrs. David)

ACADIAN BREAD ROLLS

1 (1/4-oz.) package yeast
1/4 cup warm water (110°F)
3/4 cup hot milk
1/4 cup shortening or oil
1/4 cup sugar
1¼ teaspoons salt
1 egg, beaten
4 cups all-purpose flour
Melted butter or margarine for
   brushing

Dissolve yeast in water. Mix hot milk, oil, sugar and salt in large mixing bowl. Cool to luke warm. Stir in yeast and egg. Add 2 cups flour and beat until smooth. Gradually stir in more flour until dough leaves sides of bowl. Turn dough out onto lightly floured surface and knead until smooth and elastic. Place in lightly greased bowl. Turn over once to grease upper side of dough. Cover and let rise in warm place (80-85°F) until almost double in bulk, 1-1¼ hours. Press dough down into bowl to remove air bubbles. Put a little shortening on hands. Divide dough into small pieces. Roll into balls (22, 1½-inches in diameter or 44 smaller balls). Place in shallow greased pan (pizza pan works well) with sides touching. Cover loosely with cloth. Let rise in warm place until double in bulk, 45-60 minutes. Bake in **preheated 400° oven 15-20 minutes for larger rolls, 12-15 minutes for smaller.** Brush rolls with melted butter or margarine after removing from oven.

Yield: 22-44 rolls

Linda Hebert Hollier (Mrs. Lloyd, Jr.)

JALAPEÑO CORNBREAD

1 cup yellow cornmeal
2 eggs
1/2 teaspoon salt
1/2 teaspoon baking soda
1/2 cup vegetable oil
1 cup milk
1/2 pound grated sharp cheddar
   cheese
1/2 pound grated American
   cheese
1 (17-oz.) can cream style corn
2-3 or 4 jalapeño peppers,
   chopped
1 large onion, chopped

Mix cornmeal, eggs, salt, baking soda, oil, milk, cheeses, corn, peppers and onion in large bowl. Pour into a greased 9 x 13-inch dish or pan. Bake in **preheated 350° oven 1 hour,** until tester comes out clean.

Yield: 24 servings

Melba LeBlanc LeBlanc (Mrs. George)

BOOMPS' BUTTERMILK MUFFINS

2 eggs
1 pint buttermilk
1 teaspoon baking soda
1 teaspoon baking powder
1 teaspoon sugar
1 teaspoon salt
2 tablespoons shortening,
    softened
1½ cups all-purpose flour

Beat eggs in a mixing bowl. Add buttermilk, soda, baking powder, sugar, salt and shortening. Mix until smooth. Add flour slowly until mixture thickens. Place in greased muffin pan. Bake in **preheated 375° oven 45 minutes.** Serve immediately when hot. Muffins will be soft inside with a golden crust outside.

Yield: 1½ dozen

Cloeann McDowell Clement (Mrs. John P. III)

FIG MUFFINS

1/4 cup butter, softened
1/2 cup sugar
3 eggs
2 cups mashed fig preserves
    with syrup
1 cup Old-Fashioned oatmeal,
    uncooked
1½ cups all-purpose flour
2 teaspoons baking powder
1/2 teaspoon baking soda
1/2 teaspoon salt

*Orange Spread:
1 (3-oz.) package cream cheese,
    softened
1/4 cup sifted confectioners
    powdered sugar
2 tablespoons orange juice
    concentrate

Cream butter and sugar. Add eggs and beat well after each. Add fig preserves with syrup. Stir in oatmeal and sifted flour, baking powder, soda and salt. Mix only enough to moisten dry ingredients.

Bake in buttered muffin cups in **preheated 375° oven 15-20 minutes.** Serve warm with Orange Spread.*

Cream cheese until light and fluffy. Beat in confectioners sugar and orange juice concentrate. Frost muffins.

Serve at room temperature but keep refrigerated otherwise.

Yield: 15-18 muffins

Patricia Cashman Andrus (Mrs. Robert)

ORANGE-PECAN MUFFINS

1/2 cup margarine
1 cup sugar
2 eggs
3/4 cup sour cream
1/2 teaspoon orange extract
2 cups all-purpose flour
1 teaspoon baking soda
1/2 teaspoon salt
1/2 cup chopped pecans
3 tablespoons grated orange
    rind (zest)
3 tablespoons orange juice

*Orange Icing:
2 cups confectioners powdered
    sugar
1 tablespoon melted margarine
1 tablespoon grated orange
    rind
1/4 cup orange juice

Cream margarine in large mixing bowl. Add sugar. Beat until light and fluffy. Beat in eggs. Stir in sour cream and orange extract. Sift flour, soda and salt together. Blend into batter. Add pecans, orange rind and juice. Mix well. Spoon into muffin tins coated with vegetable spray, filling each 3/4 full. Bake in **preheated 375° oven 20 minutes** or **12-15 minutes** for miniature muffin tin. Cool and ice with Orange Icing.*

Place sugar, margarine, rind and juice in top of double boiler over hot water for 10 minutes. Remove from heat. Beat icing until of good spreading consistency.

Yield: 1½ dozen large or 6 dozen small

Becky G. Daigle (Mrs. Kenneth)

OATMEAL MUFFINS

1 cup quick cooking oats
1 cup buttermilk
1 cup firmly packed brown sugar
1 egg, slightly beaten
1¾ cups all-purpose flour
1 teaspoon baking powder
1 teaspoon baking soda
1 teaspoon salt
1/2 teaspoon cinnamon
1/4 teaspoon mace
1/4 teaspoon cloves
1/2 cup vegetable oil
1/2 cup raisins

Combine oatmeal and buttermilk in small mixing bowl. Let stand. Mix sugar and egg in large mixing bowl. Combine flour, baking powder, soda, salt, cinnamon, mace and cloves. Stir into egg mixture. Add oatmeal and buttermilk mixture. Add oil and raisins. Spoon into greased muffin tins. Fill half full. Bake in **preheated 400° oven 15-20 minutes.**

Yield: 1½ dozen

Anita G. Guidry (Mrs. Owen A.)

TRUNK COFFEE CAKE

2 eggs, well beaten
1 cup sugar
2 tablespoons melted butter
Pinch of salt
3/4 cup sour milk* (buttermilk)
1 teaspoon baking soda
1 1/2 cups all-purpose flour
1 teaspoon cream of tartar

Topping:
1/4 cup melted butter
6 tablespoons sugar
1 teaspoon cinnamon

*Sour milk can be made by
adding 1 teaspoon lemon juice
or vinegar to the 3/4 cup
sweet milk.

In large mixing bowl, add sugar to beaten eggs. Stir in melted butter and salt. Stir soda into sour milk. Stir cream of tartar into flour. Alternately add milk mixture and flour mixture to egg and sugar. Stir just to combine. Do not overbeat. Pour into greased and floured 9 x 9-inch pan. Carefully spread melted butter on top and sprinkle with mixture of sugar and cinnamon.

Bake in **preheated 350° oven 35-45 minutes** until cake tester comes out clean. *This recipe was found in an old trunk dated 1932.*

Yield: 9 servings

Doreen Claire McSpadden (Mrs. Joe R.)

ALMOND COFFEE CAKE

1 cup quick oatmeal
1 1/2 cups boiling water
1/2 cup margarine, softened
1 cup brown sugar
1 cup white sugar
2 eggs
1 1/2 cups all-purpose flour
1 teaspoon baking soda
1/2 teaspoon salt
1 teaspoon cinnamon

*Frosting:
1/2 cup margarine, softened
1 cup brown sugar
1 cup grated coconut
1 teaspoon vanilla
1/4 cup slivered almonds

Pour boiling water over oatmeal in bowl or pan. Let stand 10 minutes. In a large mixing bowl, cream margarine. Add brown and white sugar and eggs. Beat until well-mixed. Add flour, baking soda, salt and cinnamon. Mix well. Add oatmeal mixture. Pour into a 9 x 13-inch greased baking dish. Bake in a **preheated 350° oven 30-35 minutes.** While cake is still hot and in dish, top with Frosting*

Cream margarine in medium mixing bowl. Add sugar, coconut, vanilla and almonds. Spread on hot cake. Place under broiler 4 minutes. Watch carefully so it does not burn.

Yield: 36 servings

Lois Riley Montgomery (Mrs. Thad, III)

APRICOT COFFEE CAKE

1/2 cup light brown sugar,
    packed
2 tablespoons butter, softened
2 tablespoons all-purpose flour
1 teaspoon cinnamon
3 cups all-purpose flour
1 1/2 teaspoon baking powder
3/4 teaspoon baking soda
1/4 teaspoon salt
3/4 cup butter, softened
1 1/2 cups sugar
4 eggs
1 1/2 teaspoons vanilla
1 cup sour cream
3/4 cup coarsely chopped dried
    apricots
1/4 cup coarsely chopped dried
    prunes
1/2 cup chopped nuts, optional
Confectioners powdered sugar,
    for sprinkling

Mix sugar, butter, 2 tablespoons flour and cinnamon in small bowl with fork until crumbly. Set streusel mixture aside. Grease and flour 10-inch tube pan. Sift together 3 cups flour, baking powder, soda and salt. Set aside. Cream butter in large mixing bowl. Add sugar, beating until light and fluffy. Add eggs, one at a time, beat until fluffy. Add vanilla. At low speed, add flour in fourths alternately with sour cream in thirds just until smooth. Gently fold in apricots and prunes and nuts, if desired. Pour 1/3 of batter into prepared pan. Sprinkle 1/3 of streusel mixture. Repeat layers twice with remaining batter and streusel. Bake in **preheated 350° oven 55-60 minutes** or until inserted cake tester comes out clean. Cool on rack 20 minutes. Remove to plate. Sift confectioners sugar over top.

Yield: 10 servings

Deborah Austin (Mrs. J. W.)

CRANBERRY ORANGE BREAD

2 cups all-purpose flour
3/4 cup sugar
1 1/2 teaspoons baking powder
1 teaspoon salt
1/2 teaspoon baking soda
1 cup coarsely chopped
    cranberries
1/2 cup chopped nuts
1 teaspoon grated orange zest
1 egg, beaten
3/4 cup orange juice
2 tablespoons vegetable oil

Combine flour, sugar, baking powder, salt and soda in bowl. Stir in cranberries, nuts and zest. In another bowl combine beaten egg, orange juice and oil. Add to dry ingredients, stirring just until moistened. Bake in a greased 9 1/2 x 5 x 3-inch loaf pan in **preheated 350° oven 50 minutes** until done. Remove from pan and cool.

Yield: 12 slices

Betsy Settle Taylor (Mrs. J.W.)

NUT BREAD

3 cups flour
1 cup sugar
1 teaspoon salt
2 teaspoons baking powder
1 cup chopped pecans
1 cup milk
1 whole egg, beaten

Sift flour, sugar, salt and baking powder into a bowl; add nuts, milk and egg. Mix. Place in 3 (3 x 6½-inch) well-greased and floured loaf pans. Or, use 4 baking powder cans filled 3/4 full. Bake in **preheated 325° oven 45 minutes** or until golden brown. Let stand 5 minutes out of oven before removing from baking tins. It is better when made a few days before you use it. Freezes nicely. Cut thin and butter to serve. *This recipe was developed by my grandmother during a time that sugar was scarce.*

Yield: 3 small loaves

Missy Hardy Abendroth (Mrs. Joe)

SAL'S LEMON NUT BREAD

1/2 cup butter, softened
1 cup sugar
2 eggs, lightly beaten
1¼ cups all-purpose flour
1/2 teaspoon salt
1 teaspoon baking powder
1/2 cup milk
1/2 cup chopped walnuts
1 tablespoon grated lemon rind

1/4 cup sugar
Juice of 1 lemon

Cream butter and sugar well in mixing bowl. Add eggs. Mix flour, salt and baking powder and add alternately with milk to creamed mixture. Add nuts and lemon zest and mix well. Pour into a greased 5¼ x 9¼ x 3-inch loaf pan. Bake in **preheated 350° oven 1 hour** or until done.

Mix sugar and lemon juice in small pan over low heat to dissolve sugar. Pour sauce over hot bread in pan. Cool in pan. Remove and slice.

Yield: 10-12 slices

Kathy Van Wie (Mrs. William)

WHOLE WHEAT BANANA BREAD

1/2 cup butter
1 cup sugar
2 eggs, slightly beaten
3 medium bananas, mashed
1 cup whole wheat flour
1 cup all-purpose flour
1/2 teaspoon salt
1 teaspoon baking soda
1/3 cup hot water
1/2 cup chopped pecans

Melt butter and blend with sugar. Mix in eggs and bananas until smooth. Mix flour, salt and soda, then add alternately with hot water. Stir in pecans. Pour into greased 9 x 5-inch loaf pan. Bake in **preheated 325° oven 1 hour and 10 minutes.**

Yield: 1 loaf

Beulah Hebert Stansbury

BANANA CAKE-BREAD

1/2 cup butter
1¼ cups sugar
2 eggs
1 teaspoon baking soda
4 tablespoons sour cream
1 cup mashed bananas
    (2-3 bananas)
1½ cups all-purpose flour
1/4 teaspoon salt
1 teaspoon vanilla

In a large mixing bowl, cream butter and sugar. Add eggs, Beat until very light and fluffy. Dissolve soda in sour cream and add to mixture. Add bananas, flour, salt and vanilla. Mix well. Pour into 5½ x 9½-inch buttered loaf pan. Bake in **preheated 350° oven 45-50 minutes.** Test for doneness with wooden pick.

Yield: 1 (5 x 9-inch) loaf

Karen Clark Fleming (Mrs. Glenn)

PRALINE BREAD

1 cup chopped pecans
1 cup Praline Liqueur, divided
1 cup butter
1 tablespoon vanilla
1 pound dark brown sugar
5 eggs
1/4 cup milk
2 cups all-purpose flour
1 teaspoon cinnamon
1/2 teaspoon baking powder
Cheesecloth for wrapping

Marinate pecans in 1/3 cup liqueur. Cream butter, vanilla and sugar in large mixing bowl. Add eggs and milk. Sift flour, cinnamon and baking powder into mixture. Add pecans and liqueur. Pour into 2 greased 5 x 9-inch loaf pans. Bake in **preheated 300° oven 60-70 minutes.**

Cool and wrap in cheese cloth, then poke holes in top of bread with wooden pick. Pour 1/3 cup liqueur over each loaf. Wrap in foil or in air-tight tin. Age 3 days in refrigerator.

Yield: 2 (5 x 9-inch) loaves

Marcelle Bienvenue, Chez Marcelle

27

the
1900s

n the first decade of the 20th Century when our nation was guided by Presidents McKinley, Theodore Roosevelt and Taft, LaFayette reached toward 6,000 citizens, with all of The Attakapas area of 17,000 turning, as flowers to the sun, toward LaFayette, capital "L" capital "F" as it was then spelled, for LaFayette had become, because of the railroad, a service and distribution center for the entire Attakapas area.

Each train that left Lafayette took local produce far beyond parish lines leaving, in exchange, hard cash. Hard cash was unique to the area—before the Civil War, during the War and its aftermath, Reconstruction.

Silver money meant that local citizens could buy those things that the trains brought to them: new food products, ready-made clothes and traveling theatrical entertainment all the way from New Orleans. Hard cash meant too that services could be purchased. What housewife would not be happy to acquire "table dressed" meats and poultry? Imagine! No more wringing a chicken's neck for the next meal. How wonderful to buy only the amount of meat needed for a given meal! No more butchering, curing, working for days so when all was said and done you didn't care if you ever saw another piece of meat.

Louis duBernard opened the very first "table dressed" butcher shop in town, starting with a meat cooler that held 100 pound blocks of ice. Later he purchased a mechanical refrigerator with an ammonia tank as the coolant. This could become very volatile if the tank pressure reached a dangerous level. Though there never was an explosion, the buildings within the square block of the butcher shop were vacated more than once in a run to safety.

It was the train that brought the Yandles and Mrs. Yandle's German baking expertise to appreciative Lafayette citizens. Appreciative because oven directions still said that *if a hand can be held without pain in a fired oven for 60 seconds, it will be a slow oven; if for 45 seconds, it is moderate; and, if for only 20 seconds, quick.* Yandle's Confectionary Store first opened in a tent on Jefferson Street but within months had moved to its own building on Jefferson. There one could choose, because one did have money now, from trays covered with white and pink pulled taffy, or peanut brittle, chocolate fudge that smothered pecans or concealed marshmallows and plates of many-layered cakes crowned with jewel-colored frostings displayed in the two show windows, all better than homemade.

The dedication, June, 1901, of the main building of Southwestern Louisiana Industrial Institute, SLII, today's University of Southwestern Louisiana, USL, was such an important day to Lafayette citizens that businesses closed for half a day and parades were held. The crowd was estimated between 3,000 and 5,000 people. By the end of the first semester 145 students from twelve parishes and two states, Louisiana and Texas, were enrolled. The first commencement, May, 1904, was so important that Southern Pacific Railroad offered special-rate tickets for those visitors attending graduation.

By 1906 the Gordon Hotel and Jefferson Theater were thriving dreams of local businessmen. Lafayette phone customers could call up to 1,000 miles away and town government was a full time operation. Street signs were erected on all corners, all houses within the city limits were numbered so the post office could easily deliver mail and, a speed limit of eight miles an hour was imposed.

It was a time of innocent expectations. A favorite recreational activity for a young lady of the time was to put on her prettiest dress, and arm in arm with her best friend, walk down to the train depot to watch the passenger train come in. Of course, more important than the arrival of the train, were the young men of the town who were also at the depot, watching the trains arrive and the pretty girls pass by. Many a Lafayette courtship was begun as the young people "walked" at the depot. The social wisdom then, is valid today:

> To catch a man, chere, just wear pretty clothes.
> Talk about, chere
> To keep a man, yes, as anyone knows
> Be a good cook!

Orpha Valentine, author
Lafayette, Its Past, People & Progress

Beverage

Appetizer

CENTENNIAL CHERRY BOUNCE

1/2 gallon Louisiana wild cherries
1/2 gallon good bourbon whiskey
2 cups sugar
2 cups water

Wash cherries and put in gallon crock or jug. Add whiskey. Cover with cheese cloth or cork loosely and set aside for 3 months or longer (mark your calendar), in a dark closet, until whiskey has absorbed cherry flavor. After 3 months, make a simple syrup of sugar and water in saucepan. Boil until thick. Cool. Pour cherry/whiskey mixture through filter paper into 1-quart bottles or decanters. To 2/3 cherry bounce add 1/3 simple syrup. If you prefer it less sweet use less simple syrup. Cork tightly. Serve in liqueur glasses.

Yield: 2½ quarts

Lucille Roy Procter Copeland (Mrs. Robert)

I can remember my grandmother, Mrs. Joseph Arthur Roy, Sr. telling me when I was a little girl how the servants would pick the wild cherries from the cherry trees and how every hostess served 'Cherry Bounce' as a liqueur. Until the day Grandma passed away she always served her guests who came to call a small slice of fruit cake and a glass of Cherry Bounce on a crystal plate centered with a lace doily. Our family still makes the liqueur when we can find the wild cherries.

Grandma's father, William Britton Bailey, was the mayor of Vermilionville in 1884. It was during his administration that the name of Vermilionville was changed to Lafayette. He was also the founder of The Daily Advertiser.

ROSEMARY'S CHERRY BOUNCE

Wild Louisiana cherries, or fresh
    bing cherries
750 ml (1 fifth) good whiskey
1¼ cup sugar

Place cherries, the measurement of 4 fingers high, in a 1-quart bottle. Add whiskey and sugar. Cover with cheese cloth or cork. Let sit 6-8 weeks before sampling. Strain, place in bottle and cork.

Yield: 1 quart

Rosemary Ham (Mrs. Howard H.)

AMARETTO LIQUEUR

4 cups sugar
8 cups water
1 fifth of grain alcohol
3½ ounces almond extract
1½ ounces vanilla (Mexican, if
    available)

Heat sugar and water in a 2½ or 3-quart pot over low flame until mixture produces small bubbles. Cool to room temperature. Add alcohol, almond and vanilla. Bottle and drink! Fills 4 fifths or 4 wine bottles and costs about $10.00.

Yield: 4 quarts

Betty Baquet Bares (Mrs. Allen)

APRICOT BRANDY

2 cups sugar
2 cups vodka
1 (12-oz.) package dried apricots

Mix sugar, vodka and apricots in a 1½-quart jar. Cover. Shake everyday for two weeks if you can last that long. Strain. Apricots can be frozen and used later in any recipe calling for dried apricots. They are also good, chopped, on ice cream with Apricot Brandy poured over the top.

Yield: 1 quart

Kay R. Darling (Mrs. Charles)

CHEZ BAILÉ CRÈME

3 large eggs
1 (14½-oz.) can sweetened
    condensed milk
1 (12-oz.) carton Coffee Rich or
    · (12-oz.) Half & Half cream
3 tablespoons chocolate syrup
1/4 teaspoon coconut extract
1½ cups Irish whiskey

Blend eggs in a large blender. While blending, add condensed milk, Coffee Rich (or Half & Half), chocolate, coconut extract and whiskey all slowly and in the order given. Chill in refrigerator. Serve in liqueur glasses. (One ice cube optional.) *A gift to the great people of Lafayette, Louisiana.*

Yield: 1 liter

Cloeann McDowell Clement (Mrs. John P., III)

OLD LOUISIANA EGGNOG

10 eggs, separated
1½ cups sugar
1½ cups good brandy
1½ cups Jamaica rum
1 cup whipping cream
1 quart milk
Nutmeg for sprinkling

Separate yolks from whites. Beat yolks thoroughly. While mixing, slowly add sugar, brandy and rum. Add cup of cream, then milk, while running mixer at slow speed. Beat egg whites until thick (not dry). Fold into above mixture until whites have completely disappeared. Pour into container to cool in refrigerator. Serve with a dash of nutmeg on top of each serving. Better to make one or two days before serving.

Yield: 2½ quarts

Patricia Freeman Hosmer

ICE CREAM EGGNOG

12 fresh eggs, separated
3/4 cup sugar, divided
1 pint bourbon whiskey or
    brandy, to your taste
2 ounces rum
1 quart heavy cream
1 pint milk
1 teaspoon vanilla extract
1 quart vanilla ice cream
Nutmeg for sprinkling

In a very large bowl beat egg yolks until thick and pale in color slowly adding ½ cup sugar. Gradually add liquors, beating constantly. Let stand. Lightly whip cream. Add milk and vanilla. Combine with yolk mixture. Beat egg whites until stiff slowly adding ¼ cup sugar. Fold egg whites into cream and yolk mixture. Chill thoroughly. Before serving, unmold ice cream and place in center of bowl. Ice cream may be placed in individual molds and floated on top of eggnog. Serve in well-chilled cups with a sprinkle of nutmeg.

Yield: 12 servings

Edna Roy Roy (Mrs. Maxime, Sr.)

EGGNOG CHERIE

6 eggs, separated
6 tablespoons sugar, divided
Whiskey to your taste, optional
1 pint whipping cream, whipped

To increase recipe:
allow
1) 1 egg per person
2) 1 pint cream per 6 eggs
3) 1 tablespoon sugar per egg

Beat egg yolks separately in mixing bowl, adding 3 tablespoons sugar. Beat until sugar is dissolved. Add whiskey to your taste, beat again. Beat egg whites in separate bowl until very stiff. Slowly add remaining 3 tablespoons sugar. Whip cream. Fold egg whites into cream, mix thoroughly. Fold in yolk mixture and eggnog is ready to serve. *From the recipe files of my grandmother, Mrs. John Cameron Nickerson.*

Yield: 6 servings

Cherie Chappuis Kraft (Mrs. Ralph)

BRANDY MILK PUNCH

1³/₄ cups simple syrup
2 cups fine brandy
3/4 cup Crème de Cacao
2 quarts whole milk
1 quart heavy cream
Freshly grated nutmeg

To make a simple syrup mix 1 cup water and 1 cup sugar in saucepan. Bring to boil, cook on low boil 5 minutes. Cool. In a 4-quart container mix brandy, Crème de Cacao, milk and 1³/₄ cups simple syrup together and refrigerate. Just before serving, whip heavy cream until it just begins to thicken, then fold into brandy mixture. Fill brandy snifters with ice. Ladle in punch mixture and grate fresh nutmeg on top of each glass. *Serve at once and be prepared for seconds or thirds! This recipe was adapted from the wonderful version served on the steamship Natchez.*

Yield: 15 (8-oz.) servings

Terry L. Thompson

BRANDY ICE

1 pint vanilla ice cream
1 ounce brandy
1 ounce dark Crème de Cacao
3 cubes of ice

Place ice cream, brandy, Crème de Cacao and ice in blender. Mix until soft and smooth. Serve in stemmed glasses.

Yield: 2 servings

Jacques Delaveau

CAFÉ au LAIT

Pour deux

1½ tablespoons sugar
1 cup boiling milk
1 cup hot, dark roast coffee
    poured into 2 coffee cups

Place sugar in small heavy pot. Cook over medium heat to caramelize, stirring constantly. At the first puff of smoke, remove sugar from heat. Add hot milk slowly to sugar, stirring to dissolve. Add to the hot coffee and stir.

Yield: coffee milk for 2

Terry L. Thompson (Mrs. Pat)

This beverage is of French origin and along with hard rolls and butter or croissants is the breakfast of France. In the Louisiana version, the sugar is caramelized, giving the drink a distinctive flavor.

CRÈME DE MENTHE

6 cups water
6 cups sugar
1 pint grain alcohol (190 proof)
1-2 ounces pure peppermint
    extract
1-3 teaspoons green food
    coloring

Bring water and sugar to boil in 3-quart saucepan. Simmer 10 minutes. Cool. Add alcohol. Starting with 1 ounce of peppermint extract, add more according to your taste. Again, starting with 1 teaspoon food coloring add more until the color you desire. Cover and let ripen 1 month, shaking occasionally. Serve in liqueur glasses or over ice cream.

Yield: 1/2 gallon

Kay R. Darling (Mrs. Charles)

Microwave directions: Place sugar and water in 2½-quart glass measuring cup. Microwave on **HIGH (100%) 22 MINUTES** or until mixture boils, stirring one time. Boil **2 MINUTES LONGER** on **HIGH (100%)**. Let cool. Follow directions above.
Jean K Durkee

KAHLÚA

2 cups boiling water
1 vanilla bean
1 (2-oz.) jar Yuban instant coffee
4 cups sugar
1 pint brandy

Bring water to a boil in large saucepan. Add vanilla bean, instant coffee and sugar. Cool. Add brandy. Pour into bottles and cover. Store in a dark place for 30 days.

Yield: 1 1/2 quarts

Myrrl Summers (Mrs. Charles H.)

MINT JULEP

3 or 4 mint leaves
1/2 teaspoon sugar, if desired
1 tablespoon brandy
Crushed ice
Bourbon whiskey
Sprigs of mint

Into a silver mint julep cup break mint leaves, add sugar and brandy. Muddle this and fill the cup with crushed ice. Fill the cup with bourbon whiskey and stir until the cup frosts. Decorate cup with sprigs of mint.

Yield: 1 cup

Lucille Roy Procter Copeland (Mrs. Robert)

VOILÂ! ORANGE LIQUEUR

1 cup 190 proof grain alcohol
1 large orange, unpeeled
White string, tape

Simple syrup:
1 cup sugar dissolved in
1/2 cup water. Place in
2-cup Pyrex measuring cup.

Microwave on **HIGH (100%)**
3 MINUTES, stir at 1 minute intervals. Cool. Add to orange mixture.

Place alcohol in wide-mouthed peanut butter jar. With white string tied around unpeeled orange, suspend orange 1/4-inch above surface of liquid. Tape string to outside of jar. Screw lid on to hold orange in place. Place jar in dark corner of cupboard for 2 weeks. Mark your calendar! After 2 weeks, remove orange. Discard orange as it will have absorbed fumes from alcohol. Juice from orange will have dripped into alcohol. Add cooled simple syrup to orange mixture. Serve in liqueur glasses. Store in air tight jar.

Yield: 1 2/3 cups

Dorothy Witte Lampshire (Mrs. Wayne)

MARDI GRAS CHAMPAGNE PUNCH

2 quarts pineapple juice
4 quarts lemon juice
3 quarts orange juice
5 pounds sugar
15 fifths champagne
7 or 8 quarts sparkling water

Mix pineapple, lemon and orange juices with sugar. Place in 5 (1/2-gallon) jars and pack in ice.

Proportions for serving in punch bowl
1/2 gallon of juice mix
3 fifths champagne
1½ quarts sparkling water

Float an ice ring in the center of the punch bowl.

Yield: 100 servings

Eva Dell Daigre (Mrs. John J.)

ROSÉ STRAWBERRY SPARKLE

40 ounces frozen strawberries, thawed (reserve 10 whole berries for garnish)
1 cup sugar
4 (fifths) rosé wine
4 (6-oz.) cans frozen lemonade, concentrated
2 (1-qt.) bottles carbonated water

Combine thawed strawberries, sugar and 1 bottle rosé wine. Let stand 1 hour, strain. Combine strained liquid and lemonade and remaining 3 bottles of wine. Pour over block of ice in punch bowl. Just before serving, add carbonated water. Float whole strawberries in punch.

Yield: 24 servings

Annette Myers (Mrs. Scott, Jr.)

SANGRIA PUNCH

3 scoops dry lemonade flavor drink mix
1 (48-oz.) can cranberry/apple drink
1 (2-quart) bottle lemon-lime soda
Fresh fruit to garnish, strawberries, lemon, lime, orange or apple slices

Dissolve lemonade in cranberry/apple drink in 2-quart container. Chill. Just before serving, pour over ice ring in punch bowl. Stir in lemon-lime soda. Add fresh fruit slices.

Yield: 3 quarts—24 punch cups

Donna Rylee (Mrs. James E.)

37

FRUIT PUNCH

3 (28-oz.) cans pineapple juice
3 (6-oz.) cans frozen orange
    juice plus water as directed
2 (6-oz.) frozen lemon juice
3 quarts gingerale

In a 2-gallon container mix pineapple juice, orange juice and lemon juice. Chill. When ready to serve add gingerale. *A recipe used in my family for weddings and teas.*

Yield: 40 cups

Maude "Muffet" Villien (Mrs. Fred)

PEPPERMINT PUNCH

2 tablespoons finely crushed
    peppermint candy
1 pint softened peppermint ice
    cream
4 cups milk
1 pint peppermint ice cream

In a large mixing bowl, mix candy, softened ice cream and milk on low speed until slushy. Pour into punch bowl or chilled glasses. Put scoops of ice cream into punch bowl or into each glass. Garnish with crushed candy or candy canes, if desired. *This is a very good punch for children. Very refreshing.*

Yield: 5½ cups

Connie Dutsch Roberts (Mrs. U.D.)

CORN BEER

1 pint fresh corn kernels
1 pint molasses
1 gallon water

Boil corn in a 6-quart pot until it is soft. Add molasses and water. Stir together well *and set it by the fire* (in a warm place). In twenty-four hours the beer will be good. When you spoon off the first beer, just add more molasses and water. The same corn will last for six months. *From the recipe files of my mother, Mrs. J.J. Fournet.*

Yield: 5 quarts beer

Paul Fournet

JELLO PUNCH

5 cups boiling water
5 cups sugar
4 (3-oz.) packages JELLO,
    any flavor
1 (6-oz.) can frozen lemonade
1 (6-oz.) can frozen orange juice
2 (46-oz.) cans pineapple juice
1 ounce almond extract
1 gallon water

Bring water to boil in 2$\frac{1}{2}$ gallon container. Add sugar and jello. Stir until dissolved. Cool slightly. Add frozen lemonade and orange juice, pineapple juice, almond and water. Pour punch into 3 (1-gallon) plastic jugs. Place in freezer. Stir or shake punch 2 times before it freezes. This can be prepared ahead. Before serving, thaw partially. Punch should have ice crystals.

Yield: 2 gallons

Bonnie Buratt

SPICED ICED TEA

18 cups water
9 tea bags
2-3 sticks cinnamon
1$\frac{1}{2}$ cups orange juice
1$\frac{1}{2}$ cups pineapple juice
3/4 cup lemon juice
2 tablespoons grated orange rind
1 tablespoon grated lemon rind
3 cups sugar mixed in 3 cups
    water
Dash of grated nutmeg
Dash of ground cloves
1/8 teaspoon ground cinnamon

Bring water to boil and add tea bags. Reduce heat, cover and steep 10 minutes. Remove from heat, add cinnamon sticks and steep 10 minutes longer. Blend in remaining ingredients, stirring carefully until sugar has dissolved. Remove tea bags after steeping another 5-10 minutes. Serve hot or cold. Can be made 1 week ahead of time and kept refrigerated. Reheat as needed.

Yield: 48 punch cups

Karen Clark Fleming (Mrs. Glenn J.)

MARGARITAS SOLIMAR

2 (6-oz.) cans frozen pink
    lemonade, concentrated
1 (6-oz.) can frozen limeade,
    concentrated
9 ounces Triple Sec
Tequila

Make the Margarita base in a pitcher with lemonade, limeade and Triple Sec. In a blender, mix equal portions of the base and tequila, usually about 5 ounces of each. Fill blender with crushed ice. Process a few seconds, then enjoy!

Yield: 4 servings

Russel and Cathy Butz

SESAME CHEESE WAFERS

1/2 cup butter, softened
2 cups shredded sharp cheese
1½ cups all-purpose flour
1/2 teaspoon salt
1/4 teaspoon red pepper
1/2 cup toasted sesame seeds

Allow shredded cheese to reach room temperature. In a mixing bowl combine cheese and softened butter. Cream well. Toast sesame seeds in heavy skillet, stirring constantly over low heat until golden brown, approximately 5 minutes. Cool. Combine cheese, butter, flour, salt and pepper. Work dough until mixture is thoroughly blended. Add sesame seeds. Pinch off small amounts of dough and make into small balls. Press down with a fork to make a wafer. Bake in a **preheated 375° oven 10 to 12 minutes.**

Yield: 4 dozen

Flora W. Rickey (Mrs. Horace, Sr.)

CHILI CHEESE ROLL

1/2 pound sharp cheese
1/2 pound mild cheese
3 ounces cream cheese
1/2 cup chopped nuts
3 cloves garlic, minced
Chili powder for rolling

Grate cheese and cream cheese and mix well with nuts and garlic. Form into long rolls and roll in chili powder. Cover with foil or wax paper and chill. Freezes well.

Yield: 4 rolls with about 60 slices

Sally Ross Moores (Mrs. John D.)

GARLIC CHEESE ROLL

1 pound Velveeta cheese
3 ounces cream cheese
1 cup chopped pecans
1 teaspoon garlic powder
Chili powder

Grate Velveeta and cream cheese together in large bowl. Add pecans and garlic powder. Blend well. Form into 2 long rolls. Sprinkle chili powder on wax paper and roll cheese rolls until well covered. Wrap each roll in aluminum foil. Chill. Freezes well. Serve on cheese board with crackers.

Yield: 20-30 slices

Evelyn Martin Chiasson (Mrs. Bob)

PARTY CHEESE BALL

1/2 cup chopped black walnuts
4 ounces blue or Roquefort
   cheese
8 ounces cream cheese
1/4 teaspoon garlic salt
1 tablespoon chopped pimiento
1 tablespoon chopped bell
   pepper

Spread walnuts in shallow pan and toast in **preheated 350° oven 6-8 minutes.** Blend cheese and cream cheese. Stir in garlic salt, pimiento and bell pepper. Chill until firm. Shape into ball. Roll in toasted walnuts. Chill until serving time. Serve with crackers.

Yield: 10-12 servings

Annette Myers (Mrs. Scott, Jr.)

ARTICHOKE DIP

2 (8½-oz.) cans artichoke hearts,
   drained well
1 cup mayonnaise
1 (0.6-oz.) packet Good Seasons
   Italian Dressing mix
1/8 teaspoon TABASCO,
   optional

Drain artichokes and chop coarsely in food processor. Add mayonnaise and Italian dressing mix. Blend until smooth. Add TABASCO if desired. Serve chilled with crackers. Dip can be prepared and refrigerated up to 2 weeks.

Yield: 1½ pints

Jill Verspoor Durkee (Mrs. Robert III)

ORANGE PECANS

1 teaspoon grated orange zest
1/4 cup orange juice
1/2 cup sugar
2 cups pecan halves

Combine rind, juice and sugar in saucepan. Bring to rapid boil and add pecans. Stir over high heat until all syrup is absorbed. Remove from heat and stir until pecans have separated. Turn out onto lightly buttered cookie sheet or aluminum foil to cool. Separate as necessary. Store in tin.

Great as appetizer, snack or dessert!

Yield: 2 cups

Karen Veillon McGlasson (Mrs. H. Edwin)

41

BRAUNSCHWEIGER BALL

1 pound Braunschweiger
    sausage (liver sausage)
2 packages green onion dip
    (Frito brand/generic)
2 tablespoons water
1 teaspoon sugar
8 ounce package cream cheese
Dash of Worcestershire sauce
Garlic powder
Dash TABASCO sauce
Parsley, snipped

In food processor combine sausage, dry green onion dip, water and sugar. Blend together.

Turn mixture out onto wax paper.

Form ball by wrapping wax paper around sausage mixture. Chill well. In another bowl blend cream cheese, Worcestershire sauce, a few sprinkles of garlic powder and TABASCO sauce. With spatula frost chilled Braunschweiger Ball with the cream cheese mixture. Cover with snipped parsley.

Chill. Serve with rounds of rye bread, Melba toast or crackers.

Yield: 30-50 servings

Doreen Claire McSpadden (Mrs. Joe R.)

SNAPPY CHEESE RING

5-6 slices bacon, cooked and
    crumbled
1 pound sharp cheese, grated
3/4 cup mayonnaise
1 medium onion, grated
2 green onion tops, chopped
1 clove garlic, minced
1/2 teaspoon TABASCO sauce
1 cup strawberry preserves
Lettuce leaves
Green grapes
Crackers

Combine bacon, grated cheese, mayonnaise, grated onion, onion tops, garlic, and TABASCO sauce. Chill in a 1-quart greased mold several hours. When firm turn out onto a platter of lettuce leaves. Garnish with grapes. Serve on a cracker topped with strawberry preserves.

Yield: 8-10 servings

Betty LeBlanc Ellison (Mrs. Guy, Jr.)

SMOKED OYSTER DIP

8 ounces cream cheese, softened
2 tablespoons mayonnaise
1 tablespoon Worcestershire sauce
1/8 teaspoon red pepper
5 drops TABASCO sauce
1 (3³/₄-oz.) can smoked oysters, finely chopped in oil

Mix softened cream cheese, mayonnaise, Worcestershire, red pepper and TABASCO together in small bowl. Blend in chopped oysters and oil from can. Serve in small bowl with crackers.

Yield: 1¹/₂ cups dip

Lillian Myers (Mrs. Scott, Sr.)

SMOKED OYSTER LOG

1 (8-oz.) package cream cheese
1 teaspoon Worcestershire sauce
1/2 teaspoon garlic powder
1/2 teaspoon onion powder
1/4 teaspoon salt
1/2 teaspoon black pepper
1/4 teaspoon red pepper
1 tablespoon lemon juice
1 flat tin small smoked oysters

Garnish:
Chopped fresh parsley
Pimiento slices
Black olive slices

In food processor or by hand, whip cream cheese and all seasonings until well-blended. On a sheet of aluminum foil, spread cheese mixture in 9 x 13-inch rectangle. Place foil on cookie sheet. Drain oil off smoked oysters. Chop oysters coarsely and sprinkle over cream cheese pressing in somewhat. Place tray in freezer for 10-15 minutes so cheese begins to firm again. Check once in a while. Remove from freezer and roll up jelly roll fashion beginning with short end and removing foil as log grows. Gently roll log in fresh chopped parsley and place on serving tray. Decorate with pimiento and olive slices, store in refrigerator until serving time. Arrange crackers on sides to serve.

Yield: 20 servings

Patricia Cashman Andrus (Mrs. Robert M.)

PINWHEELS

1 (8-oz.) package, 6-8 boiled ham slices
3 ounces cream cheese, room temperature
1 (15-oz.) can asparagus spears, drained

Spread each slice of ham with soft cream cheese. Place an asparagus spear across end of ham slice. Roll up firmly, jelly roll fashion. Chill well. Slice into 1/4-inch slices.

Yield: 50 servings

Elizabeth C. Montgomery (Mrs. Denbo)

OYSTER ARTICHOKE RAMEKIN

3 dozen raw oysters, with liquid
4 tablespoons butter
2 tablespoons flour
1 clove garlic, minced
1 1/2 tablespoons chopped green
  onion tops
6 cooked or canned artichoke
  hearts, drained and chopped
1/4 cup dry sherry
1/2 cup Italian seasoned bread
  crumbs
1/2 teaspoon salt
1/4 teaspoon red pepper
1/8 teaspoon each thyme and
  oregano
6 slices lemon

Check oysters for shells, drain and reserve liquid. Cut oysters in half if large. Make roux with butter and flour. Stir together in 3-quart saucepan over medium heat until color of peanut butter. Add oysters to roux. Stir over medium heat until edges curl. Add garlic, onion tops and artichokes. Slowly add 3/4-cup reserved oyster liquid and simmer 10 minutes. Add sherry, then bread crumbs until consistency of a chowder (not too dry). Add salt, pepper, thyme and oregano. Place mixture into individual ramekins with a slice of lemon on top. Bake in **preheated 400° oven 10-15 minutes** or until bubbly.

Yield: 6 servings

Betty Richard Butcher (Mrs. Thomas Sr.)

Microwave directions: Follow directions above. Place 6 ramekins on a 12-inch glass plate. Microwave on **HIGH (100%) 5-6 MINUTES.** *Jean K Durkee.*

CRABMEAT ARTICHOKE

2 (8 1/2-oz.) cans artichoke hearts,
  drained
2 (8-oz.) cans sliced water
  chestnuts, drained
2 (6-oz.) cans claw crabmeat,
  drained
1 (0.6-oz.) package Good
  Seasons Italian dressing mix
1/4 teaspoon salt
1/4 teaspoon TABASCO sauce
8 ounces cream cheese,
  softened
Paprika for sprinkling

Chop artichokes and water chestnuts fine. Add crabmeat, seasoning mix, salt and TABASCO sauce. Stir into softened cream cheese. Refrigerate several hours or overnight. Serve in dish with crackers or melba toast. Sprinkle top with paprika.

Yield: 1 quart

Yvonne Richard (Mrs. Leo)

CRAB STUFFED MUSHROOMS

30 medium mushrooms
8 ounces fresh lump white
   crabmeat
3/4 cup dry bread crumbs
1 bunch green onions, finely
   chopped
1 tablespoon chopped parsley,
   fresh or dried
1 teaspoon salt
1 teaspoon red pepper
1½ cups grated Monterey Jack
   cheese
1 cup butter, divided
2-3 tablespoons dry white wine

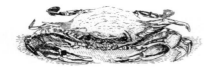

Pop stems off mushroom caps and store for future use. Clean caps by washing quickly under running water. Drain upside down on towels and pat dry. Run fingers through crab meat to remove shells. In a bowl mix crumbs, green onions, parsley, salt, red pepper and cheese with crabmeat. Toss lightly but well. Melt 3/4 cup butter and pour over stuffing. Toss well again. Melt remaining 1/4 cup butter in shallow baking pan or glass dish large enough to hold mushroom caps. Add wine to pan and swirl to mix with butter. Lightly pack each cap with stuffing, rounding off tops. Place in buttered pan and bake in a **preheated 350° oven** until caps look dark and juicy and tops are lightly browned, **about 15-20 minutes.** Serve about 3 per person with toast triangles on side. Divide buttery sauce in bottom of pan over toast points for added treats!

Yield: 10 servings

Patricia Cashman Andrus (Mrs. Robert)

GONE MUSHROOMS

1 (8-oz.) can water chestnuts
2 pounds fresh mushrooms,
   cleaned and stemmed
1/2 cup butter
1 cup seasoned bread crumbs
1 teaspoon chopped parsley
1/2 cup Parmesan cheese,
   grated
Salt & pepper to taste
1/4 teaspoon garlic powder
1/2 teaspoon onion powder

Place water chestnuts in food processor with steel blade and finely chop. Clean and stem mushrooms. Melt butter in frying pan. Add mushrooms and sauté 1 minute on medium heat. Remove mushrooms from pan with slotted spoon. To the remaining butter in skillet add bread crumbs, parsley, Parmesan cheese, chopped water chestnuts, salt, pepper, garlic and onion powder. Heat over low heat until it forms a paste. Remove from heat. Stuff mushrooms and serve immediately.

Yield: 12 servings

Karin Leigh David (Mrs. Irvin L.)

MINIATURE CRAWFISH BALLS

1 pound crawfish tails, ground
1/2 fresh cayenne pepper,
    ground or 1/2 teaspoon
    dried crushed red pepper
1/4 cup finely chopped parsley
1/4 cup finely chopped green
    onion tops
1/4 cup finely chopped bell
    pepper
2 teaspoons salt
2 teaspoons red pepper
1 egg, beaten
1/2 cup plain bread crumbs

In a bowl or food processor, mix ground craw-fish tails, cayenne pepper, parsley, onion tops, bell pepper, salt and red pepper. Add egg and bread crumbs and mix thoroughly. Form this mixture into miniature balls.

Hint: Coat hands with salad oil to make roll-ing of balls easier.

Place on lightly greased cookie sheet. Bake in a **preheated 375° oven 12-15 minutes.** *These can be frozen then baked as needed.*

Yield: 50 crawfish balls

Deanna Theriot Dupuis (Mrs. Burton)

CRAWFISH MOLD

1 pound crawfish tails, cooked
    and seasoned
Creole seasoning for sprinkling

1/2 cup water
1 envelope unflavored gelatin
1 (8-oz.) package cream cheese
1 cup whipping cream
1/3 cup mayonnaise
1 bunch green onion tops,
    chopped
2 ribs celery, chopped
1/2 bell pepper, chopped
10-12 jalapeño stuffed green
    olives, sliced
1 teaspoon salt
1 teaspoon white pepper
1/4 teaspoon Accent
1/4 teaspoon 1812 wine sauce

Cook crawfish according to package direc-tions. **Microwave directions:** Make slits on top of bag and place on microsafe plate. Microwave on **MEDIUM HIGH (70%) 5 MIN-UTES.** Season gently with Creole seasoning after removing crawfish from bag. Set aside.

Heat water and gelatin in small saucepan, or **microwave directions:** in a 2-cup glass measure on **HIGH (100%) 1 MINUTE,** until smooth. Using a large mixer bowl blend cream cheese and cream until smooth. Add gelatin mixture, mayonnaise, onion tops, celery, bell pepper, olives and cooked crawfish. Stir gently and add salt, white pepper, Accent and 1812 wine sauce. Pour into greased or Pam sprayed 5 or 6-cup mold. If a 4-cup crawfish mold is used, the remaining mixture can be molded in an oblong platter. This can be used as a base for the unmolded crawfish. Serve with a small knife and crackers.

Yield: 15-20 servings

Marilyn Abendroth Tarpy (Mrs. Robert)

46

TOLLEY'S SHRIMP DIP

24 ounces cream cheese,
   softened
1 medium onion, grated
2 cloves garlic, minced
Juice of 1 lemon
2 tablespoons Lea & Perrins
1 tablespoon minced parsley
1/4 teaspoon salt
1/8 teaspoon black pepper
1/8 teaspoon red pepper
Liquid from 1 (4$^1/_2$-oz.) can
   shrimp
3 (4$^1/_2$-oz.) cans cooked and
   peeled shrimp

Soften cream cheese in microwave on **HIGH (100%) 20 SECONDS.** Place in large mixing bowl along with onion, garlic, lemon juice, Lea & Perrins, parsley, salt, pepper, shrimp liquid. Beat until light and fluffy. Add whole shrimp to mixture. Blend on low speed until shrimp are coarsely chopped.

Serve hot or cold with crackers or chips.

Yield: 1 quart

Tolley Davis Odom (Mrs. James)

CRABMEAT BITES

1/4 pound butter
1 (5-oz.) jar Old English
   cheese spread
1/4 teaspoon garlic salt
1 (6-oz.) can crabmeat
6 English muffins, split in half

Soften butter and cheese. Mix together with garlic salt in a small bowl.

Rinse canned crabmeat with cold water and freshen with a squeeze of lemon before using. (This step is not necessary if using fresh crabmeat.) Add crabmeat to mixture and blend well. Spread crab mixture on 12 English muffin halves. Place in the freezer 10 or 15 minutes to make cutting easier; or, until you are ready to use them. Cut into eighths and place on greased cookie sheet. Bake in a **preheated 400° oven for 10 to 15 minutes** until they start to bubble. *Enjoy!*

Yield: 96 tiny pieces

Jean G. Leland (Mrs. Rodney C.)

Sue S. Sullivan (Mrs. Joseph D.) gives an alternate method for serving **Crabmeat Bites.** *Cut English muffins in quarters and sprinkle with seasoned salt. Follow baking directions above.*

HOG HEAD CHEESE

Water seasoned with
1/3 cup salt
1 tablespoon red pepper
1 tablespoon black pepper
20 pound cleaned hog head,
    with nose, eyes, mouth and
    ears removed. Ask butcher
    for neck
Small pork shoulder for
    additional meat
1 cup finely chopped onion tops
1 cup minced parsley
2 medium onions, finely chopped
1 teaspoon black pepper
1 teaspoon red pepper
Salt to taste

Fill large gumbo pot half full with hot water. Season with salt, red and black pepper. Add head, neck and shoulder. Boil until tender and meat falls off the bone. Remove from heat and remove bones. Reserve stock. Grind meat medium fine. Put meat in roasting pan. Add onion tops, parsley and onions. Skim grease or fat off stock. Add 1½ cups stock to mixture. Add black and red pepper and salt to taste. Simmer until onions are tender and stock has reduced. Place in a greased 9 x 13-inch dish. Refrigerate. Hog Head Cheese is ready to serve when it has jelled.

Yield: 24 servings

Philomene Credeur Hebert
Linda Hebert Hollier

CHICKEN GLACÉ

5 chicken breasts
Salt and pepper
4 (1/4-oz.) packages unflavored
    gelatin
3 ounces cold water
29 ounces chicken broth
1 medium onion, finely chopped
3 ribs celery, finely chopped
1 bell pepper, finely chopped
1 clove garlic, minced
1/4 cup chopped green onion
    tops
1/4 cup minced parsley
1 (4-oz.) jar diced pimiento,
    drained
2 teaspoons salt
1 teaspoon red pepper

Cook chicken in 4 cups of water well seasoned with salt and pepper.

Bone chicken and chop fine in food processor. Strain and reserve broth. Soften gelatin in cold water and some broth. Heat broth to a boil in 3-quart saucepan. Add onion, celery, bell pepper and garlic. Simmer 5 minutes. Add gelatin. Let cool. Add finely chopped chicken, onion tops, parsley, pimiento, salt and pepper. Fill 2 (1-quart) well-greased ring molds. Serve with crackers. *Better if made 2 days ahead. Tastes like hog head cheese.*

Yield: 2 (1-quart) molds

Elizabeth C. Montgomery (Mrs. Denbo)

Microwave shortcut: Place chicken breasts in 2-quart glass or ceramic casserole. Add 4 cups water seasoned with salt and pepper. Microwave on **HIGH (100%) 10 MINUTES** until chicken is cooked. Bone and chop chicken fine. Continue with directions above. *Jean K Durkee*

PAT'S SUMMER SAUSAGE

2 pounds lean ground beef
1 cup water
1 teaspoon freshly ground black
    pepper
1 tablespoon whole peppercorns
1 tablespoon garlic juice or
    powder
1 tablespoon liquid smoke
1 tablespoon onion powder
2 tablespoons Morton's Tender
    Quick curing salt
2 teaspoons TABASCO sauce
    or 1/2 teaspoon cayenne
    pepper

Day 1: Combine all ingredients mixing well with hands or in a food processor. Shape into 3 or 4 rolls and wrap each in plastic wrap. Refrigerate at least 24 hours.

Day 2: Remove wrap and place rolls on rack in shallow pan. Bake in **preheated 300° oven 60 minutes.** Turn sausage over every 15 minutes. Cool then wrap in plastic wrap and foil. Refrigerate or freeze. Cut into thin slices and arrange on plate with Horseradish Mayonnaise.*

Yield: 3 (2/3 lb.) rolls or 4 (1/2 lb.) rolls

*Horseradish Mayonnaise:
1/2 cup sour cream
1/2 cup mayonnaise
1 tablespoon prepared
    horseradish sauce
1 teaspoon Dijon mustard
1/4 teaspoon salt

Combine sour cream, mayonnaise, horseradish, mustard and salt. Place in airtight jar. Refrigerate until used.

Yield: 1 cup

Patricia Cashman Andrus (Mrs. Robert)

SALAMI MAXINE

5 pounds ground beef
1 tablespoon mustard seed
1 tablespoon garlic powder
2 teaspoon hickory salt
2 teaspoons sugar
2 tablespoons Morton's Tender
    Quick curing salt

Mix all ingredients thoroughly in a large bowl. Cover tightly and refrigerate for 3 days. Mix thoroughly once a day. After 3 days, shape meat into 5 small loaves 2½-inches thick. **Bake in preheated 200° oven 3½-4 hours.** Roll loaves several times during cooking.

Yield: 50 slices

Maxine Rinne (Mrs. Carl)

SUMMER SAUSAGE MARJORIE

4 pounds ground beef
2 cups cold water
3 tablespoons curing salt—
    Morton's Tender Quick
2 teaspoons garlic powder
2 teaspoons onion powder
2 teaspoons seasoned red
    pepper
2 teaspoons dry crushed red
    pepper
2 teaspoons coarse ground
    black pepper

Place meat in a large bowl with a fitted cover. Dissolve Tender Quick curing salt in 2 cups cold water. Add to meat. Mix in garlic powder, onion powder, red and black pepper. Dip in with both hands and blend thoroughly and completely. Cover bowl and refrigerate 24 hours. During the next 24 hours mix again 2 times to help the curing salt and spices flavor and produce a nice color in the meat. Divide meat into four equal portions and roll each into long-shaped rolls 2-3 inches in diameter. Wrap in aluminum foil. Punch holes in bottom of foil so grease will drain out. Place on roasting pan and rack. Bake in a **preheated 320° oven 1 hour.** Remove foil, **lower oven to 200° and continue to bake 3 hours.** Roll sausages on rack every half hour so they keep the rounded shape. After baking, cool and dry thoroughly with paper towels. Wrap in aluminum foil and refrigerate. Use within a week or two, or freeze.

Yield: 4 (1-pound) sausages

Marjorie B. Cloninger (Mrs. R.D.)

Microwave directions for cooking 1 pound of sausage at a time. Cut one sausage roll into 2 (1/2-lb.) rolls. Place the 2 rolls on a microsafe rack. Cover with wax paper. Microwave on **MEDIUM HIGH (70%) 15 MINUTES.** Roll sausages over on rack 2 or 3 times. *Jean K Durkee*

DRY ROASTED PECAN HALVES

2 cups pecan halves
Boiling water to cover pecans
1 tablespoon salt or Creole
    seasoning

Drop pecan halves in boiling water to cover. Boil 2 minutes. Drain. Spread pecans in shallow pan and roast uncovered in **preheated 275° oven 30 minutes.** Sprinkle with salt and/or Creole seasoning.

Yield: 2 cups

Anne R. Meleton (Mrs. Pierce)

MEAT PIE FILLING

1 pound lean ground pork
1½ pounds lean ground beef
   (grind pork and beef
   together)
2 tablespoons oil
2 teaspoons red pepper
2 teaspoons black pepper
1 teaspoon chili powder
1 teaspoon salt
2 tablespoons oil
1 tablespoon butter
2 medium onions, finely chopped
4 cloves garlic, minced
2 cups chopped green onion tops
1 cup chopped bell pepper
1/4 cup chopped parsley
2 tablespoons flour
1/4 cup chicken broth

In skillet cook pork and beef in oil until mealy. Drain off fat. Add red and black pepper, chili powder and salt. In a large Dutch oven heat oil and butter. Add onion, garlic, onion tops, bell pepper and parsley. Cook and stir over medium heat until vegetables are limp. Add meat mixture, flour and chicken broth. Cook over medium heat until meat is done, stirring often. Cover and let stand 1 hour to mellow. Chill in refrigerator before placing on pastry. Filling can be frozen in small packages. See page 52 for pastry recipe.

Yield: Filling for 80-100 pies

Barbara Hopkins Mangum (Mrs. James A.)

Microwave shortcut: Place 2½ pounds of beef and pork in plastic colander over glass bowl. Cover with wax paper. Microwave on **HIGH (100%) 9-10 MINUTES.** Stir meat twice during cooking. Season meat and set aside. Discard fat. Continue recipe above. *Jean K Durkee*

MARINATED SHRIMP

1½ pounds peeled shrimp
2 cups sliced onion
1/2 cup red hamburger relish
1/4 cup salad oil
3/4 cup white vinegar
2 tablespoons capers with liquid
1/2 teaspoon celery seed
3 dashes TABASCO sauce
1/8 teaspoon salt
1/4 teaspoon garlic powder

Boil shrimp in salted water about 15 minutes or until pink. Drain. Arrange shrimp in a 2-quart dish with sliced onion and red hamburger relish.

Mix together salad oil, vinegar, capers, celery seed, TABASCO sauce, salt and garlic. Pour over shrimp mixture. **Marinate 24 hours.** Serve with wooden picks as an appetizer.

Yield: 10 servings of 3-4 shrimp

Margret D. McCoy (Mrs. Medford)

Microwave directions: Place shrimp in a 2-quart glass dish. Sprinkle with Creole seasoning. Do not add water or salt. Cover. Microwave on **HIGH (100%) 5 to 7 MINUTES** or until shrimp are pink. Shake dish to rearrange shrimp after 3 minutes cooking time. Proceed with directions above. *Jean K Durkee*

51

CAJUN MEAT & OYSTER PIE

1/4 cup oil
1/4 cup flour
1 pound ground round beef
1/2 pound ground lean pork
1 large onion, minced
1 small bell pepper, minced
4 cloves garlic, minced
1/4 cup chopped green onion
    tops
1/4 cup chopped parsley
1 pint oysters, chopped and
    drained
2 teaspoons salt
1/2 teaspoon red pepper

Heat oil in skillet. Add flour. Stir until roux becomes dark brown. In another skillet brown beef and pork. Add onion, bell pepper, garlic, onion tops and parsley. Sauté until vegetables are wilted. Add chopped oysters, salt and pepper to taste. Add roux and simmer on low heat 20 minutes, stirring occasionally. Set aside and cool. See recipe below.

Prepare pastry. Place 1 tablespoon meat mixture on 36 (3-inch) pastry rounds. Fold over and crimp edges together with fork. Bake in **preheated 375° oven 25 minutes** until golden brown. For a large meat pie, place mixture in 9-inch pastry. Bake in **preheated 375° oven 50 minutes.**

Yield: 36 individual or 1 large pie

Yvonne Anderson Champagne
(Mrs. George J., Jr.)

PASTRY FOR MEAT PIES

3 cups biscuit mix
1/2 teaspoon red pepper
1/8 teaspoon salt
3 tablespoons shortening
8-9 tablespoons iced water

Stir biscuit mix, red pepper and salt together with fork. Cut in shortening with pastry blender or 2 knives. Sprinkle water until dough can be worked into ball. Divide in half. Roll out very thin, cut into 3-inch rounds. Place 1 tablespoon meat filling in center. Fold in half. Crimp open edges together with fork tines. Bake on ungreased sheet in **preheated 375° oven 20-25 minutes** or until golden.

Yield: 3 dozen

Yvonne Anderson Champagne
(Mrs. George, Jr.)

CHICKEN TARTS

1 (3-lb.) chicken, cut into pieces
1¹/₂ cups water
1/2 teaspoon vinegar
1/2 teaspoon sugar
1 teaspoon salt
2 teaspoons red pepper
2 teaspoons black pepper
1/2 cup margarine
1 cup chopped onion tops
1 cup finely chopped onion
1/2 cup chopped bell pepper
3 ribs celery, chopped
2 tablespoons chopped parsley
1 clove garlic, minced
3 tablespoons flour

Place chicken, water, vinegar and sugar in heavy covered pot. Cook until tender. Cool, bone and chop chicken fine. Return to broth in pot. Add salt, red and black pepper. Simmer covered 40 minutes.

Heat margarine in large heavy pot. Add onion tops, onion, bell pepper, celery, parsley, garlic. Stir constantly. Cook until vegetables are tender. Add 1/2 cup chicken broth. Cover. Simmer 40 minutes. Stir occasionally. Add chicken. Simmer 20 minutes. Mix flour with small amount of broth to make a paste. Add to chicken mixture to thicken. Remove from heat. Let stand covered 1 hour. Chill overnight.

Yield: filling for 100 tarts

Edna J. Hopkins (Mrs. Thomas B.)

Microwave directions: Place chicken, water, vinegar and sugar in 3-quart ceramic casserole. Cover. Microwave on **HIGH (100%) 20 MINUTES.** Cool, bone and chop chicken fine. Return to broth, season. Cover. Microwave on **HIGH (100%) 10 MINUTES.** Melt margarine in 8-cup glass measure and add vegetables. Microwave on **HIGH (100%) 6 MINUTES.** Add chicken and 2 tablespoons broth. Microwave on **HIGH (100%) 5 MINUTES.** Add flour to thicken. Chill overnight. *Jean K Durkee*

PASTRY FOR TARTS

2 cups all-purpose flour
2 teaspoons salt
3/4 cup shortening
1 egg
1/2 cup cold water
Paprika

Sift flour and salt together twice. Cut in shortening until mealy. Shake egg and cold water in jar. Add to mealy mixture. Roll out on floured surface and cut with biscuit cutter or hamburger patty mold. Place small amount of meat mixture to one side, fold over; cleat together with fork prongs. Place on oiled cookie sheet. Brush over top with pastry brush dipped in oil. Pierce top crust only. Sprinkle top with paprika. Bake in **preheated 375° oven 10 minutes** until brown.

Yield: Pastry for 50 tarts

Edna J. Hopkins (Mrs. Thomas B.)

53

the
1910s

A t the beginning of Lafayette's first century, the railroad had just crossed the Atchafalaya and penetrated the prairies that lay just west of the town. In its pristine state, the prairie was a wildlife paradise with lush grasslands, marshes, and ponds where millions of ducks, geese, rails, cranes, and shorebirds came to winter. The sandhill crane, whooping crane, and prairie chickens had nested in the prairies but were extirpated with the coming of civilization. Deer became scarce because everyone carried a gun and a few shells to add wild meat to the diet. Rangy cattle that roamed the unfenced prairie and backyard hogs provided most of the meat for the country boucheries and the town butcher shops.

On the national scene William Howard Taft was one of two presidents in the 1910s. However, it was Woodrow Wilson who led us through the years of World War I. When our country entered the war a mass meeting was held in the Jefferson Theater. There, all patriotic speeches were delivered in French and at the conclusion both The Star Spangled Banner and La Marseillaise were sung with fervor.

In the next twenty years a string of rice mill towns followed the railroad line across the state. Ducks and geese still migrated in great numbers to the expanding rice fields, where locals and city folk made creeps at night and tried to kill the most with the least shots. In late summer, young mottled ducks that gathered in large flocks were a favorite target. On the burned and grazed cattle range, the papabotte (upland plover), dormeur (dowitchers), and other shorebirds were hunted on horseback and buggy for the market and food.

It was not until the advent of the gas engine and the automobile in the 1920s and 1930s that sport hunting became popular. Yankee and local investors, hoping to make a killing in agriculture or muskrats, bought up huge tracts of marsh, later organized hunting clubs to make the best of a bad deal—until oil came along.

Roads were bad and river boats slow so saltwater fish, crabs, shrimp, and oysters rarely got to Lafayette. Before intensive agriculture, the Vermilion River was clearer, and provided catfish, sac á lait (crappie), bream, and largemouth bass for the frying pan, garfish for fish balls, and gaspergou (freshwater drum) for the pot of court bouillon. Crawfish were caught when a rainy season made the swamps and ponds the ideal environment for a population explosion of crawfish. The day of levees and water control, crawfish traps, outboard motors, and a world market was in the far future.

Jacob M. Valentine, Jr.
Biologist
U.S. Fish & Wildlife Service, retired

Fish

Shellfish

FRIED CATFISH

1½—2 pounds farm raised
    catfish fillets
Salt, pepper, garlic powder and
    TABASCO sauce
Prepared yellow mustard
1 cup yellow cornmeal, lightly
    seasoned with salt and
    pepper
3 tablespoons flour
Cooking oil for deep frying

Season fillets with salt, pepper, garlic powder and TABASCO sauce. Coat fillets generously with mustard, but don't overdo it. Cut fillets into bite-size pieces. Dredge pieces in seasoned cornmeal mixed with flour. Deep fry in about 2 inches of cooking oil in heavy skillet or Dutch oven at 350° until golden brown and crisp. Serve at once with tartar sauce.

Yield: 4-6 servings

Keith E. Courrégé

BROILED POND CATFISH FILLETS

6 catfish fillets
Lemon pepper, garlic powder,
    red and black pepper
1/3 cup butter or margarine
1 tablespoon minced parsley
1/3 cup chopped green onions
1/2 pound fresh shrimp,
    chopped, seasoned with salt
    and pepper
1 cup crabmeat
1½ cups diced bread crumbs
2-3 tablespoons chicken broth
1 tablespoon dry white wine
Melted butter and lemon juice

Pass the Sauce Please:
1/2 cup butter, melted
Juice of one lemon
1 tablespoon finely chopped
    parsley
1/8 teaspoon garlic powder

Rinse and dry fillets. Season with lemon pepper, garlic powder, red and black pepper. Set aside. Melt butter in saucepan. Add parsley and green onions. Sauté 2-3 minutes. Add seasoned shrimp, cook until pink. Add crabmeat and bread crumbs. Add chicken broth and wine to moisten mixture. Place fillets in pan lined with foil. Broil in **preheated broiler 3 minutes.** Turn fillets over. Baste with butter and lemon juice. Spread dressing over each fillet and **broil 5 minutes longer.**

Mix butter, lemon juice, parsley and garlic powder together. Warm and serve sauce with broiled catfish.

Yield: 6 servings

Georgina Bertrand Baquet (Mrs. George)

FRESH FLOUNDER WITH CRAB STUFFING

4 whole large flounder, 1-pound each, heads removed
Salt, black and red pepper for sprinkling
1/2 cup butter
1 bunch green onions, thinly sliced
1 pound fresh white lump crabmeat
1/2 cup torn or coarsley chopped parsley
Juice of 1/2 lemon
2 tablespoons melted butter
8 lemon slices

Wash and pat dry each flounder. Using a sharp knife, make a slit along backbone from head opening almost to tail on dark, thick side of flounder. Lift flesh off bone with fingers to form a pocket. Sprinkle inside of pockets and both sides of fish with salt, red pepper and black pepper. Arrange flounder, pocket side up, on well buttered baking sheets with rims.

Melt butter in heavy sauté pan over medium heat. Sauté green onions 2 minutes. Pick over crabmeat for shells. Lightly toss crabmeat and parsley with onions. Remove from heat. Salt very lightly. Sprinkle red and black pepper to taste.

Gently place crab mixture equally inside 4 flounder pockets. Sprinkle lemon juice over each fish. Baste fish with melted butter. Arrange lemon slices on top of crab in pockets.

Bake in **preheated 350° oven 20 minutes.**

Yield: 4-6 servings

Patricia Cashman Andrus (Mrs. Robert)

BAKED FLOUNDER WITH GRAPES

1 1/2 pounds fillet of flounder
2 tablespoons butter
1/4 cup finely chopped green onion tops and bulbs
1 teaspoon salt
1/2 teaspoon pepper
1/2 cup dry white wine
3 tablespoons butter
3 tablespoons flour
3/4 cup heavy cream
1 cup green grapes

Cut fish into 6 serving-size portions. Place butter in a 7 x 11-inch baking dish; melt in a 350° oven until bottom of dish is coated. Sprinkle green onions in dish. Place fish in one layer over green onions. Season with salt and pepper. Pour wine over fish. **Bake in preheated 350° oven 20 minutes.** After fish is cooked, drain liquid. Measure 1/4 cup and reserve for sauce. To make the sauce, melt butter in a saucepan. Add flour to make a paste. Stir in fish/wine stock. Add cream and grapes. Place over low heat until thickened, stirring constantly. Pour sauce over hot fish on serving platter.

Yield: 4-6 servings

Sue B. Alves

STUFFED FLOUNDER FILLET

1 pound flounder fillets, fresh
  or frozen
Salt and red pepper
2 tablespoons butter
1 tablespoon flour
1/2 cup evaporated milk
1 small onion, finely chopped
2 tablespoons chopped celery
2 tablespoons butter
1/8 teaspoon garlic powder
1/8 teaspoon oregano
1 teaspoon salt
1/4 teaspoon red pepper
1/2 cup cooked rice
1/3 cup cracker meal
1 egg, well beaten
1 cup white crabmeat
1 hard cooked egg, minced
1 tablespoon melted butter
1 tablespoon lemon juice

Dry fish on paper towels. Season well with salt and pepper.

Refrigerate.

Melt butter in small saucepan. Add flour, blend well. Add milk, cook and stir until white sauce thickens. Set aside. Sauté onion and celery and butter until tender in another saucepan. Add garlic powder, oregano, salt and pepper. In a bowl combine cooked rice, cracker meal, white sauce, onion mixture, beaten egg, crabmeat and cooked egg. Place fish on greased foil on cookie sheet. Spread stuffing on fish fillets. Fold half of fillet over stuffing. Brush with melted butter and lemon juice. Fold foil over and seal. Bake in **preheated 350° oven 35 minutes.** Uncover last 10 minutes. Garnish with lemon wedges.

Yield: 2 servings

Myrtle Landry Simms' FUN COOKING GUIDE

GASPERGOU BOUILLABAISSE

7 or 8 pound gou fish, cut into
  7 or 8 pieces
Salt, cayenne pepper
3 tablespoons vegetable oil
1 large onion, sliced
1 large bell pepper, sliced
1/2 cup chopped green onion
  tops
1/2 cup chopped parsley
2 (16-oz.) cans tomato sauce
1 (6-oz.) can tomato paste
1 (10-oz.) can Ro-tel tomatoes
  and green chilies, blended
Salt and pepper

Season fish with salt and cayenne pepper. Place oil in large Dutch oven. Layer half the seasoned fish, onion, bell pepper, onion tops and parsley and 1 can tomato sauce. Add all tomato paste and Ro-tel tomatoes. Repeat layers ending with tomato sauce. Cover. Cook on low heat 2 hours. Stir by shaking pot— never a spoon. Season. *Gaspergou is found mostly in bayou water in south Louisiana. Fishermen frequently find this type of fish in their nets.*

Yield: 8 servings

Verlie T. Bourdreaux (Mrs. Walter)

POACHED RED SNAPPER
Bellevue Plantation

1 (4-5 lb.) or 2 (2-2¹/₂ lb.) whole
   red snapper or red fish,
   cleaned
Cheesecloth to wrap fish
1¹/₂ quarts water
2 lemons, sliced
1 medium onion, coarsely
   chopped
5 sprigs parsley
1 bay leaf
1 cup white wine
1 tablespoon salt
2 teaspoons red pepper
2 teaspoons whole cloves
1/8 teaspoon thyme

In a large pot or fish poacher bring water and all seasonings to boil. Wrap cleaned fish in cheesecloth and place in seasoned water. Cover with lid. Reduce heat and simmer 20 minutes. Fish will be cooked when it flakes easily with a fork. Lift fish from pot, remove cheesecloth and serve with Garlic & Mustard Sauce.*

*Garlic & Mustard Sauce:
1 clove garlic, minced
1 cup mayonnaise
1 tablespoon lemon juice
1 teaspoon prepared yellow
   mustard
1 teaspoon creole mustard
1/2 teaspoon mixed dried herbs

Blend garlic, mayonnaise, lemon juice and mustard in food processor or blender. Pour in serving dish and sprinkle with herbs. Chill before serving.

Yield: 4 servings

Tolley C. Davis (Mrs. F.H., Sr.)

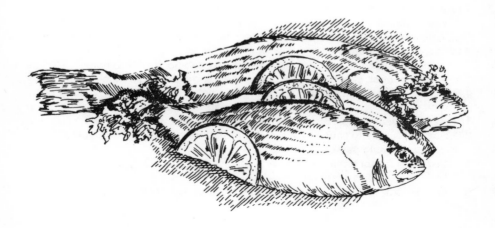

DUCK KEY BROILED FISH

3 pounds fish fillets
10 tablespoons teriyaki sauce
2 tablespoons Worcestershire
sauce
Juice from 1/2 lemon
3 green onions, chopped
5 cloves garlic, chopped
3/4 pound butter, divided
Tony Chachere's Creole
Seasoning for sprinkling

Marinate fish in plastic bag with teriyaki sauce, Worcestershire sauce and lemon juice. Refrigerate overnight while turning occasionally to insure complete marination. In a skillet sauté green onions and garlic in 1/4 cup butter. Add remaining butter, cover and simmer 20 minutes.

Season fish sparingly on both sides with Tony Chachere's Creole Seasoning. Dip fish fillets in garlic-butter mixture and place on hot BBQ grill or hot black iron skillet for 3 minutes. Turn fillets over and cook other side for 1-2 minutes longer. *This recipe was created in the Florida Keys by Louisiana Cajuns.*

Yield: 6 servings

Ted M. Breaux

BAKED RED SNAPPER

1/2 cup vegetable oil
3 medium onions, chopped
3 ribs celery, chopped
1 (6-oz.) can tomato paste
1 (16-oz.) can whole tomatoes,
chopped with liquid
2 medium bell peppers, chopped
6 cloves garlic, minced
Salt to taste
Pepper to taste
Red pepper to taste
1 tablespoon sugar
3 medium whole red snapper
3 tablespoons Worcestershire
sauce
1 sliced lemon and juice
1/2 cup chopped parsley

Sauté onion and celery in oil. Add tomato paste, tomatoes, bell pepper, garlic, salt, pepper, red pepper and sugar. If sauce is too thick add water a little at a time. Cover and simmer 1½ hours, stirring occasionally. Rinse and dry fish. Salt and pepper inside and out. Pour cooled tomato mixture over fish in a large baking dish. Add Worcestershire, lemon juice, lemon slices and parsley. Bake in **preheated 350° oven 20-30 minutes** or until fish flakes easily with a fork. *This is just one of the many ways my mother, who is of French descent, cooked fresh fish my dad would catch. Fishing and hunting were his hobbies and he fished in the basin at Henderson for over 60 years.*

Yield: 4-6 servings

Patricia Shelton Cella (Mrs. Eugene)

61

STUFFED RED SNAPPER

2 (1½-lb.) whole red snapper
Salt and pepper

*Stuffing:
1/2 pound raw or canned shrimp
1 (7-oz.) can crabmeat
2-3 slices stale bread
1/4 cup butter
1/2 bunch green onion tops,
   chopped

Sauce:
1/2 cup butter
2 onions, chopped
2 ribs celery, chopped
1½ bunches green onion tops,
   chopped
2 cloves garlic, chopped
2 teaspoons salt
1/2 teaspoon pepper
1 (10-oz.) can Ro-tel tomatoes
   and chilies, pureed
1 (6-oz.) can tomato paste
2 teaspoons dry mustard
1½ teaspoons prepared basic
   roux

Clean, rinse and dry fish. Sprinkle inside and out with salt and pepper. Refrigerate.

If using raw shrimp, cook in shells in well-seasoned water until shrimp are pink. Peel, chop and mix with crabmeat in a bowl. Dice bread and soak in water. Squeeze. Add to crab/shrimp mixture. Sauté onion tops in butter in small saucepan. Add to crab/shrimp mixture. Set aside in refrigerator.

Melt butter in Dutch oven. Add onion, celery, onion tops and garlic. Sauté until onions are soft. Add salt, pepper, tomatoes, tomato paste, mustard and roux. Cover. Simmer sauce 4 hours, stirring occasionally. Add water if sauce is too thick. Place Stuffing* in fish. Pour red sauce over fish. Bake in **pre-heated 350° oven 1 hour.** Spoon baste every 15 minutes until done.

Yield: 8 servings

Andrew W. Keller

Microwave shortcut: To make sauce, melt butter in microwave in an 8-cup glass measure on **HIGH (100%) 1 MINUTE.** Add onion, celery, onion tops and garlic. Micro-wave on **HIGH (100%) 10 MINUTES.** Add salt, pepper, tomatoes, tomato paste, mustard and prepared roux. Cover with wax paper. Microwave on **HIGH (100%) 24 MINUTES,** stirring at 6 minute intervals. Add water if sauce is too thick. Pour sauce over stuffed fish and follow recipe above. *Jean K Durkee*

SNAPPER PARMESAN

1 pound fillet of red snapper,
    sea bass (grouper) or red fish
1 (8-oz.) bottle Creamy Italian
    dressing
1/4 cup margarine
1/2 medium onion, chopped
2 tablespoons lemon juice
Salt and pepper
Parmesan cheese, grated
Italian seasoned bread crumbs
Paprika

Cut fish into serving pieces. Coat fish with Creamy Italian dressing. Place fish on a baking dish or pan. In a small saucepan, sauté onion in margarine. Add lemon juice and pour mixture over fish. Add salt and pepper to taste. Sprinkle liberally with Parmesan cheese, bread crumbs and paprika. Bake in **preheated 425° oven 16-18 minutes** or until fish flakes easily with a fork.

Yield: 2 servings

Janie Boyd Tew (Mrs. Billy)

Microwave Directions: Place fish fillets coated with Creamy Italian dressing in a glass baking dish. Melt margarine in a 2-cup glass measure. Add onions. Microwave on **HIGH (100%) 3 MINUTES.** Add lemon juice and pour mixture over fish. Sprinkle with pepper (salt after cooking), Parmesan, bread crumbs and paprika. Cover with wax paper. Microwave on **HIGH (100%) 4-6 MINUTES.** Rearrange fish in the dish once during cooking time. *Jean K Durkee*

TUNA FISH PIE

3 tablespoons butter
3 tablespoons chopped onion
1 cup chopped bell pepper
3 tablespoons all-purpose flour
1²/₃ cups milk
1/2 teaspoon salt
1 tablespoon lemon juice
1 (10-oz.) can tuna, drained

*Cheese Rolls:
1¹/₂ cups all-purpose flour
3 teaspoons baking powder
1/2 teaspoon salt
1/8 teaspoon pepper
2 tablespoons shortening
1/2 cup milk
3/4 cup grated cheddar cheese
2 ounce jar sliced pimiento,
    drained and chopped

Melt butter in a medium saucepan. Add onion and pepper. Cook over low heat until soft. Add flour. Stir until well-blended. Add milk slowly, stirring constantly until thick and smooth. Add salt, lemon juice and tuna. Pour into buttered 7 x 11-inch baking dish. Cover with Cheese Rolls* and bake in **preheated 400° oven 12-15 minutes** or until brown.

Sift flour, baking powder, salt and pepper into a mixing bowl. Add shortening and mix with a fork. Add milk to make soft dough. Toss lightly on floured board until smooth. Roll out into a rectangle 8 x 12 inches. Sprinkle with cheese and pimiento and roll as jelly roll. Slice 1 inch thick and lay on tuna fish mixture with ring side up. Follow baking directions above. *From the recipe files of my mother, Mrs. Tom Ball.*

12 servings

Katherine Ball Broussard (Mrs. Fernand S.)

CRABMEAT AU GRATIN I

4 tablespoons butter
4 tablespoons flour
2 cups milk
2 ounces chopped pimiento,
    drained
1/4 cup chopped onion tops
1 tablespoon chopped parsley
1/2 teaspoon garlic powder
1/2 teaspoon Accent
1/2 teaspoon Worcestershire
    sauce
1 teaspoon salt
1/4 teaspoon white pepper
1 bell pepper, chopped
1 onion, chopped
2 ribs celery, chopped
2 tablespoons butter
1 pound white lump crabmeat
1 cup grated cheddar cheese
Butter slices for top

Melt butter in medium saucepan. Stir in flour to blend. Add milk. Cook white sauce over medium heat until thick. Add pimiento, onion tops, parsley, garlic powder, Accent, Worcestershire, salt and pepper. Sauté bell pepper, onion and celery in 2 tablespoons butter in skillet. Add to white sauce. Drain crabmeat on paper towels. Place crabmeat in buttered 7 x 11-inch baking dish. Pour sauce over crabmeat. Sprinkle with grated cheese. Dot top with butter. Bake in **preheated 350° oven 30 minutes.**

Yield: 6-8 servings

Beulah D. Stephan (Mrs. John E.)

CRABMEAT AU GRATIN II

1/2 cup margarine
1/2 onion, diced
2 ribs celery, diced
3 tablespoons diced bell pepper
2 tablespoons flour
1 cup milk
3 tablespoons chopped green
    onion tops
3 tablespoons minced parsley
1 teaspoon salt
1/4 teaspoon red pepper
1/2 teaspoon garlic powder
1 cup grated jalapeño cheese
1 pound white crabmeat
1 cup bread crumbs
Bread crumbs and grated cheese

Melt margarine in saucepan. Add onion, celery and bell pepper. Sauté until vegetables are tender. Add flour and milk. Mix well. Cook over medium heat, stirring constantly until thick. Add onion tops, parsley, salt, pepper, garlic powder and grated jalapeño cheese. Mix well. Add crabmeat. Stir in bread crumbs until thick. Place in buttered 2-quart casserole. Top with additional bread crumbs and grated cheese. Bake in **preheated 350° oven 15-20 minutes,** until bubbly hot.

Yield: 4-6 servings

Anita G. Guidry (Mrs. Owen A.)

CRABMEAT OLIVIER

2 tablespoons butter, melted
2 tablespoons all-purpose flour
1 cup milk
2 ounces grated sharp cheddar
    cheese
1½ teaspoons salt
1/4 teaspoon Worcestershire
    sauce
1/4 teaspoon red pepper
1/8 teaspoon white pepper
1 dash TABASCO sauce
Grated rind of 1/2 lemon
1 small onion, grated
1 pound lump crabmeat
4 stuffed olives, chopped
1 (4-oz.) can sliced mushrooms,
    drained
1/4 cup chopped green onion
    tops
4 sprigs parsley, chopped
1/4 cup seasoned bread crumbs

Melt butter in saucepan over low heat. Add flour to make a paste. Slowly add milk. Stir until smooth. Cook over medium heat until mixture bubbles and thickens. Add grated cheese to hot white sauce. Season with salt, Worcestershire sauce, red pepper, white pepper, TABASCO, lemon rind and onion. Pour sauce over crabmeat. Mix carefully so lumps will not break. Add olives, mushrooms, onion tops and parsley. Place in 6 individual ramekins. Sprinkle bread crumbs on top. Bake in **preheated 350° oven 15 minutes** or until bubbly. Serve at once.

Yield: 6 servings

Virginia Buchanan Olivier (Mrs. Dan)

CRABMEAT FELIX

5 tablespoons butter
3 tablespoons flour
1½ cups milk
1/4 teaspoon white pepper
1 pound white lump crabmeat
1 (4-oz.) jar diced pimiento,
    drained
1/4 cup chopped green onion
    tops
1 tablespoon chopped bell
    pepper
1 teaspoon salt
1 teaspoon onion powder
1/2 teaspoon red pepper
Seasoned bread crumbs
Paprika

Melt butter in a small saucepan. Add flour stirring to blend. Add milk and white pepper. Cook over medium heat until white sauce is thick. In a mixing bowl, combine crabmeat, pimiento, onion tops, bell pepper, salt, onion powder and red pepper. Add white sauce to crab mixture. Pour into a 1½-quart baking dish. Sprinkle top with bread crumbs and paprika. Bake in **preheated 350° oven 25 minutes.**

Yield: 6 servings

Billie Ruth Demanade (Mrs. Felix)

CRAB & SHRIMP EARLEEN

4 tablespoons butter
4 tablespoons all-purpose flour
1 cup milk
1 egg yolk, beaten
1¹/₂ teaspoons salt
1/8 teaspoon white pepper
1/4 pound Swiss cheese, grated
4 tablespoons butter
1/2 cup chopped green onion
　　tops
1/2 cup chopped celery
1/2 cup chopped red bell pepper
　　(green will do)
1/2 pound small fresh
　　mushrooms
1 pound peeled raw shrimp
1 teaspoon lemon juice
1 pound white crabmeat
1/4 cup sherry

In a medium saucepan make a cream sauce by melting 4 tablespoons butter and adding flour. Whisk to blend. Add milk and stir until thickened. Whisk in egg yolk, salt and pepper. Add cheese. Stir slowly to blend. In a large pot melt 4 tablespoons butter. Add onion tops, celery, bell pepper, mushrooms and shrimp. Sauté until vegetables are limp and shrimp is pink. Add cream sauce and lemon juice. Simmer 3 minutes. Gently stir in crabmeat and sherry. Heat thoroughly. Serve in pastry shells.

Yield: 6 servings

Earleen Guice (Mrs. Derrick)

SEAFOOD STUFFED EGGPLANT

2 medium eggplant
1 medium onion, chopped
1/4 cup chopped fresh parsley
1/4 cup chopped bell pepper
2 cloves garlic, minced
3 tablespoons bacon fat
4 slices bread
1 cup cooked, well-seasoned
　　shrimp, peeled
1 (3.6-oz.) can smoked oysters,
　　drained
1 (6¹/₂-oz.) can crabmeat,
　　drained
1/2 teaspoon salt
1/4 teaspoon red pepper
2 tablespoons seasoned bread
　　crumbs
2 tablespoons grated Parmesan
　　cheese

Cut eggplant in half lengthwise. Carefully scoop out pulp, leaving shells intact. Chop pulp. Cook pulp in small amount of boiling salted water until tender. Drain well. In a large skillet sauté onion, parsley, bell pepper and garlic in bacon fat until tender. Remove from heat. Add eggplant, mix well. Soak bread in water; squeeze out excess. Add bread to eggplant mixture along with shrimp, oysters, crabmeat, salt and pepper. Spoon stuffing into eggplant shells. Combine bread crumbs and cheese. Sprinkle over top. Place eggplant in shallow pan with 1/4-inch hot water. Bake in **preheated 350° oven 30 minutes.**

Yield: 4 servings

Patricia Cashman Andrus (Mrs. Robert)

STUFFED CRABS à la FREDA

1 cup (1/2 pound) butter
1 cup chopped onions
1 cup chopped celery
1 cup chopped bell pepper
1 cup fresh bread crumbs,
    Pepperidge Farm white
    bread suggested
1 cup Half & Half cream
1/3 cup chopped green onion
    tops
1/3 cup chopped parsley
Salt, black and red pepper to taste
2 pounds lump crabmeat
Bread crumbs for sprinkling
Butter for top

Melt butter in large Dutch oven. Add onions, celery, bell pepper. Sauté 15 minutes on low heat. Add bread crumbs and cream. Continue to cook 5 minutes more. Add onion tops, parsley, salt, black and red pepper to taste. Mix well. Gently fold in lump crabmeat. Heat thoroughly, 5-10 minutes. Spoon mixture into 12 crab shells. Top with bread crumbs. Dot top with butter. Place shells on cookie sheet. Bake in **preheated 350° oven 10-15 minutes.** *Always a favorite dish with family and friends of Dr. & Mrs. Edgar Breaux.*

Yield: 12 servings

Alfreda Williams Dugas

Microwave warm-up: HIGH (100%) **1 MINUTE** per 1 individual crab shell.
Jean K Durkee

COASTAL CRAB CHOPS

6 tablespoons butter
2 medium onions, minced
1 small bell pepper, chopped
2 pounds crabmeat
3 eggs, beaten
1/2 cup chopped green onion
    tops
1/2 cup chopped parsley
1 teaspoon lemon juice
1 teaspoon Worcestershire
    sauce
1 teaspoon salt
1 teaspoon red pepper
1/2 teaspoon black pepper
12 boiled crab claws

White Sauce:
4 tablespoons butter
1/4 cup flour
4 tablespoons heavy cream
1/2 cup seasoned bread crumbs

Melt butter in heavy skillet. Add onion and bell pepper. Sauté until onion is soft. Add crabmeat, eggs, onion tops, parsley, lemon juice, Worcestershire, salt, red and black pepper. Cook 10 minutes over medium heat. Make a thick white sauce in a small saucepan. Melt butter, stir in flour to blend. Add cream. Cook until thick. Pour into crab mixture. Add more cream if mixture is dry. Refrigerate 2 hours to firm. Shape crab mixture into a *chop*. Insert boiled crab claw into chop. Pat dry bread crumbs on both sides, fry in deep fat until golden brown. These chops can also be baked on a cookie sheet in **preheated 350° oven 20 minutes.**

Yield: 6-8 servings

Alida "Sis" Talley (Mrs. Bill)

CRAB IN RAMEKINS

1/2 cup butter
1/3 cup chopped onion
1/3 cup chopped celery
1 tablespoon chopped green
    bell pepper
2 tablespoons chopped parsley
1 (10¾-oz.) can cream of
    mushroom soup
1/4 cup milk
1½ cups Pepperidge Farm
    stuffing mix
1 teaspoon dry mustard
1/4 teaspoon salt
1/4 teaspoon cayenne pepper
1 pound white crabmeat
Seasoned bread crumbs for
    sprinkling

In a large skillet melt butter. Add onion, celery, bell pepper and parsley. Sauté until tender. Remove from heat. Add mushroom soup, milk, stuffing mix, mustard, salt and pepper. Stir until well blended. Fold crabmeat gently into mixture. Spoon into 8 ceramic crab-shaped ramekins.

Sprinkle bread crumbs on top. Bake in **pre-heated 350° oven 25 minutes.**

Yield: 8 servings

Bettye Welch (Mrs. W. T.)

Microwave directions: Melt butter or margarine in an 8-cup glass measure. Add onion, celery, bell pepper and parsley. Microwave on **HIGH (100%) 3 MINUTES.** Add remaining ingredients. Continue to microwave on **HIGH (100%) 1-2 MINUTES** until heated through. Spoon crabmeat mixture into 8 ramekins. Sprinkle bread crumbs on top. Place 4 ramekins in microwave at a time. Microwave on **HIGH (100%) 4 MINUTES.** Repeat with remaining 4 ramekins. *Jean K Durkee*

C'EST BON CRABE

2 eggs beaten
1/2 cup mayonnaise
1 tablespoon prepared mustard
1 tablespoon Worcestershire
    sauce
1/4 teaspoon TABASCO sauce
1/2 teaspoon salt
1/4 teaspoon red pepper
1 small onion, finely diced
1 tablespoon finely diced bell
    pepper
1/2 cup cracker meal
1 pound white crabmeat

Beat eggs in mixing bowl. Add mayonnaise, mustard, Worcestershire, TABASCO, salt, pepper, onion, bell pepper and cracker meal. Mix thoroughly. Fold in crabmeat. Place in 2-quart round casserole or individual crab shells. Bake in **preheated 325° oven 15-20 minutes** until hot and bubbly.

Yield: 4-6 servings

Beverly Crain (Mrs. Jim H.)

MUSHROOM SOUFFLÉ ROLL

1¹/₂ pounds mushrooms, finely
   chopped
6 egg yolks
1/2 cup butter, melted
1/2 teaspoon salt
1/4 teaspoon white pepper
2 tablespoons lemon juice
6 egg whites
5 sautéed mushroom caps,
   garnish
2 tablespoons parsley

*Crab Filling:

1 pound white crabmeat, drained
   and all shells removed
1 tablespoon butter
2 ounces cream cheese
1 cup sour cream
1/2 teaspoon salt
1/4 teaspoon white pepper
1/2 teaspoon lemon juice

*Hollandaise Sauce à la Microwave:

1/2 cup butter or margarine
2 tablespoons lemon juice
3 egg yolks, beaten
1/4 teaspoon salt
1/4 teaspoon white pepper

Chop mushrooms in food processor. Wring out moisture in towel or paper towel. Beat yolks until fluffy in mixing bowl. Add melted butter, salt, pepper, lemon juice and chopped mushrooms. Beat egg whites until they form soft peaks. Fold into mushroom mixture. Grease a 11 x 17 x 1-inch jelly roll pan. Line with greased waxed paper. Pour mixture into prepared pan. Spread evenly. Bake in **pre-heated 350° oven 15 minutes,** or until soufflé starts to pull away from sides of pan. Remove from oven. Cover with 2 overlapping sheets of waxed paper. Invert onto another cookie sheet. Cool 5 minutes, remove top sheet of paper. Sauté crab in butter. Stir in cream cheese and sour cream. Add salt, pepper and lemon juice. Spread Crab Filling* on soufflé. Starting with long side, roll jelly roll fashion. Place roll on long narrow platter. Garnish with sautéed mushroom caps placed down the center. Sprinkle with parsley. Pour hot Hollandaise Sauce* over top. Serve hot or cold slices.

Yield: 12 servings

Felicia Mallet Elsbury (Mrs. Joe W.)

Melt butter in 2-cup Pyrex measuring cup on **HIGH (100%) 1 MINUTE.** Stir in lemon juice, eggs, salt and pepper. Microwave on **HIGH (100%) 45 SECONDS,** beat with whisk at 15 second intervals. *Jean K Durkee*

CORKY'S CRAWFISH PIE

Perfect Pie Crust:
1/2 cup instant (Wondra) flour
1/4 cup chilled unsalted butter,
    cut into 1-inch cubes
1/4 cup solid vegetable
    shortening
1/2 teaspoon salt
1/4 cup cold liquid (lemon or
    orange juice with water)
All-purpose flour for board

Crawfish Pie Filling:
1/2 cup margarine
1 large onion, chopped
1 medium bell pepper, chopped
3 tablespoons all-purpose flour
1 (10-oz.) can Ro-tel tomatoes
    and green chilies, blended
1 teaspoon sugar
1 teaspoon salt
1½ pounds crawfish tails, peeled
2 ounces crawfish fat

In a mixer or food processor blend instant flour, butter, shortening and salt until mixture is crumbly and size of small peas. Add cold liquids and mix until dough comes clean from bowl and forms a ball. Flatten dough into an 8-inch circle. Enclose in plastic wrap and refrigerate 30 minutes. Place dough on lightly floured surface. **Hint:** Roll dough between 2 sheets of lightly floured wax paper. Roll to fit a 10-inch pie plate.

Melt margarine in a large skillet. Add onion and bell pepper and sauté 15 minutes or until vegetables are tender. Stir in flour. Add tomatoes, sugar and salt. Simmer until mixture has thickened, about 10 minutes. Stir to prevent sticking. Add crawfish and fat. Simmer uncovered 10 minutes. Add another tablespoon of flour if needed for thickness. Pour crawfish mixture into prepared unbaked pie shell. Bake in a **preheated 400° oven 30 to 45 minutes** or until crust is brown. Let set 15-20 minutes before cutting to serve.

Yield: 8 servings

Corky Daigre Hutchison (Mrs. James)

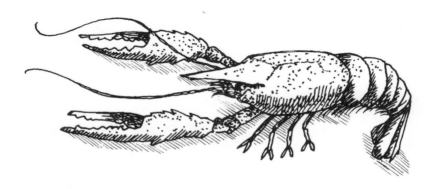

CRAWFISH PIE PATRICIA

2 (9 or 10-inch) pie shells,
  unbaked
1 cup butter
3/4 cup all-purpose flour
2 onions, chopped
2 cloves garlic, minced
1/2 cup chopped celery
1/2 bell pepper, chopped
2 small bunches green onions,
  bulbs and tops chopped
  separately
1/4 cup tomato puree, fresh
  preferably
2½ cups water or chicken stock
1½ teaspoons salt
1/4 teaspoon red pepper
1/2 teaspoon black pepper
1/2 teaspoon sweet basil
2 pounds crawfish tails, peeled
2 ounces crawfish fat
2-3 tablespoons cornstarch
1 small bunch parsley, chopped

Prepare your favorite pastry.

Melt butter in large saucepan. Add flour and brown lightly. Add onion, garlic, celery, bell pepper and green onion bulbs. Sauté 10-12 minutes, stirring constantly over medium heat. Add tomato puree, water, salt, red and black pepper and basil. Stir well. Cover and simmer 25-30 minutes, stirring frequently. Puree mixture in food processor with steel blade, in batches. Return to same pot. Add crawfish tails and fat. Cook 5 minutes to heat crawfish. Stir in 2-3 tablespoons cornstarch mixed with enough water to make a paste. Add green onion tops and parsley. Adjust seasoning. Pour crawfish mixture in bottom crust of prepared pie dough. Roll second pie dough and cover pie. Seal edges and cut slits in top. Bake in **preheated 375° oven 15 minutes.** Reduce temperature to **350°** Bake **15-20 minutes** or until brown.

Yield: 8-10 servings

Patricia Cashman Andrus (Mrs. Robert)

CRAWFISH ÉTOUFFÉE

1 large onion, chopped
1/3 large bell pepper, chopped
1/4 cup margarine
1/3 cup crawfish fat
3 tablespoons catsup
1 teaspoon salt
1/4 teaspoon red pepper
1 heaping tablespoon cornstarch
  mixed with 1/3 cup water
1 pound peeled crawfish tails
1/4 cup chopped parsley
1/4 cup green onion tops

Sauté onion and bell pepper in margarine in 3-quart saucepan. Add crawfish fat. Cover and cook over medium heat 10-15 minutes. Add catsup, salt, pepper and cornstarch paste. Blend well and cook 5 minutes, stirring occasionally. Add crawfish. Cover and cook 5 minutes. Remove from heat and stir in parsley and chopped onion tops. Serve over steamed rice.

Yield: 4 servings

Mary Alice Richard Robin (Mrs. Herbert)

CRAWFISH CARDINALE CRÊPES

12 (6-inch) crêpes
1/2 cup butter
1 medium onion, chopped
2 cloves garlic, minced
1 tablespoon chopped parsley
4 tablespoons all-purpose flour
2 cups heavy cream
1/2 teaspoon salt
Freshly ground black pepper,
     to taste
1/2 teaspoon cayenne pepper
1/4 teaspoon mace
1/4 teaspoon allspice
1/4 teaspoon ground cloves
2 small bay leaves, minced
3 tablespoons cognac
3 tablespoons dry white wine
3 cups peeled crawfish tails,
     boiled with salt and pepper
Finely minced parsley
Finely minced green onion

Follow Basic Crêpe recipe on page 164. In a heavy sauté pan melt butter and gently sauté onion, garlic and parsley until onion is transparent. Add flour, blending well. Stir constantly 3-4 minutes to form a light yellow roux. Add cream, salt, black and cayenne pepper, mace, allspice, cloves, bay leaves, cognac and wine. Bring mixture to boil. Reduce heat and simmer 5 minutes. Remove from heat and puree sauce in blender. Reheat sauce in sauté pan. Add crawfish tails. Cook over medium heat 8 minutes. Stuff crêpes with crawfish tails and a small amount of sauce. Place 3 crêpes on each serving plate. Top with remaining sauce and sprinkle with a mixture of parsley and green onion which has been sautéed in a small amount of butter. Serve at once.

Yield: 12 crêpes (4 servings)

Terry L. Thompson (Mrs. Pat)

CRAWFISH FETTUCINE

1¹/₂ cups margarine
3 medium onions, finely chopped
2 medium bell peppers, finely
     chopped
1/4 cup all-purpose flour
4 tablespoons dehydrated
     parsley
3 pounds crawfish tails, peeled
1 pint Half & Half cream
1 pound Velveeta cheese, cut
     into small pieces
2 teaspoons jalapeño relish
2 cloves garlic, minced
Salt, red and black pepper
     to taste
1 pound fine fettucine noodles,
     cooked
Parmesan cheese for sprinkling

Melt margarine in a large saucepan. Add onions and bell pepper. Cook covered until tender, approximately 15-20 minutes. Add flour. Cover and cook approximately 15 minutes, stirring frequently to prevent sticking. Add parsley and crawfish tails. Cook covered 15 minutes, stirring frequently. Add cream, cheese, jalapeño relish, garlic, salt and pepper. Cover and cook on low heat 30 minutes, stirring occasionally. Cook fettucine according to package directions. Mix crawfish mixture and fettucine noodles thoroughly. Pour mixture into two 3-quart greased casseroles. Sprinkle top with Parmesan cheese. Bake in **preheated 350° oven 15-20 minutes** until heated through.

Yield: 16 or more servings

John J. Daigre

CRAWFISH SUPREME

1 cup vegetable oil
2 cups chopped celery
1 cup chopped onion
1 cup chopped green onion tops
1 cup chopped bell pepper
1 cup chopped parsley
4 cups water
2 pounds cleaned crawfish tails

*Cheese Sauce:
3/4 cup butter
3/4 cup all-purpose flour
2 cups evaporated milk
1 1/2 cups grated cheddar cheese
2 tablespoons white wine
1 tablespoon salt
2 teaspoons red pepper
1/2 teaspoon black pepper

In heavy 4-quart pot heat oil. Add celery, onion, bell pepper and parsley. Sauté until wilted. Add water and bring to boil. Simmer 45 minutes uncovered. Stir occasionally. Add crawfish. Cover and simmer 15 minutes. In 2-quart saucepan melt butter and blend in flour. On medium heat add milk slowly until blended. Stir in cheese and wine. If mixture is too thick add more wine. Add Cheese Sauce* to crawfish mixture. Season with salt and pepper. *May be served in shells or ramekins. Also delicious as a dip with fancy crackers.*

Yield: 4 quarts

Virginia Davidson (Mrs. J. J., Jr.)

CRAWFISH TARTS à la MICROWAVE

1/2 cup vegetable oil
1/2 cup all-purpose flour
1 onion, chopped
2 ribs celery, chopped
1/2 bell pepper, chopped
1/4 cup crawfish fat
1 pound crawfish tails, peeled
    and cut into pieces
1 tablespoon chopped green
    onion tops
1 tablespoon chopped celery
    leaves
1 teaspoon salt
1/2 teaspoon red pepper
1/4 teaspoon white pepper
1/2 teaspoon garlic powder
Baked pastry shells, 50 bite-size
    or 12 (3-inch) tart size

Mix oil and flour together until completely blended in a 4-cup Pyrex measuring cup. Microwave on **HIGH (100%) 6-7 MINUTES,** or until roux becomes a dark brown color. Quickly add onion, celery and bell pepper. Microwave on **HIGH (100%) 3 MINUTES.** Pour roux into 2-quart glass dish. Add crawfish fat, crawfish, onion tops, celery leaves, salt, red and white pepper and garlic powder. Cover. Microwave on **HIGH (100%) 4 MIN-UTES,** stirring at 2 minutes. Cool, fill baked pastry shells. Tarts can be frozen or refrigerated at this point. When ready to serve, bake in **preheated 400° conventional oven 20 minutes** or, remove from foil pie forms and microwave on **HIGH (100%) 30 SECONDS** per tart or 3 bite-size tarts.

Yield: 50 small or 12 large tarts

Recipe developed by Mrs. Marie Angelle and converted to microwave by her son, Msgr. Robert Angelle.

OYSTER PIES

6 tablespoons flour
3 tablespoons oil
3 tablespoons butter or
    margarine
2 ribs celery, chopped
6 green onions, chopped
1/2 bell pepper, chopped
1 medium yellow onion, chopped
1 clove garlic, minced
2 tablespoons chopped parsley
1 1/2 teaspoons salt
1/2 teaspoon black pepper
1/2 teaspoon red pepper
6 dozen oysters, drain and
    reserve liquid
12-16 (3-inch) frozen unbaked
    pastry shells, partially baked

In Dutch oven make a roux with flour, oil and butter. Cook over medium heat, stirring until golden brown. Add celery, green onions, bell pepper, onion, garlic and parsley. Sauté until vegetables are wilted. Add salt, pepper and oyster liquid. Cook slowly until very thick. Drain oysters on paper towels and cut in half. Add to mixture and simmer 5 minutes or until edges curl. If oysters thin mixture too much, remove oysters with slotted spoon, and reduce liquid over high heat until very thick again. Return oysters to sauce. Let cool before filling partially baked pastry shells. Pies can be refrigerated or frozen at this time and baked just before serving in **preheated 300° oven 20 minutes.**

Yield: 12-16 pies

Judith Mouton Hebert (Mrs. Henry P., Jr.)

Microwave reheating: Remove pies from foil pie forms. Microwave on **HIGH (100%)** **1 MINUTE** per pie. *Jean K Durkee*

RUSTY'S OYSTER STEW

2 tablespoons oil
1 fist size onion, finely chopped
2 cloves garlic, finely chopped
3 cups hot water
1 rib celery, finely chopped
1/3 cup finely chopped parsley
2 tablespoons oil
2 tablespoons all-purpose flour
1 pint raw oysters with liquid
    (strained)
1 teaspoon salt
1/2 teaspoon black pepper
1/3 teaspoon red pepper
Steamed rice for 4 servings

In a large skillet or heavy 2-quart pot, sauté onion and garlic in oil. Add hot water, celery and parsley. Cover and simmer.

Make a light brown roux with oil and flour in a small skillet. Add roux to vegetable mixture in large pot and bring to boil. Add oysters and liquid and bring to boil. Add salt, black and red pepper. Taste and add more seasoning if you prefer. Cover and simmer 30-40 minutes. Serve in bowls over steamed rice.

Yield: 4 servings

Warren Lenox Brown, Jr. (Rusty)

OYSTERS BROUSSARD

36 fresh oysters with liquid
3 cloves garlic, minced
1 cup canned tomatoes, drained and pureed
1/2 cup dry bread crumbs
2 (8¹/₂-oz.) cans artichoke hearts, drained and pureed
1 cup whipping cream
1/4 cup finely chopped celery
1-1¹/₄ teaspoons salt
1/8 teaspoon cayenne pepper
1/2 pound white crabmeat
1/2 pound mushrooms, finely chopped
3 tablespoons melted butter
1/2 cup minced green onion tops
1/4 cup chopped parsley
1/2 pound ham, finely chopped
1/4 cup sherry
1 cup Parmesan cheese
Lemon wedges

Place oysters in colander to drain. Reserve liquid. Wash 36 oyster shells or miniature scallop shells. Set aside. Combine garlic, tomatoes, bread crumbs, artichokes, cream, celery, salt and cayenne in large saucepan, mixing well. Bring to boil; cover and simmer 15 minutes, stirring occasionally. Sauté crabmeat and mushrooms in butter 5 minutes. Add crabmeat/mushroom mixture, onion tops, parsley, ham and sherry to artichoke mixture. Stir well. Simmer 5 minutes, stirring occasionally. Remove from heat. Cover and chill 1-2 hours. Place 1 oyster (or 2 small) in each shell. Moisten each with 1 teaspoon reserved oyster liquid. Spoon chilled mixture evenly over top. Place filled shells on a bed of rock salt on baking sheet. Bake in **preheated 450° oven 8 minutes.** Sprinkle each oyster with 1 teaspoon Parmesan cheese. Bake **5 minutes** until cheese melts and browns slightly. Serve with lemon wedges. *This recipe won a silver medal in the 1983 Acadiana Culinary Classic.*

Yield: 36 servings

Joe Broussard

OYSTER JAMBALAYA

2 medium onions, chopped
1/2 cup butter
1 cup long grain rice, uncooked
1½ teaspoons salt
1 teaspoon seasoned pepper
2 cups oyster water (water can
    be added to oyster water)
32-36 medium raw oysters
1/2 cup chopped green onions
1 tablespoon chopped parsley
3 tablespoons butter

In a heavy 4 or 5-quart pot sauté onions in butter until medium brown. Add rice, salt and pepper to onions and fry medium brown. Add oyster water and cover tightly. Simmer until rice is almost *swollen* but not done. Add oysters, cover and simmer 15 minutes or until oysters and rice are cooked. Add green onions and parsley. Dot with butter. *This recipe was given to me by my grandmother, Mrs. William B. Torres of Franklin, LA, when I was a bride 30 years ago.*

Yield: 6 servings

Hascal R. Hardy (Mrs. Irby)

SCALLOPED OYSTERS

1 cup white bread crumbs
2 cups oysterette cracker crumbs
1 cup melted butter (only)
3 tablespoons finely chopped
    green onions
1 quart oysters; drain and reserve
    liquid
Salt, black pepper, cayenne
    pepper for sprinkling
4 tablespoons heavy cream
3/4 cup oyster liquid

Mix bread and cracker crumbs with butter and green onions. Place thin layer in bottom of buttered 2-quart oblong baking dish. Cover with half the oysters. Season with salt and pepper. Add half of cream and half of the oyster liquid. Repeat layers of oysters, seasonings, cream and oyster liquid. Top with remaining crumbs.

Bake uncovered in **preheated 400° oven 30 minutes.**

Yield: 10-12 servings

Missy Hardy Abendroth (Mrs. Joe)

OYSTER AND CHICKEN JAMBALAYA

1 (3-lb.) chicken, cut up
1/4 cup cooking oil
1 onion, chopped
1/2 cup chopped bell pepper
1/2 cup chopped celery
2 cloves garlic, minced
Oyster juice and water to make
   3½ cups
5 chicken bouillon cubes
2 cups raw long grain rice
3 dozen oysters, cut in half
1/4 cup chopped green onion
   tops
1/4 cup chopped parsley
2 teaspoons Worcestershire
   sauce
3 tablespoons chopped sweet
   red pepper, (optional)
1½ teaspoons salt
1/2 teaspoon black pepper
1/4 teaspoon red pepper
1/2 teaspoon powdered thyme
   or 1½ teaspoons leaves
2 bay leaves

In a heavy Dutch oven brown chicken well in oil. Cover and simmer 15-20 minutes. Stir once or twice. Bone chicken, cut into bite-sized pieces and set aside. In same Dutch oven wilt onion, bell pepper, celery and garlic. Add oyster juice, softened bouillon cubes, rice, oysters, chicken, onion tops, parsley, Worcestershire, red bell pepper, salt, black and red pepper, thyme and bay leaves. Stir, cover, and bake in **preheated 350° oven 1 hour.** Uncover and stir gently with a fork. If too moist, leave uncovered, reduce oven heat to 225° and cook for 15-20 minutes longer.

Yield: 8-10 servings

Keith E. Courrégé

MAW MAW'S SHRIMP AND CABBAGE

3 cups cooked rice
2 pounds unpeeled shrimp
1 (2¹/₂-3 lb.) cabbage, finely
    shredded
1 pound butter
1 cup finely chopped green
    onions
1 cup finely chopped onions
1 cup finely chopped celery
1/2 cup finely chopped parsley
1/4 cup finely chopped fresh
    jalapeño peppers
6 cloves garlic, minced
1 tablespoon salt
1 tablespoon red pepper

Cook rice. In large pot barely cover shrimp with water seasoned with two teaspoons salt and one teaspoon red pepper. Steam 10 minutes. Remove shrimp and peel. Add cabbage to shrimp juice and cook until wilted. Drain, reserving liquid. In a large skillet sauté onions, celery, parsley, peppers and garlic in butter until wilted. Mix peeled shrimp, rice, cabbage, vegetables, salt and pepper in 5-quart casserole and add 2 to 3 cups of shrimp/cabbage juice. Bake uncovered in a **preheated 350° oven 50-60 minutes.**

This recipe has been in the Fred Leger family for over eighty years. P.S. Believe me, one pound of butter!

Yield: 12 servings

Phillip Arleigh Lank

SHRIMP ADELE

1/2 cup butter
2 cloves garlic, minced
1 bunch green onion tops and
    bulbs, finely chopped
36 jumbo shrimp, peeled,
    seasoned with salt, white
    pepper and cayenne pepper
1 quart heavy cream
1/2 cup chicken broth
3 ounces cream sherry
2 tablespoons basil
1 (16-oz.) can whole tomatoes,
    run through processor
1/4 cup water
2 tablespoons cornstarch
Salt and pepper to taste
1/2 bunch parsley, finely
    chopped

Melt butter in a large pot. Add garlic and green onions. Sauté until soft. Add seasoned shrimp and gently toss until they turn light pink. Add heavy cream, chicken broth, sherry, basil and tomatoes. Cook 15 minutes. Thicken with a paste of 1/4 cup water and 2 tablespoons cornstarch. Check seasoning and add salt and pepper to taste. Add parsley and serve in small bowls or ramekins.

Yield: 6 servings

Marcelle Bienvenue

AMARETTO SHRIMP

1/2 cup butter
1 medium white onion, finely
    minced
1 pound large shrimp, peeled,
    leave tail on and butterfly
1/2-1 cup Amaretto liqueur
1 cup blanched sliced almonds
1/2 teaspoon salt
Chopped parsley

Melt butter in skillet until golden brown. Add onions. Sauté until transparent. Add shrimp and stir fry 5 minutes until pink. Add Amaretto, almonds and salt. Cook 1½ minutes until bubbly. Serve in a scallop shell or ramekin with a sprinkle of chopped parsley.

Yield: 4 servings

Sous Chef Bryan Richard
Chez Marcelle

SHRIMP CREOLE

1/2 cup butter
3 tablespoons all-purpose flour
1 large onion, chopped
1/2 bell pepper, chopped
3 cloves garlic, chopped
1 (8-oz.) can tomato sauce
1 cup water
1 bay leaf
1½ teaspoons sugar
1/2 teaspoon red pepper
1/4 teaspoon lemon juice
1/8 teaspoon TABASCO sauce
Seasoned salt and black pepper
    to taste
2 pounds raw medium shrimp,
    peeled
1 tablespoon chopped parsley
Cooked white rice
Chopped green onion tops

Make a light roux with butter and flour in a 5-quart Dutch oven. Add onion, bell pepper and garlic. Sauté over medium heat until vegetables are limp. Stir in tomato sauce, water, bay leaf, sugar, red pepper, lemon juice, TABASCO, seasoned salt and black pepper. Simmer on medium low heat 30 minutes. Add shrimp and parsley. Cover. Cook 25 minutes or until shrimp is tender. Serve over hot rice. Top with chopped green onion tops.

Yield: 4-6 servings

Hascal Hardy (Mrs. Irby)

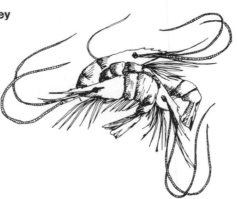

RITZY SEAFOOD EGGPLANT

3 medium eggplant, peeled and
    diced
1/4 cup butter or margarine
1 large onion, chopped
1 medium bell pepper, chopped
2 ribs celery, chopped
1 teaspoon garlic powder
1/2 cup water
1 pound peeled and deveined
    shrimp
1 pound crabmeat
1/4 cup butter or margarine
1 tablespoon all-purpose flour
1 cup milk
1/2 teaspoon salt
1/4 teaspoon white pepper
1/4 cup sliced mushrooms
1/4 cup chopped parsley
1/4 cup chopped onion tops
1/4 cup chopped celery leaves
1½ teaspoons salt
1/2 teaspoon red pepper
1/4 teaspoon black pepper
1/4 teaspoon TABASCO sauce
8 ounces Ritz crackers, crushed
    (keep 1 cup for topping)
Butter to dot top
Paprika for sprinkling

Prepare eggplant and set aside.

Melt butter in a 4-6 quart saucepan. Sauté onions, bell pepper and celery in butter until soft. Add eggplant, garlic powder and 1/2 cup water. Cover and simmer until eggplant is very tender. Add shrimp and crabmeat and simmer 10 minutes.

To make a white sauce, melt butter in a medium saucepan over low heat. Add flour and cook 1 minute, stirring constantly. Over medium heat, add milk stirring constantly, until thick and bubbly. Stir in salt, white pepper and mushrooms. 1 (10¾-oz.) can cream of mushroom soup may be substituted for white sauce.

Add white sauce to eggplant mixture. Stir in parsley, onion tops, celery leaves, salt, pepper, TABASCO and crushed crackers. Place in a 9 x 13-inch baking dish. Top with 1 cup crushed crackers. Dot with butter and sprinkle with paprika. Bake in **preheated 350° oven 30 minutes.** *C'est bon, chère!*

Yield: 10-12 servings

Karleen Guilbeau Barry (Mrs. J. Robert, Jr.)

This is a recipe from Madame Sauce Piquante, Karleen Guilbeau Barry, author of **Madame Sauce Piquante's Cookbook.** *It was adapted from a beef and eggplant dressing recipe given to her by her Nanaine (godmother), Mrs. Joe Lalonde.*

SHRIMP AND PEPPERS ÊLÉGANT

2 pounds peeled shrimp
Garlic powder, lemon pepper,
   cayenne pepper for
   sprinkling
3/4 cup butter (1 1/2 sticks)
4 cloves garlic, minced
1/2 cup minced parsley
1/2 cup minced green onion tops
1/2 pound mushrooms, sliced
2 medium large bell peppers,
   sliced into strips
1/2 cup Chablis (white wine)
2 tablespoons cornstarch
1 teaspoon salt
1/2 teaspoon cayenne pepper

Season peeled shrimp with garlic powder and pepper. Cover and refrigerate 4 hours or overnight. In a skillet melt butter. Add garlic, parsley, onion tops and mushrooms. Sauté 10 minutes or until wilted. Add shrimp. Stir for 3 minutes, cover and simmer 5 minutes. Add bell pepper slices. Mix wine and cornstarch and add to thicken mixture. Add salt and pepper. Simmer covered 5 minutes. *This elegant dish may be served over baked fish or as a dip with melba rounds, or over rice as a main course!*

Yield: 6 servings

Betty Baquet Bares (Mrs. Allen)

SHRIMP AND RICE ROCKEFELLER

1 cup chopped onions
2 tablespoons butter
12 ounces raw shrimp, peeled
   and cut in half
1 (10³/₄-oz.) can mushroom soup,
   undiluted
1 cup grated Swiss cheese
1/4 cup sherry wine
3 cups cooked rice
1 (8-oz.) can water chestnuts,
   drained and chopped
2 (10-oz.) packages frozen
   chopped spinach, cooked
1 tablespoon lemon juice
1/4 cup grated Parmesan
   cheese, divided
1 teaspoon salt
1 teaspoon red pepper
1/2 teaspoon black pepper

In a 3-quart sauce pan sauté onions in butter. Add shrimp, cook until pink. Stir in mushroom soup, cheese and sherry. Heat thoroughly until mixture is warm. Add cooked rice, water chestnuts, drained spinach, lemon juice and 2 tablespoons Parmesan cheese. Add salt, red and black pepper. Pour into a greased shallow 2-quart dish. Sprinkle remaining Parmesan cheese over top. Bake in **preheated 350° oven 30 minutes.**

Yield: 6-8 servings

Mrs. Lloyd J. Faulk

GRILLED SHRIMP KABOB

5 pounds fresh large shrimp,
   peeled
1 tablespoon garlic powder
1 teaspoon seasoned salt
1 teaspoon cayenne pepper
1 tablespoon lemon-parsley salt
   or, (4 tablespoons Creole
   seasoning could be substituted for the above
   seasonings)
1 pound fresh mushrooms
2 large onions, cut into pieces
3 bell peppers, cut into strips
1 cup melted butter
1/2 cup lemon juice
1 tablespoon Creole seasoning
1 teaspoon garlic powder

Peel and rinse shrimp. Keep shrimp on ice or refrigerated until ready to place on skewers.

Mix seasonings to your desired taste. Pat shrimp on paper towels until only slightly wet. Lightly coat shrimp with seasoning. Place 5-6 shrimp on wooden skewers alternating with mushrooms, onions and bell peppers. Melt butter in saucepan (or 2-cup glass measure in microwave). Add lemon juice, Creole seasoning and garlic powder. Place shrimp kabobs over medium coals or gas grill. As shrimp are cooking, brush on butter mixture. Cook until shrimp are pink.

Yield: 30 kabobs

Laila Michelle Asmar

ACADIAN PEPPERED SHRIMP

1½ cups butter
3 cloves garlic, finely minced
2 whole bay leaves, preferably
   Louisiana Sweet Laurel,
   crushed fine
2 teaspoons rosemary
1/2 teaspoon basil
1/2 teaspoon oregano
1/2 teaspoon salt
1/2 teaspoon cayenne pepper
1/2 teaspoon freshly ground
   nutmeg
1/2 tablespoon paprika
5 tablespoons freshly ground
   black pepper
2 tablespoons freshly squeezed
   lemon juice
3 pounds whole fresh shrimp in
   shell, heads removed

In a large, heavy sauté pan, melt butter. Add all other ingredients except the shrimp and cook over medium heat, stirring, about 20 minutes. Add shrimp to the sauce, mix thoroughly and cook over medium heat 6-8 minutes, or just until the shrimp turn pink. Serve at once. Add some of the sauce with each portion. It is marvelous to *sop up* with a slice of French bread. Have a lot of napkins on hand. *This is a recipe to satisfy the Acadian love of spicy foods and the plentiful shrimp we are blessed with. This dish is a perfect example of the Cajun touch of spicy food which is not just 'hot,' but a wonderful combination of many tastes mingling together.*

Yield: 4-6 servings

Terry L. Thompson (Mrs. Pat)

SHRIMP SCAMPI ANNE

30 jumbo shrimp (1½-lbs.)
1/4 cup olive oil
Salt, black and red pepper,
    to taste
3 large cloves garlic, minced
1/3 cup chopped parsley
1/3 cup seasoned bread crumbs
8 tablespoons melted butter
1/3 cup white wine, optional
Dash TABASCO sauce
Cooked linguine
1/4 cup mixture of freshly grated
    Romano and Parmesan
    cheese

Slit shrimp down the back leaving tail tip section of shell on the shrimp. Devein, wash and dry shrimp. Arrange shrimp, single layer, in 10-inch square dish. Pour olive oil evenly over shrimp. Sprinkle to coat with salt, black and red pepper, garlic, parsley and bread crumbs. Cover dish and bake in **preheated 300° oven 20 minutes.** Pour butter, TABASCO and wine evenly over shrimp. Bake uncovered 5 minutes longer or until done. Do not overcook; the shrimp will toughen. Serve over cooked linguine and top with grated cheese. *A dry wine is a good choice with this dish!*

Yield: 4-6 servings

Marilyn Anne Jones Breaux (Mrs. Paul)

CHINESE STYLE FRIED SHRIMP

1 pound medium shrimp

Marinade:
1 teaspoon salt
1/2 teaspoon sugar
3 tablespoons sherry or dry
    white wine
1 clove garlic, minced
1 tablespoon chopped ginger
    root
2 or 3 cups peanut oil

Batter:
1 cup self-rising flour
3/4 cup water
1 egg, slightly beaten
1/2 teaspoon salt
1/4 cup oil

Peel and devein shrimp leaving last segment of tail-shell intact. Lay flat and cut, from inside curve, not quite all the way through. Press shrimp flat. In 2-quart bowl place shrimp with marinade of salt, sugar, wine, garlic and ginger root for 1 hour or more. Stir often to keep shrimp covered with marinade.

Heat oil, 350°-375°, in wok or heavy, deep pot. Make a batter of flour, water, egg, salt and oil in smaller bowl. Dip shrimp into batter. Try not to get batter on tail-shell.

Fry shrimp several at a time without crowding in pot. Fry until golden brown. Drain on paper towels when done. Serve immediately.

Yield: 6 servings

Keith E. Courrégé

the
1920s

he 1920s was a decade when the citizens of the nation elected four presidents, Wilson, Harding, Coolidge and Hoover and over 10,000 citizens made Lafayette one of the largest towns in southwest Louisiana. Because Lafayette was the railroad and educational center for the surrounding towns, she attained the name "hub city."

Lafayette was indeed a hub city during the flood of May, 1927. As the only high ground, Lafayette became the refuge center for the Attakapas area when the Mississippi River became a fast, muddy rush of water, 50 to 100 miles wide.

Lafayette citizens, through the Red Cross kitchens, prepared and served 50,000 meals daily. In one day volunteers prepared 18,600 sandwiches. A typical meal prepared by the camp kitchen included 3,000 loaves of bread, 1,400 pounds of meat, 400 pounds of rice, 400 pounds of beans, and 150 gallons of milk. The bread was furnished locally. Cattle purchased from refugees were slaughtered for meat.

In the Twenties industries started forming. These included railroad repair shops, blacksmith shops, ice cream manufacturers, bottling works, sash and door factories, cotton oil mills, drug preparations, syrup mills, perfume manufacturers, bakeries, tank manufacturers and small isolated oil companies. Many of these industries have disappeared from the scene.

Tourism was heavily promoted during the 1920s and Lafayette soon became the tourist center of south Louisiana. Tall banana trees and giant live oaks were abundant. Spanish moss hung from the trees forming a tapestry for the lazily flowing Teche and Vermilion bayous, providing scenic tranquillity for both visitors and natives. Local citizens developed beautiful gardens and flower trails including the annual "Azalea Trail" festivity still honored each spring.

The tourists who came particularly appreciated the local cooking. Gumbos? How do you make a gumbo? Often they purchased The Lafayette Cook Book which offered chicken and oyster gumbo, crab gumbo and okra gumbo on the opening recipe page. This cookbook was compiled in 1922 by the members of Circle 1 of the Methodist Episcopal Church South in Lafayette, Louisiana. Mrs. T. B. Hopkins, Jr. wrote for the committee, "In collecting the recipes for this book we drew upon the resources of Lafayette's best cooks...through the publication of The Lafayette Cook Book our women may become renowned for their knowledge of the art of cookery." Today, our cooks, men as well as women, are indeed renowned!

Crawfish, used for years only as bait, were now being sold at grocery stores, roadside stands and fish markets. Before long, the now famous crustacean was the favorite seafood of the entire area.

At this time too, popular entertainment came often by train from performances in New Orleans. Entertainers such as Will Rogers, Eddie Cantor, John Barrymore and Al Jolson appeared at the original Jefferson Opera House built in 1906 and later called The Azalea Theatre. Because they could not duplicate the natural beauty in Hollywood, film companies came to the area for location shots. The most famous movie, "Evangeline" starring Delores Del Rio, was filmed in 1928.

Shady oaks and flowing bayous, pink azaleas and red camellias, flooded green rice fields and earth-orange sweet potatoes made Lafayette a dream on film and in reality.

L. C. Melchior
The Nostalgia Man

Gumbo-Soup

Game

ROUX

The microwave will brown my roux
And even do the gaspergou.
Now if you like to stir a lot,
Just cook yours in a black iron pot.

2/3 cup oil
2/3 cup flour

2 cups onion, chopped
1 cup celery, chopped
1/2 cup green bell pepper,
chopped
4 cloves garlic, minced
1/4 cup parsley, chopped
1/4 cup green onion tops,
chopped
Approximately 1/4 cup hot water

Mix oil and flour together in a 4-cup measure. Microwave uncovered on **HIGH (100%) 6-7 MINUTES.** Stir at 6 minutes—Roux will be a light brown at this time and will need to cook 30 seconds to 1 minute longer to reach the dark brown color so important in making Louisiana gumbos and stews. The Roux will be very hot, but usually the handle on your glass measuring cup will stay cool enough to touch. Add onion, celery and bell pepper to Roux in measuring cup. Stir and return to Microwave. Sauté on **HIGH (100%) 3 MINUTES.** Add garlic, parsley and green onion to Roux, stir and return to microwave. Sauté on **HIGH (100%) 2 MINUTES.** You should have about 3¾ cups of Roux now. If any oil has risen to the top, pour this off. Slowly add enough hot tap water to bring Roux to the 4-cup mark. Stir and you will have a smooth dark Roux in only 12 minutes. Roux freezes very well and you are ready at any time to put together a delicious gumbo or stew.

ROUX is an equal mixture of oil and flour that is browned and used as a thickening base for many of the South Louisiana dishes such as stews, gumbos, etouffees and sauce piquantes. It not only thickens, but it also gives a different, quite distinct flavor due to the browning of the flour.

From: Tout de Suite à la Microwave I
Jean K Durkee

CHICKEN FILÊ GUMBO

1 (3-4 lb.) chicken, cut up
Salt and pepper
1/2 cup vegetable oil
1/2 cup flour
1 large onion, minced
1/2 cup minced celery
1/3 cup minced bell pepper
2 cloves garlic, pressed
2 tablespoons Worcestershire
  sauce
1 teaspoon TABASCO sauce
1/2 teaspoon salt
1/2 teaspoon pepper
1/2 teaspoon red pepper
1 bay leaf
3 quarts hot water
1 pound smoked pork sausage,
  sliced into 1/4-inch rounds
1/2 cup sliced green onion tops
1/2 cup minced parsley
Steamed rice for serving
2 tablespoons filé

Clean and season chicken pieces with salt and pepper. Heat oil in Dutch oven. Add chicken, brown evenly, remove and set aside. Make roux by adding flour to hot oil in pot. Stir constantly over medium heat until the color of dark coffee with cream and smells like browned flour. Stir onion, celery, bell pepper and garlic into roux. Add chicken and cook until vegetables are tender. Add Worcestershire sauce, TABASCO, salt, black and red pepper and bay leaf. Add hot water. Cover and simmer 1 hour. Add sausage, remove bay leaf, cover and simmer 1 more hour. Skim off excess fat then add green onion and parsley. Simmer 10 minutes. Serve in bowls over steamed rice. Place 1/2 teaspoon filé on rim of each bowl or pass filé to be sprinkled on gumbo.

Yield: 10-12 servings

Helen Walker Poydras

TASSO OKRA GUMBO

3/4 cup oil
3/4 cup flour
2 medium onions, chopped
4 cups water
20 ounces frozen cut okra,
  thawed
10 ounces Ro-tel tomatoes and
  green chilies, blended
2 pounds Tasso (smoked pork)
4 whole chicken breasts, skinned
6 drumsticks, skinned
1 teaspoon salt
1/2 teaspoon red pepper
3 dashes TABASCO sauce
Steamed rice

In a Dutch oven heat oil and flour stirring until roux becomes dark brown. Add onions, sautéing until tender. Add water a little at a time, stirring. Add okra, tomatoes, Tasso, raw chicken, salt, and pepper. Simmer 1 hour or until Tasso is tender. Taste and add TABASCO sauce. Serve in bowls over steamed rice.

Yield: 8 servings

Lola Soileau Busby (Mrs. Ben R.)

CHICKEN AND OYSTER GUMBO

1/2 cup oil
1/2 cup flour
1 (4-5 lb.) chicken, cut into pieces
1 large onion, minced
1 large bell pepper, minced
1 quart cold water
3 quarts boiling water
Salt, black and red pepper
    to taste
1 tablespoon chopped parsley
2 tablespoons chopped onion
    tops
2 tablespoons minced celery
4 tablespoons Worcestershire
    sauce
50 oysters (canned lobster may
    be substituted)
1 teaspoon filé
Boiled rice for serving

Heat oil in 2 gallon pot. Add flour stirring to make a dark brown roux. Add chicken and stir every minute for 10 minutes. Add onion and bell pepper and let brown 2 minutes. Add quart of cold water. When mixture boils add 3 quarts boiling water, salt and pepper. Let boil slowly until chicken begins to get tender, about 3 hours. Add parsley, onion tops, celery and Worcestershire. Boil 10 minutes. Skim off fat. Oysters should be put in when gumbo is done and allowed to come to one good boil. Remove from fire and sift in filé, stirring continuously. Reheat just to boiling point. Serve with boiled rice. *From the recipes of my father, Walter B. Gordy.*

Yield: 1 ½ gallons

Matthew B. Gordy

CHICKEN OKRA GUMBO

1/2 cup vegetable oil
2 quarts fresh okra, sliced thinly
1 (4-5 lb.) hen, cut into pieces
    and seasoned with salt and
    pepper
3 tablespoons vegetable oil
3 tablespoons flour
1 cup chopped onions
1/2 cup chopped celery
1 bell pepper, chopped
1 clove garlic, minced
2 large fresh tomatoes or
    1 (15-oz.) can whole
    tomatoes, chopped
2 quarts water or chicken stock
1 tablespoon salt
1/2 teaspoon red pepper
1/4 teaspoon black pepper
1 pound smoked pork sausage,
    cut into 1-inch pieces

Heat oil in skillet. Add okra. Cover and cook slowly 30-40 minutes until okra is tender. In Dutch oven sear seasoned chicken in 3 tablespoons oil until brown. Remove chicken and set aside. In remaining oil add flour, stirring constantly until brown roux forms. Add onion, celery, bell pepper and garlic. Cook on low heat until onions are transparent. Add tomatoes. Cook until well blended. Add okra, chicken, water, salt, red and black pepper. Cover. Cook over medium heat 2½-3 hours or until chicken is tender. More water may need to be added. If desired, add sausage to gumbo during the last 30 minutes. Serve over cooked rice.

Yield: 6-8 servings

Alice Veillon Lasseigne

LENTEN SHRIMP & EGG GUMBO

3/4 cup vegetable oil
3/4 cup all-purpose flour
2 medium onions, finely chopped
1¹/₂ bell peppers, finely chopped
3 large cloves garlic, minced
1 pound raw shrimp with shells
1 bay leaf and onion peelings
Cheesecloth
3¹/₂ quarts water
1¹/₂ tablespoons salt
1¹/₂ teaspoons cayenne pepper
1/2 teaspoon black pepper
10 hard cooked, peeled eggs
1/4 cup chopped green onion
1/4 cup chopped parsley

Heat oil in Dutch oven and add flour. Stir to make a dark brown roux. Add onion, bell pepper and garlic. Cook until vegetables are soft. Peel shrimp. Wrap shells in cheesecloth square with onion peelings and bay leaf. Tie securely. Place shells along with 3¹/₂ quarts water in large pot. Bring to boil and boil 20 minutes. Discard bag of shells and add shrimp stock slowly to roux. Add salt and pepper. Simmer 40 minutes. Add shrimp and simmer 10 minutes. Add peeled whole eggs. Simmer 5 minutes. Check seasoning and add green onion and parsley.

Yield: 10 servings

Patricia Cashman Andrus (Mrs. Robert M.)

DUCK & OYSTER GUMBO GORDY

2/3 cup shortening
4-6 ducks, cut into pieces, seasoned with salt and pepper
2/3 cup all-purpose flour
2 large onions, finely chopped
1 large bell pepper, finely chopped
3 cloves garlic, chopped
2 quarts water
2 teaspoons salt
1 teaspoon red pepper
5 dashes TABASCO sauce
1 cup finely chopped celery
1/3 cup chopped parsley
2/3 cup chopped green onion tops
1/2 cup red wine (one cheese glass)
1 quart raw oysters and liquid
2 tablespoons Worcestershire sauce
Boiled rice for serving
Filé for sprinkling

In Dutch oven melt shortening until hot. Sear ducks then transfer ducks to large gumbo pot. To remaining hot oil in Dutch oven, add flour. Stir constantly over medium high heat until roux is **dark, dark** brown. Add onion, bell pepper and garlic. Stir and cook until vegetables are soft. Add water, salt, red pepper and TABASCO. Cook on low heat 30 minutes. Pour this mixture over ducks in gumbo pot. Add more water, if necessary. Cover. Boil slowly until ducks begin to get soft. Skim off grease. When ducks are cooked, remove from pot. Bone ducks and return meat to gumbo. *Throw away the bones.* Add celery. Boil slowly 1 hour. Add parsley, green onion tops and red wine. Cook 15 minutes. Add oysters and oyster liquid. Bring to brisk boil, then cut off heat. Check seasonings. Add Worcestershire sauce and serve over boiled rice. Filé may be sprinkled on at the table. *From the recipe files of Walter Brown Gordy, Sr."*

Yield: 10 servings

Matthew B. Gordy

SEAFOOD GUMBO

2 cups vegetable oil
2 cups all-purpose flour
4 cups chopped onion
2 cups chopped celery
1 cup chopped bell pepper
2 tablespoons minced garlic
5 pounds raw shrimp in shells
Cheese cloth
7 quarts water
2 (2-oz.) packages dried shrimp
2 (10-oz.) jars oysters and liquid
1 tablespoon salt
2 tablespoons cayenne pepper
Black pepper to taste
Creole seasoning to taste
2 pounds white crabmeat
2 pounds claw crabmeat
1/2 cup chopped green onion
    tops
1/2 cup chopped parsley
Cooked rice for serving

Heat oil in Dutch oven. Add flour, stirring over medium heat to make a brown roux. Add onion, celery, bell pepper and garlic. Cover. Sauté slowly until onions are tender. Peel shrimp. Wrap shells in cheese cloth square. Tie securely. Place shells (may be added loose and strained later) along with 7 quarts water in 2 1/2-3 gallon gumbo pot. Bring to boil and boil 20 minutes. Discard bag of shells. Add roux, oyster liquid and dried shrimp to stock in gumbo pot. Stir and simmer 1 hour uncovered. Add salt, pepper and Creole seasoning. Season well! Add fresh shrimp and crabmeat. Cook over medium heat. When shrimp are pink, add oysters, onion tops and parsley. Cook 15 minutes over low heat. Taste for seasoning. Serve in bowls with cooked rice along with hot French bread.

Yield: 24 servings

Carolyn Camardelle (Mrs. Gabe)

SEAFOOD GUMBO à la BOUDREAUX

1 1/2 cups vegetable oil
1 2/3 cups all-purpose flour
4 quarts water
3 pounds peeled shrimp
2 pounds crabmeat
1 tablespoon salt
2 teaspoons red pepper
1/2 teaspoon black pepper
1 pint oysters, drained
1/2 cup chopped green onion
    tops
1/2 cup chopped parsley
Cooked rice for serving

Heat oil in heavy skillet. Stir in flour to make a dark brown roux. Heat water in 6-quart pot. Add roux and bring to boil. Boil 30 minutes. Add shrimp, crabmeat, salt and pepper to taste. Cook over medium heat 30 minutes. Add oysters, onion tops and parsley. Cook 15 minutes. Add more water if too thick. Serve with cooked rice.

Yield: 10 servings

Verlie T. Boudreaux (Mrs. Walter)

91

CRAB STEW à la GORDY

24 whole crabs, boiled in highly seasoned water. Clean crabs, but leave fat as it adds much to the flavor. Reserve liquid. Remove claw meat to add later.
1/2 cup vegetable oil
1/2 cup flour
1 large onion, chopped fine
1 small bell pepper, chopped fine
2 cloves garlic, chopped
1 (16-oz.) can whole tomatoes, chopped with liquid
1 (8-oz.) can tomato sauce
1 quart hot water
1 slice of lemon, diced
1/2 cup minced celery
2 tablespoons dry parsley flakes
2 dashes TABASCO sauce
2 teaspoons salt
1/2 teaspoon red pepper
1/8 teaspoon black pepper
1/3 cup chopped green onion tops
1/3 cup red wine (1/2 cheese glass)
1 tablespoon lemon juice
1 tablespoon Worcestershire sauce
Cooked rice for serving

In a Dutch oven, heat oil until hot. Add flour. Stir over medium high heat until roux is **dark, dark** brown. Add onion, bell pepper and garlic. Cook and stir until vegetables are soft. Add tomatoes and tomato sauce. Stir well and simmer covered 10 minutes. Add hot water, lemon, celery, parsley, TABASCO, salt, red and black pepper. Cover. Simmer 45 minutes. Place cleaned crab bodies in a large cooking pot. Pour roux mixture over crabs. Add liquid from boiled crabs. Bring to boil and add enough hot water to cover crabs. Check seasoning. Add salt and pepper to taste. Add onion tops and wine. Cook uncovered on low heat 30-40 minutes. Stir every 5 minutes. Turn heat off. Add lemon juice and Worcestershire. Seine crabs out of stew. Place in separate bowls on table. Add claw meat to stew and bring to boil. Serve over cooked rice. *From the recipe files of Walter Brown Gordy, Sr.*

Yield: 12 servings

Matthew B. Gordy

Microwave directions: In a 4-cup Pyrex measuring cup mix oil and flour together completely. Microwave on **HIGH (100%) 5 MINUTES** stir and continue to microwave on **HIGH (100%) 1 MINUTE** longer until roux is a dark brown color. Quickly add onion, bell pepper and garlic. Microwave on **HIGH (100%) 3 MINUTES.** Pour roux into a 4 or 5-quart ceramic dish. Stir in tomatoes and tomato sauce. Cover. Microwave on **HIGH (100%) 3 MINUTES.** Add hot water, lemon, celery, parsley, TABASCO, salt, red and black pepper. Cover. Microwave on **HIGH (100%) 11 MINUTES.** Pour roux mixture over crab bodies and continue recipe as above. (Recipe may be completed in microwave if larger dish is available.) *Jean K Durkee*

CRAB AND LOBSTER BISQUE

3 tablespoons butter
1 medium onion, chopped
3 tablespoons flour
1½ tablespoons tomato paste
3 cups chicken broth
3 cups cream or Half & Half
    cream, room temperature
2 cups crabmeat and/or lobster
1/4 cup chopped parsley
1/2 cup sauterne wine
1 teaspoon salt
1/2 teaspoon cayenne pepper

Sauté butter and onion on low heat in a 4-quart pot. Stir often. Cook until onion is soft. Stir in flour. Add tomato paste, mixing well. Add chicken broth. Cook 40-50 minutes on low heat, stirring often. Slowly add cream, stir to mix well. Add crab and/or lobster, parsley and wine. Cook slowly over low heat 10 minutes. Season with salt and pepper.

Yield: 6 to 8 (cup-size) servings

Marilyn Ann Jones Breaux (Mrs. Paul)

CRAB AND ARTICHOKE BISQUE

1 bunch green onions, finely
    minced
1 clove garlic, finely minced
1 (8½-oz.) can artichoke hearts,
    crushed by hand
1/2 cup Chablis wine
1 bay leaf
2 teaspoons white pepper
1 teaspoon nutmeg
1/2 teaspoon salt
1/4 teaspoon cayenne pepper
1 quart strained chicken stock
1 pint Half & Half cream
1 pound lump crabmeat, picked
    clean
1/4 cup cornstarch
Paprika for sprinkling

In a 3 or 4-quart saucepan sauté green onions, garlic and artichokes in Chablis wine, or a dry white wine. Add bay leaf, white pepper, nutmeg, salt and cayenne pepper. Simmer 5 minutes. Add chicken stock (reserve 1/2 cup to be mixed with cornstarch), cream and crabmeat. Simmer 15 minutes. Thicken with cornstarch dissolved in reserved chicken stock, add gradually to the hot soup until desired texture is achieved. Garnish with paprika.

Yield: 15-20 small servings

Bryan Richard
Sous Chef Chez Marcelle

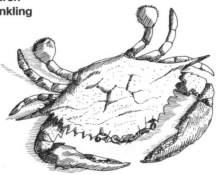

CRAWFISH BISQUE

1/2 cup vegetable oil
1/2 cup all-purpose flour
1 large onion, minced
1 rib celery, minced
1 clove garlic, minced
2 quarts boiling water
1 teaspoon salt
1/2 teaspoon red pepper
1/8 teaspoon black pepper
Pinch sugar
4 ounces crawfish fat
2 pounds crawfish tails in fat,
    peeled, seasoned with
    Creole seasoning
1/2 cup chopped parsley
4 green onion tops, chopped
6 hard cooked eggs
Stuffed crawfish heads

Heat oil in large Dutch oven. Add flour stirring to make a dark brown roux. Add onion, celery and garlic. Sauté until onions are soft. Add water slowly and bring to low bowl. Boil gently 30 minutes. Add salt, pepper, sugar and crawfish fat. Simmer 1 hour, covered. Add crawfish tails. Cook on medium heat 15 minutes. Remove from heat. Add parsley and onion tops. Serve in bowls with hard cooked eggs and stuffed crawfish heads.

Yield: 2 quarts

Jill Verspoor Durkee (Mrs. Robert R., III)

STUFFED CRAWFISH HEADS

60 crawfish heads, cleaned
1/4 cup cooking oil
1 large onion, minced
2 ribs celery, minced
2 medium bell peppers, minced
3 cloves garlic, minced
1/2 pound crawfish tails, peeled
4-5 slices stale bread or
    1 small French bread loaf,
    toasted
2 cloves garlic, minced
1 tablespoon salt
1/2 teaspoon black pepper
1/2 teaspoon red pepper
1/4 pound crawfish tails, peeled
Seasoned bread crumbs
Steamed rice for serving

Heat oil in large pot. Add onions, celery, bell pepper and garlic. Sauté until wilted. Grind 1/2 pound crawfish tails and bread in food processor. Add to sautéed vegetables. Add garlic, salt, black and red pepper and 1/4 pound crawfish tails. Cook 5-8 minutes, stirring. Cool and stuff crawfish heads, packing tightly. Roll stuffed heads in thin layer of bread crumbs. Place on baking sheet with rim. Bake in **preheated 375° oven 15-20 minutes.** Add to bisque. Serve with steaming rice.

Yield: 60 stuffed heads

Mrs. Marie Angelle

GOULASHSUPPE de LAFAYETTE

3 tablespoons vegetable oil
1 cup chopped onions
1 pound lean stew meat
1 tablespoon all-purpose flour
1 teaspoon paprika
1/2 teaspoon garlic powder
1/2 teaspoon red pepper
1/2 teaspoon caraway seed
1/2 teaspoon marjoram
1 or 2 teaspoons salt
5 tablespoons tomato puree
40 ounces beef broth
4 small potatoes, 3 cups peeled
    and finely diced

Heat oil in Dutch oven or large pot. Add onions and sauté until clear, not brown. Trim fat from meat and finely dice. Add meat to onions. Sprinkle flour over meat, stirring to blend. Lower heat while adding paprika, garlic powder, red pepper, caraway seed, marjoram, salt and tomato puree. Stir in beef broth, canned or use 2 tablespoons instant beef granules to 40 ounces water. Bring to boil and add diced potatoes. Cover and cook on medium heat until potatoes are cooked, 20-30 minutes. Serve in soup bowls. *This is our Lafayette version of a soup we enjoyed while skiing in Austria with 30 Louisiana friends.*

Yield: 6-8 servings

Robert R. Durkee, Jr.

CURRY CREAM SOUP

2 medium onions, chopped
2 ribs celery, chopped
2 red Delicious apples, chopped
3 tablespoons butter
2 tablespoons curry powder
1/4 cup all-purpose flour
4 cups chicken stock
1/2 teaspoon salt
1/8 teaspoon each—chili
    powder, cayenne pepper,
    paprika
2 cups heavy cream
1 cup chopped cooked chicken
18 avocado slices

In a large saucepan sauté onions, celery, apples in butter until soft but not brown. Add curry powder and sauté 2 minutes longer. Stir in flour. Add chicken stock a little at a time. Add salt, chili powder, cayenne, and paprika. Simmer 5 minutes. Purée in blender, about half at a time until smooth. Chill. Just before serving add cream and chopped chicken. Serve in 6 bowls and garnish with avocado slices.

Yield: 6 servings

Jilles P. Verspoor

CATFISH COURT BOUILLON

2 pounds catfish fillets, cut into
    chunks, seasoned with salt,
    lemon pepper, coarse black
    pepper & cayenne pepper
1/2 cup butter
1 large onion, chopped
1/2 bell pepper, chopped
3 "toes" garlic, minced
2 tablespoons prepared roux
1 (10-oz.) can Ro-tel tomatoes,
    blended with liquid
1 (8-oz.) can tomato sauce
1 bay leaf
1 teaspoon Worcestershire
    sauce
1½ cups chicken or fish stock
1/4 cup red wine
1/3 cup chopped parsley
1/3 cup chopped onion tops

Season catfish with salt, lemon pepper, coarse black pepper and cayenne pepper. Refrigerate 2 hours. In Dutch oven melt butter. Add onion, bell pepper and garlic. Sauté over low heat 30 minutes. Add roux, tomatoes, tomato sauce, bay leaf and Worcestershire sauce. Cook 15 minutes. Add stock and wine. Cover. Simmer until oil rises to the top, 45 minutes. Add fish, parsley and onion tops. Simmer covered 30 minutes on low heat. Serve with cooked rice.

Yield: 6-8 servings

Betty Baquet Bares (Mrs. Allen)

REDFISH COURT BOUILLON

3-4 pounds redfish fillets
Salt and red pepper
1/2 cup cooking oil
1/2 cup flour
1 large onion, minced
1 large bell pepper, minced
1/3 cup minced celery
1 (16-oz.) can tomatoes, mashed
    with juice
1/2 lemon, cut in round slices
2 tablespoons Worcestershire
    sauce
3 cups boiling water
1/2 cup red wine
1½ teaspoons salt
1/2 teaspoon black pepper
1/3 cup chopped green onion
    tops
1/3 cup chopped parsley

Slice fish in 1½-inch slices and season with salt and red pepper. Set aside in refrigerator. Heat oil in 4½-quart Dutch oven and add flour. Stir until roux is dark brown. Add onion, bell pepper and celery, Allow to brown, stirring often for 12 minutes. Add tomatoes and cook 2 minutes. Add lemon, Worcestershire, boiling water, wine, salt and pepper. Cover and simmer 1 hour. Add fish, cover and cook an additional 30 minutes. Add green onion tops and parsley. Serve with boiled rice. *From the recipe files of Walter B. Gordy.*

Yield: 10 servings

Matthew B. Gordy

*A similar recipe was submitted by **Beulah Punch.** She adds 8 ounces tomato sauce and omits celery.*

CRAB CORN BISQUE

1 pound butter
1 small white onion, chopped
2 (10-oz.) packages frozen
  cream corn or fresh corn
  from 6 ears
1 pint Half & Half cream
1 pint milk
1 pound white crabmeat
1 tablespoon instant flour
1/2 teaspoon salt
1/2 teaspoon white pepper
Chopped chives and chopped
  parsley for garnish

In a medium saucepan sauté onion in butter. Add corn, cream, milk and crabmeat. Bring to boil. Simmer 10 minutes. Thicken with flour. Season to taste with salt and pepper. Garnish with chives and parsley. Serve in cup-size servings.

Yield: 8 servings

Alma B. Stuller (Mrs. G. F.)

GASPERGOU FISH COURT BOUILLON

5 pounds gaspergou fillets
  or any firm fish
Mixture of:
  4$^1/_2$ teaspoons salt
  1 teaspoon each black
  pepper, red pepper, Accènt
  and 3/4 teaspoon thyme
2 tablespoons Louisiana hot
  sauce
3 slices bacon
3 ribs celery, minced
3 cups finely chopped onions
1 large bell pepper, finely
  chopped
10 cloves garlic, minced
6 tablespoons Basic Roux
1 cup hot water
1 (8-oz.) can tomato paste
1 (10-oz.) can Ro-tel tomatoes
  and green chilies, blended
1 teaspoon sugar
1 teaspoon Kitchen Bouquet
2 thin slices of lemon
6 cups water
4 tablespoons minced parsley
6 tablespoons minced onion tops

Cut fish into 2-inch pieces. Mix seasonings together. Sprinkle half the mixture on fish fillets. Sprinkle hot sauce on fish. Cover and refrigerate 3 hours or more. Cook bacon in 8-quart pot 5 minutes over medium heat. Add celery, onion, bell pepper and garlic. Cook until onions are wilted. Add Basic Roux dissolved in hot water, tomato paste, tomatoes, sugar, Kitchen Bouquet and lemon slices plus remainder of salt, pepper, thyme, and Accènt mixture. Add 6 cups water. Cover and cook over medium heat 1½ hours. Add fish and cook uncovered 20-25 minutes. Add parsley and onion tops. Serve with cooked rice. *When I moved on Cherry Street as a bride in 1923, my neighbors, Lucy and Paul Goulas, told me I must learn to cook like the French people. This was their recipe.*

Yield: 12 servings

Bessye Evans Faulk (Mrs. J. W.)

CHAMPAGNE CAMEMBERT SOUP

4 tablespoons butter
1 tablespoon all-purpose flour
1 cup chicken stock
1/2 pint whipping cream
5 ounces milk
6 tablespoons butter
4 1/2 ounces Camembert cheese
    cut into small pieces with
    rind on
5 ounces champagne
Salt and white pepper to taste
Chopped parsley for garnish

In a large saucepan melt 4 tablespoons butter. Stir in flour until well blended. Add chicken stock and whisk until just before mixture boils. Remove from heat. Add cream and milk. Return to heat and bring to just before boiling point again. Remove from heat. Add 6 tablespoons butter, Camembert cheese and champagne. Stir over medium heat until cheese has melted. Season with small amounts of salt and pepper. Garnish with parsley. *An elegant soup to serve your guests.*

Yield: 4 servings

Cloeann McDowell Clement (Mrs. John P.)

MA BRYANT'S CORN SOUP L'ACADIEN

6 medium slices (1 lb.) pickled
    pork
1 large onion, chopped
2 tablespoons chopped green
    pepper
3 cups fresh or frozen whole
    grain corn
1 (10-oz.) can Ro-tel tomatoes
    and green chilies, blended
1 (16-oz.) can whole tomatoes,
    undrained and chopped
6 cloves garlic, chopped
3 tablespoons chopped parsley
1/2 cup chopped green onion
    tops
Salt to taste

Brown meat lightly in large heavy pot. Add onions and green peppers. Sauté until tender. Add corn, Ro-tel tomatoes and green chilies, tomatoes, garlic, parsley and green onion tops. Sauté for 5 minutes. Add water and bring to boil. Cover, lower heat, and let simmer 30-45 minutes. Additional water may be added if soup is too thick. Salt to taste.

Yield: 6-8 servings

Alida "Sis" Talley (Mrs. Bill)

CREAM OF TOMATO SOUP

2 cups canned tomatoes
1/2 cup butter
1/2 cup all-purpose flour
4 cups milk
1½ teaspoons salt
3/4 teaspoon white pepper

Simmer tomatoes and liquid in medium sauce-pan 15 minutes. Puree in food processor, then pour through sieve. Melt butter in 3-quart saucepan. Stir in flour. Add milk slowly to blend. Cook until white sauce is thick. Add salt, pepper and hot tomato juice. Serve hot with plain or cheese crackers.

Yield: 10 servings

Virgie Ewell Heard Wallis (Mrs. Hugh C.)

TURTLE SOUP WITH MADEIRA

3/4 cup unsalted butter
1/2 cup flour
1/2 pound smoked ham, cut into
    1/2-inch cubes
2 pounds Terrapin or Snapper
    turtle meat, cubed
1 cup chopped onion
2 large tomatoes, chopped
    (preferably Creole tomatoes)
1/4 cup chopped celery
3 tablespoons minced parsley
4 cloves garlic, minced
2 teaspoons salt
1 teaspoon ground black pepper
1/2 teaspoon cayenne pepper
1 whole bay leaf, minced
1/2 teaspoon thyme
1/2 teaspoon ground cloves
1/2 teaspoon allspice
1/4 teaspoon mace
1/4 teaspoon grated nutmeg
3 cups rich brown stock
2 cups rich poultry stock
1 tablespoon Worcestershire
    sauce
1 tablespoon fresh lemon juice
1/2 cup Madeira
Chopped, hard boiled eggs

In a large 5-quart pot melt butter over low heat. Add flour, stirring constantly and cook over low heat, stirring until a smooth light brown roux is formed, about 10-15 minutes. Add ham, turtle meat, onion, tomatoes, cel-ery, parsley and garlic. Mix well. Continue cooking over low heat, stirring until vegeta-bles are lightly browned. Add salt, black pep-per, cayenne pepper, bay leaf, thyme, cloves, allspice, mace and nutmeg. Blend well. Add stocks. Stir to blend well. Raise heat to high and bring to a boil. Lower heat and simmer 2 hours, covered. Stir from time to time with wooden spoon. Just before serving, stir in Worcestershire sauce, lemon juice and Madeira. Ladle into individual soup plates and garnish with chopped egg. *Turtle soup has long been a favorite Cajun dish, the main ingredient being readily available.*

Yield: 8-10 servings

Terry L. Thompson (Mrs. Pat)

OYSTER ROCKEFELLER SOUP

1 medium onion, finely minced
5 cloves garlic, minced
2 ribs celery, minced
3 cups chicken stock
2 cups cooked spinach, pureed
    in processor or blender
2 pints oysters and oyster liquid
2 pints Half & Half cream
3/4 cup freshly grated Parmesan
    or Romano cheese
1/3 cup cornstarch dissolved in
1/2 cup Pernod
1 tablespoon anise seed
Salt and pepper to taste
Lemon slices for garnish

In a 4 or 5-quart pot sauté onion, garlic and celery for 5 minutes in a little of the chicken stock. Add puree of spinach and simmer 5 more minutes. Add remaining chicken stock and the oyster liquid (oysters will be added later). Slowly add cream and blend well. Cook for 10 minutes, stirring constantly. Add grated cheese, whisking constantly. Thicken with cornstarch dissolved in the Pernod. When soup is hot and thick, remove from heat and add drained oysters. Add anise seed, salt and pepper and serve with a garnish of thin lemon slice.

Yield: 6-8 servings

Bryan Richard
Sous Chef Chez Marcelle

LENTIL SOUP

1 pound lentils
2 quarts water
1 large onion, chopped
1 bell pepper, chopped
2 small carrots, chopped
1 clove garlic, minced
2 bay leaves
Picnic ham bone with meat or
    1 pound smoked sausage
2 teaspoons salt
1 teaspoon pepper

Sort and wash lentils. Place in large Dutch oven and cover with water. Soak overnight. Drain. Add 2 quarts water, onion, bell pepper, carrots and garlic which have all been finely chopped. Add bay leaves and ham, salt and pepper. Cook on medium heat 2 hours. If using sausage, add during the last half hour, and add more salt. Remove half the lentils, mash and return to pot to thicken soup. *Very good served over rice. Freezes well.*

Yield: 8-10 servings

Virgie F. Wallace (Mrs. Wayne)

A handful of lettuce leaves, put to the boiling soup, will imbibe the grease and fat; then, when removed, will leave it clear and free.

CREAM OF EGGPLANT SOUP

2-3 medium eggplants, peeled
    and diced
1 tablespoon salt
6 tablespoons butter
1 large onion, diced
1 cup diced tomatoes
2 quarts chicken stock
2 quarts whipping cream
2 tablespoons oil
2 tablespoons all-purpose flour
1 teaspoon curry powder
1 teaspoon white pepper
1/2 teaspoon red pepper
Salt to taste

Place peeled and diced eggplant in colander. Sprinkle with salt. Let sit 30 minutes. Rinse. In a 5-quart pot melt butter. Add eggplant, onion and tomatoes. Sauté five minutes. Add stock and cream. Bring to a boil. Simmer 15 minutes. Heat oil in small skillet. Add flour, stirring to make a blond roux (light tan). Gradually whip blond roux into soup until desired consistency. Add curry, white and red pepper and salt to taste.

Yield: 12 servings

Chef Joseph Gonsoulin,
Chez Marcelle

VEGETABLE BEEF SOUP

3 pounds stew meat
2 pounds soup meat with bones
1/2 pound ham pieces
6 quarts water
1 medium onion, quartered
1 rib celery, cut into pieces
2 (14½-oz.) cans whole peeled
    tomatoes with liquid,
    mashed
3 (8-oz.) cans tomato sauce
1 tablespoon salt
1 teaspoon pepper
1 cup diced carrots
2 medium size onions, chopped
2 cups chopped celery
1 cup diced turnips
1 cup chopped bell pepper
8 green onions, chopped fine
4 cups chopped cabbage
2 cups diced potatoes
6 tablespoons chopped parsley
2 pounds frozen whole kernel
    corn

Place stew meat, soup bones and ham in large 8-quart soup pot. Cover with 6 quarts water. Bring to boil, simmer 5 minutes or more. Skim off scum. Add onion, celery, tomatoes, tomato sauce, salt and pepper. Bring to a boil then lower heat. Simmer until meat is tender. Add carrots and onions. Let cook while preparing celery, turnips and bell pepper. Add to soup and let cook while preparing green onions, cabbage, potatoes, parsley and corn. Taste for seasoning, may need more salt and pepper. Simmer 30-45 minutes until vegetables are tender. *My mother gave us her recipe for Vegetable Soup when we were first married and I couldn't cook. I added the ham pieces and more corn to the recipe."*

Yield: 8-10 servings

Carolyn Shewmake Camardelle (Mrs. Gabe)

101

ALLIGATOR SAUCE PIQUANTE

2-3 pounds alligator meat
Tex-Joy steak seasoning
2/3 cup shortening
1 cup all-purpose flour
3 large onions, chopped
6 ribs celery, chopped
1 large bell pepper, chopped
1 (8-oz.) can tomato sauce,
    could substitute (10-oz.) can
    Ro-tel tomatoes, mashed
1 (6-oz.) can tomato paste
1 tablespoon red pepper, omit if
    using Ro-tel tomatoes
Hot water
1/4 cup chopped green onion
    tops
1/4 cup chopped parsley
Cooked rice for serving

Cut meat into small pieces. Remove all tallow. Season with steak seasoning. Brown meat in Dutch oven or black pot using 1 tablespoon shortening. Remove meat. Melt 2/3 cup shortening in pot and add flour. Stir until dark brown. Add onion, celery and bell pepper. Sauté on low fire until onions are clear. Stir in tomato sauce and tomato paste, continue to cook 2 minutes. Add water gradually (2-3 cups at a time) until the consistency of gumbo. Cook 30 minutes. Add meat. Cover. Cook 60 minutes until meat is tender. Add onion tops and parsley, cover until served. Serve over rice. *Wild ducks, fish or game can be substituted for alligator meat.*

Yield: 6 servings

Robert M. Arceneaux

MICROWAVED ALLIGATOR

2 alligator-tail chops about
    1/2-inch thick
1 teaspoon Season-All
1 medium onion, sliced

Season alligator chops with Season-All (Lemon Pepper can be substituted). Place in a 1 1/2-quart dish and microwave on **HIGH (100%) 5 MINUTES,** uncovered. Arrange onion slices over chops, cover with plastic wrap and **MICROWAVE ON LOW (30%) 20 MINUTES.** Allow to stand 5 minutes before serving.

LSU Cooperative Extension Service

ALLIGATOR CHILI

1 pound alligator meat, diced
2 tablespoons vegetable oil
1 large onion, diced
1 large bell pepper, diced
1 clove garlic, minced
1 (16-oz.) can pinto beans
1 (10-oz.) can Ro-tel tomatoes
    and chilies, blended
1 (6-oz.) can tomato paste
Salt and pepper to taste
1 teaspoon cumin
1 diced jalapeño pepper
1 cup dark red wine

In Dutch oven boil diced meat in water seasoned with salt and pepper 20 minutes. Drain and set aside. In same pot add oil, onion, bell pepper and garlic. Sauté until onions are tender. Add pinto beans, tomatoes, tomato paste, salt, pepper, cumin and jalapeño. Cook on medium low heat 40 minutes. Add alligator meat. Cook on low heat 3 hours. Add wine last 30 minutes.

Yield: 6 servings

Cloeann McDowell Clement (Mrs. John P.)

BREAST OF WILD DUCK

4 wild duck breasts, skinned
    and boned
1/2 cup red wine
1/4 cup vegetable oil
1/4 cup soy sauce

Marinate boned duck in a mixture of wine, oil and soy sauce for 3 hours. Pat dry. Broil duck on preheated rack of broiling pan 5 inches from heat. Broil 7 minutes on each side. Transfer to board and let stand 5 minutes. Slice diagonally against grain. Serve with **Wild Game Sauce.***

*Wild Game Sauce:
3/4 cup red currant jelly
2 teaspoons Dijon mustard
1 1/2 teaspoons red wine vinegar
1 teaspoon soy sauce
3/4 teaspoon Worcestershire
    sauce
1/4 teaspoon ground cumin
1/8 teaspoon pepper

In small saucepan combine jelly, mustard, vinegar, soy sauce, Worcestershire sauce, cumin and pepper. Heat over low heat, stirring until jelly has melted. Transfer to heated sauce boat. Serve with Breast of Wild Duck.

Yield: 2/3 cup sauce

Yvonne Booth (Mrs. Barrett E.)

Microwave shortcut: Place all ingredients for **Wild Game Sauce** in a 2-cup Pyrex measuring cup. Microwave on **HIGH (100%) 1 MINUTE**, stirring at 30 seconds.
Jean K Durkee

VERNA'S QUAIL ON TOAST

8 quail, cleaned
4 slices bacon, each cut into
    4 pieces
Salt and pepper for sprinkling
1/2 cup oil
1 cup finely chopped onions
1 (8-oz.) can sliced mushrooms
    and liquid
1/2 cup water
1/3 cup finely chopped celery
    leaves
Salt and pepper to taste
8 slices toasted white bread
4 large cloves garlic, halved
2 tablespoons minced parsley

Make slit with sharp knife in top of each side of breast. Insert 1/4 slice bacon in each slit. Salt and pepper quail inside and out. Lightly brown quail on both sides in oil in heavy Dutch oven. Remove quail from pot. Add onions and sauté until brown. Add mushrooms and liquid, water, celery and salt. Return quail to pot, breast down. Cover. Simmer until tender, about 1 hour. Taste gravy. Add salt and pepper if needed. When ready to serve, toast bread and rub with cut garlic. Spoon 2 tablespoons gravy and mushrooms over bread. Sprinkle with parsley and place a quail on top. *From the recipe files of my mother.*

Yield: 6-8 servings

Verna LeBlanc Butcher (Mrs. Warren)

FRIED QUAIL

12 quail, cleaned
Salt, black and red pepper, garlic
    powder for sprinkling
2 cups buttermilk
2 tablespoons flour
2 cups flour, more may be
    needed for coating
Salt, red and black pepper, garlic
    powder for coating
Seasoned bread crumbs for
    coating
Vegetable oil for deep frying

Sprinkle quail with salt, pepper, and garlic powder. Pour buttermilk into large bowl. Add 2 tablespoons flour to thicken. Add quail, cover and set aside 4 hours. Place flour, salt, red and black pepper and garlic powder in brown paper bag. Shake bag well to mix. Remove quail from buttermilk, drain slightly. Place all quail in paper bag. Shake well to coat. Dip each quail back into buttermilk and roll in bread crumbs. Deep fry in 250°-300° oil until crumbs turn golden brown.

Yield: 6 servings

Duke Needham

DOVE-DOLPHIN

24 doves, cleaned, inside & out
Salt, pepper and herb seasoning,
    (McCormick's) for sprinkling
1/2 pound bacon, cut into strips
1/2 cup butter
2 large onions, chopped
1/2 bell pepper, chopped
3 cloves garlic, chopped
1 1/4 cups beef broth
1/2 cup red wine
1 (4-oz.) can mushrooms, bits
    and pieces

Season doves with salt, pepper and herb seasoning. Wrap with bacon and secure with toothpick through breast. Melt butter in Dutch oven on top of stove. Brown doves in butter. Add onion, bell pepper and garlic. Cook over low fire until clear and tender, approximately 15 minutes. Add broth, simmer 2 hours. During last hour add wine and mushrooms. Check seasoning. Add salt and pepper to taste. *Beulah Mouton first taught me the preparation of game cookery. She felt the secret of tender game was long, slow cooking. Patience produces perfection.*

Yield: 8 servings

Ann Humphries LeJeune (Mrs. Womack)

ROAST WILD DUCK

3 wild ducks
Salt, red and black pepper for
    sprinkling
1 orange, cut into slices with rind
1 apple, cut into slices with peel
1 jalapeño pepper, cut into
    3 strips
1 bell pepper, cut into 3 strips
3 small whole onions
1 cup vegetable oil
2 large onions, chopped
2 bell peppers, chopped
3 ribs celery, chopped
2 cloves garlic, minced
Salt and pepper
1/2 cup water

Clean ducks well. If frozen thaw at room temperature or in refrigerator (never in water). Season highly with salt, red and black pepper, inside and out. In the cavities place orange and apple slices, jalapeño pepper, bell pepper strips and whole onions. Close with picks or by stitching.

Heat oil in large Dutch oven. Brown ducks slowly, but thoroughly. Remove from pot and set aside. Add onion, bell pepper, celery and garlic. Sauté until vegetables wilt. Return ducks to pot. Add a small amount of water at a time. Add salt and pepper to taste. Cover tightly and cook over low heat 3 hours, or until tender.

Yield: 3 servings

Blanche Gauthier

VENISON ROAST CHATEAU

6-8 pound venison roast
Salt, garlic salt, black and red
    pepper, lemon & herb salt
2 large onions, sliced into rings
1 large bell pepper, sliced into
    strips
2 cups hearty Burgundy wine

Rub roast well with salt, garlic salt, black and red pepper, and lemon and herb salt. Place roast in pan. Cover roast with onions and bell pepper. Pour wine over roast and cover with foil. Marinate in refrigerator 24 hours, turning every 8 hours. Bake in same pan in marinade under foil tent in **preheated 350° oven 3 hours** or until well done. Serve hot.

Yield: 12-16 servings

Sterling Womack LeJeune

VENISON BEER STEW

4 slices bacon
2 pounds boneless venison, cut
    into bite-size pieces
1/4 cup flour
1 (16-oz.) can tomatoes,
    chopped with liquid
1 (12-oz.) can beer
1 medium onion chopped
2 teaspoons instant beef bouillon
1 teaspoon sugar
1/2 teaspoon crushed thyme
1/2 teaspoon black pepper
1/8 teaspoon red pepper
3 medium carrots, cut up
2 small turnips, peeled and
    cut into wedges
1 celery rib, cut up
1 cup frozen peas
Creole Seasoning
TABASCO
Dill weed

In large heavy pot cook bacon until crisp. Drain. Crumble and set aside. Keep 2 tablespoons of drippings in pot. Coat venison with flour and brown in pan drippings. Add tomatoes with liquid, beer, onions, bouillon, sugar, thyme and red and black pepper. Bring to boil, reduce heat, cover and simmer 1¼ hours. Add carrots, turnips and celery. Simer 30 minutes. Add peas, cook 5 minutes more. Stir in bacon. Season to taste with Creole seasoning, TABASCO and dill weed.

Yield: 4 servings

Judith Montgomery Skelton (Mrs. Roland)

FRIED QUAIL LEJEUNE

12 cleaned quail
1 quart buttermilk
2 teaspoons TABASCO sauce
4 tablespoons Worcestershire
  sauce
3 eggs, whipped
1/2 cup milk
1 cup Italian seasoned bread
  crumbs
1 cup all-purpose flour
Salt, pepper, garlic salt and
  paprika
1/2 cup butter or more
1/2 cup margarine or more

Marinate quail overnight in buttermilk, TABASCO and Worcestershire sauce. Pat quail dry and dip them in a mixture of egg and milk. Roll quail in bread crumbs and then flour that has salt, pepper, garlic salt and paprika added to it. Fry quail in large skillet with half butter and half margarine. Grease should cover about half the bird at a time. Fry 15 minutes or until brown. Do not fry too long as they will get tough.

Yield: 12 servings

Sterling Womack LeJeune

DEER SHISH KABOB

2¼-3 pounds venison, cut into
  chunks, allow 4 chunks per
  skewer or stick
1 (8-oz.) bottle Italian dressing
3/4 pound fatty bacon
2 large bell peppers, cut into
  1-inch pieces
5 small yellow onions, quartered
  or 20 small white onions
Barbecue sauce of your choice
  for basting, optional

Place deer meat in a large bowl. Cover with Italian dressing and marinate covered over night. Prepare bell pepper, onion and bacon. With skewers impale deer meat, bacon, bell pepper and onion. Always keep bacon touching deer meat. Alternate until skewer is filled.

Cook on slow heat or barbecue pit until bell peppers start to wilt then remove from fire. *You can baste with a barbecue sauce of your choice while cooking. I prefer Jack Miller's.*

Yield: 10 servings

Duke Needham

the
1930s

he decade of the Thirties watched our nation recover from The Depression, Herbert Hoover finish his term as President of the United States and FDR begin his elected and unprecedented four consecutive terms.

This Lafayette in which I spent my childhood had a population of 15,000 in the 1930s and we could walk anywhere. My father, a salesman, owned a car and a favorite evening ride was to "make a pass" down Main Street, past the new Abdalla's or stopping at Heymann's Drugstore for a chocolate milk (Hershey's syrup was not yet in stores).

Once a week I donned black sateen tights, a white cotton blouse and a large red bow to join other children at Miss LeBlanc's School of Dance. And, daily during the summer months I sat on the front porch steps of our Washington Street home waiting for "Poor Boy" Landry who came around with a snowball stand attached to his bicycle. We children supplied our own cups and spoons (paper cups were not yet available). The "snowball man" was Hulo Landry who, along with his wife, opened a small family seafood restaurant on St. John Street in 1932. They remained in this location until 1936, when they moved "out of town" to Pinhook Road. There they built a restaurant then known as "Poor Boy's Riverside Inn" which extended over the Vermilion River. Seafood has been the house staple since those days in downtown Lafayette with broiled flounder and stuffed flounder heading the list of the most popular items served.

Learning of the new canning plant the Trappey family established in New Iberia, several businessmen from Lafayette invited Mr. Trappey to look over a site on the Vermilion River as a potential location for an extension of the business. At that time, in 1930, Trappey canned okra, blackberries, figs, snap beans and especially peppers. Trappey decided to move his pepper drier to the Lafayette site. It was there that he developed a new process for canning the Louisiana yam.

We bought Mercurochrome and castor oil at the Vermilion Drug Store and large penny candies from jars at Piccione's combination store and cobbler shop where a dime's worth got the buyer "lagniappe." Our neighbors, the Grimmers, owned the first coffee roasting plant in the community. Grimmer's Coffee supplied premiums, and I still have my premium champagne glasses from that era.

In the mid-thirties I joined other young girls at Mt. Carmel Academy where the nuns taught us reading and writing and a fear of God! For celebrations at the Cathedral we were dressed as angels, complete with wings and halos, leading the processions. I also discovered Keller's Bakery in a small green wooden building where individual pies sold for a nickel! My favorite was pineapple, and Mr. Keller bagged two of them every time he saw me approaching.

All through the month of December Santa Claus came to Heymann's, stood in a side window and drew a ticket which named the winner of all the toys in the window. He was the only Santa Claus in town!

Such was the Lafayette of The Thirties.

Marguerite Richard Lyle (Mrs. Mike)
U.S.L. Faculty member
Lafayette Parish School Board member

Rice~Eggs

NEW YEAR'S PORK JAMBALAYA

1 pound smoked sausage, sliced
    1/4 inch thick
1 pound lean pork chunks, cut
    into 1-inch cubes
Tony's Creole seasoning
1/4 cup oil
1 large onion, chopped
1/4 cup chopped bell pepper
1/4 cup chopped celery
1 cup water
1 cup chicken or beef broth
1/4 cup margarine
1½ teaspoons salt
1/4 teaspoon black pepper
1/4 teaspoon red pepper
2 tablespoons minced pimiento
1 cup uncooked rice
1 (16-oz.) can black-eyed peas,
    drained
1/3 cup chopped parsley
1/3 cup chopped green onion
    tops

In a heavy 4-quart pot, brown sausage and pork, seasoned with Creole seasoning, in hot oil. Add onion, bell pepper and celery. Cover and cook on medium heat 30 minutes or until pork is almost done. Skim off excess oil. Add water, broth, margarine, salt, black and red pepper and pimiento. Bring mixture to a boil. Add rice, stir and add black-eyed peas. Cover and cook 30 minutes or until rice is cooked. Add parsley and onion tops the last 5 minutes. *My daughters and I concocted this recipe one New Year's Day and it's become a family favorite. This recipe can be doubled and tripled successfully.*

Yield: 6 servings

Betty Baquet Bares (Mrs. Allen)

SHRIMP JAMBALAYA

1/4 cup margarine
1 cup chopped onion
1/2 cup chopped bell pepper
1/4 cup chopped celery
1 cup chopped fresh mushrooms
1 teaspoon finely chopped chives
1 pound shrimp, peeled
1 teaspoon minced parsley
2 teaspoons salt
2 teaspoons green hot sauce
1 teaspoon Worcestershire
    sauce
1½ cups rice
1½ cups water

In 4-quart pot with tight fitting lid, melt margarine. Add onion, bell pepper and celery. Sauté for 15 minutes. Add mushrooms and chives. Cook 5 minutes. Peel, devein and chop shrimp coarsely. Add shrimp, parsley, salt, hot sauce, Worcestershire, rice and water. Stir well. Cook on medium heat, stirring frequently. Cook until all liquid has been absorbed. Reduce heat to simmer. Cover tightly and steam 30 minutes, stirring once or twice.

Yield: 4 servings

Genevieve Albarado (Mrs. Larry)

PUDDIN'S DIRTY RICE

2 pounds lean ground beef
1/2 pound Owens pork sausage
2 (10¾-oz.) cans cream of
  mushroom soup
2 soup cans water
1 (2.75-oz.) box dry onion soup
  mix
1/2 cup chopped green onion
  tops
1 cup finely chopped celery
1½ medium bell peppers,
  finely chopped
1/2 cup finely chopped white
  onion
2 cups uncooked long grain rice
1 teaspoon salt
1/2 teaspoon red pepper
1/4 teaspoon black pepper

Combine beef, pork, soup, water, onion soup mix, onion tops, celery, bell pepper, onion, rice, salt, red and black pepper in large bowl. Mix together with your hands (roll up your sleeves). Place in 4½-quart Dutch oven. Cover. Bake in **preheated 350° oven 1 hour 30 minutes.** Stir well at 45 minutes. Continue to cook covered.

Yield: 25 servings

Herbert "Puddin" Robin

EGGPLANT RICE DRESSING

2 medium eggplants (2 lbs.),
  peeled and diced
1 large onion, chopped
1 cup chopped celery
2 medium bell peppers, chopped
8 cloves garlic, minced
1 teaspoon salt
1 cup water
3 cups cooked rice
1½ pounds ground pork
2 teaspoons salt
1 teaspoon black pepper
1/2 teaspoon red pepper
Bread crumbs for sprinkling

Boil eggplant, onion, celery, bell pepper, garlic, salt and water in Dutch oven until vegetables are tender. Cook rice in separate pot. Place meat in small skillet, brown in its own fat. Drain and add to cooked vegetables. Cook meat and vegetables to a thick consistency. Add rice, salt, black and red pepper. Place in buttered 2-quart round glass casserole dish. Sprinkle top with bread crumbs. Bake in **preheated 350° oven 15 minutes.**

Yield: 12 servings

Marie Louise Comeaux Manuel (Mrs. John D.)

Microwave shortcut: After mixture has been placed in 2-quart glass dish, microwave on **HIGH (100%) 4 MINUTES.** *Jean K Durkee*

CAJUN RICE DRESSING

1 pound gizzards, cleaned
1/4 pound chicken, duck or
    turkey liver
1/4 cup bacon or pork sausage
    drippings
2 large onions, chopped fine
1 bell pepper, chopped fine
3 cloves garlic, minced
2 ribs celery, chopped fine
3 cups poultry stock
1 teaspoon salt
1/4 teaspoon cayenne pepper
Freshly ground black pepper
    to taste
4 cups hot cooked rice
    (cooked in salted water)
1/4 cup chopped parsley
1/3 cup finely sliced green
    onion tops

Using a hand grinder, grind the gizzards and livers. Heat the drippings in a sauté pan and sauté the gizzards and livers, stirring often until well browned. Add more drippings if necessary to prevent sticking. Add onion, bell pepper, garlic and celery and continue to sauté until vegetables are wilted. Add stock, salt, black pepper, cayenne pepper and scrape bottom of pan to release all browned bits of meat glaze. Cook over medium heat until thickened, 1-2 hours. Immediately before serving, fold in hot rice, chopped parsley and sliced green onions.

Yield: 10-12 servings

Patricia Cashman Andrus (Mrs. Robert)

MIRLITON SHRIMP RICE DRESSING

4-6 mirlitons (vegetable pears
    or chayote)
4 slices bacon, chopped
1 medium onion, chopped
1 bunch green onions, chopped
1/2 bunch parsley, chopped
2 pounds raw shrimp, peeled
1/2 cup butter
3/4 cup seasoned bread crumbs
2 eggs, beaten
1 (10-oz.) can Ro-tel tomatoes
    and green chilies, mashed
1 (14-oz.) can tomatoes, 1 cup
    drained and mashed
3 cups cooked rice
2 teaspoons salt
1/2 teaspoon red pepper
Bread crumbs for top

Boil mirlitons in lightly salted water 20 minutes. Peel, remove pit and finely chop. In a large Dutch oven sauté bacon, onion, green onion and parsley 2 minutes. Add shrimp. Stir and cook until pink. Add butter, stir until melted. Stir in bread crumbs and chopped mirlitons. Add eggs, tomatoes, cooked rice, salt and pepper. Mixture may remain in pot to bake or be transferred to 4-quart casserole serving dish. Sprinkle top with bread crumbs. Bake in **preheated 350° oven 30-45 minutes.**

Yield: 12 servings

Marilyn A. Tarpy (Mrs. Robert)

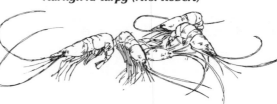

113

KELLY'S WILD RICE

1 (8-oz.) package wild rice
10½ ounces canned beef
    consommé
1 (6-oz.) can sliced mushrooms,
    broiled in butter
1/2 cup butter, sliced
Salt

Rinse wild rice in hot water. Bring consommé to boil. Pour over drained rice. Leave overnight or 6 hours in a 2-quart glass or ceramic dish. Add mushrooms and slices of butter. Cover. Microwave on **HIGH (100%) 6 MINUTES.** Stir. Continue to microwave covered on **LOW (30%) or DEFROST FOR 50 MINUTES,** stirring at 10 minute intervals. Taste before adding salt. Don't overcook. Rice should have texture. *Super with game—from recipe files of W. A. Kelly, M.D.*

Yield: 4 servings

Paul A. Barefield

NUTTY WILD RICE

1 (6-oz.) package long grain and
    wild rice mix
2 tablespoons butter
1 cup diced Canadian bacon
1/2 cup sliced green onion tops
    and bulbs
1 clove garlic, minced
1/4 cup dry white wine
1/4 cup chopped fresh parsley
1/2 teaspoon salt
1/8 teaspoon pepper
1 (8-oz.) can sliced water
    chestnuts, chopped
1 cup chopped pecans

Prepare wild rice mix according to package directions. In a large skillet, melt butter and add Canadian bacon, onion and garlic. Sauté 5 minutes, until onion is tender. Stir in wine, parsley, salt and pepper. Add water chestnuts, pecans and cooked rice. Toss lightly and heat throughout. Serve immediately or place in buttered 2-quart oven-proof dish. Cover. Bake in a **preheated 350° oven 20 minutes.**

Yield: 6-8 servings

Patricia Cashman Andrus (Mrs. Robert M.)

Microwave directions: Follow directions above. After spooning rice mixture into a 2-quart glass dish, microwave on **HIGH (100%) 4-5 MINUTES.** *Jean K Durkee*

RED BEANS AND RICE

2 tablespoons oil
1 pound ground lean beef
1 large onion, chopped
1/4 cup chopped bell pepper
2 teaspoons salt
1 tablespoon chili powder
1/2 teaspoon black pepper
1/2 teaspoon cayenne pepper
1 (16-oz.) can whole tomatoes, undrained and coarsely chopped
1 cup water
1 1/2 cups raw long grain rice
1 (15-oz.) can red kidney beans (Trappey's)

In a large skillet brown meat in hot oil over medium high heat. Drain well. Add onion and bell pepper. Cook over low heat until wilted. Add salt, chili powder, black pepper and cayenne pepper.

Stir chopped tomatoes and water into meat mixture. Simmer 10 minutes. Remove from fire. Add rice and red beans. Place in a 9 x 13 x 2-inch glass baking dish. Cover and seal tightly with foil. Bake in a **preheated 350° oven 1 hour.**

Remove from oven, fluff mixture with fork, cover and let steam for 10 minutes. If rice is not completely cooked, continue baking 15 minutes longer. Fluff again and let sit covered 10 minutes.

Yield: 6-8 servings

Grace Jenkins Boudreaux (Mrs. Wallace)

MARDI GRAS RED BEANS AND RICE

2 pounds dried red beans
4 onions, quartered
2 pounds Tasso, cut into 1-1 1/2-inch pieces. Ham and ham bone may be used in place or along with Tasso.
3 quarts water
Salt and pepper to taste
1 whole garlic florette (pod) unpeeled and left whole
Cooked white rice for serving

Wash red beans. Do not soak. Place beans and quartered onions in 6-quart soup pot. Add Tasso and/or ham bone, 3 quarts water, salt and pepper to taste and whole garlic florette (pod). Bring to boil. Cover and simmer 2 hours. Stir occasionally. Add more water if it seems too thick. Continue to simmer 1 1/2-2 hours. Beans should be well cooked but not mushy. A thick gravy will form to use over cooked white rice. *At table, pass a container of white wine vinegar. A small amount may be poured over beans by those who want it.* Serve with hot French bread.

Yield: 8-10 servings

Betty Brownsberger Palmintier (Mrs. D. J.)

RICE PILAF ON THE BAYOU

1 cup margarine
8 ounces canned sliced
    mushrooms, drain and
    reserve liquid
8 whole green onions, chopped
2 teaspoons oregano
1 teaspoon salt
2 cups Uncle Ben's converted
    raw rice
3 (10¾-oz.) cans beef bouillon
2 cups water plus liquid from
    mushrooms

In a large skillet or sauté pan, heat margarine. Add mushrooms, green onions, oregano and salt. Sauté until onions are soft. Stir in rice and brown lightly. Add bouillon, water and mushroom liquid. Pour into a 9 x 13-inch baking dish or 3-quart casserole. Cover with foil and bake in **preheated 450° oven 45 minutes.** Stir with fork to fluff. Continue to bake uncovered **15 minutes.** After removing from oven stir again and cover until serving time.

Yield: 8-10 servings

Karen Veillon McGlasson (Mrs. H. Edwin)

CREOLE RICE CALAS

1½ cups cooked rice, moderately
    hot
1 tablespoon (1 package) dry
    yeast
1/2 cup warm water
1 teaspoon sugar
3 eggs, beaten
1½ cups sifted, all-purpose
    unbleached flour
1/2 teaspoon salt
1/2 teaspoon vanilla
1/4 teaspoon freshly grated
    nutmeg
1 tablespoon + 2 teaspoons
    sugar
Cooking oil for deep fryer
Powdered sugar for dusting
Syrup or honey

Cook rice your favorite way.

Dissolve yeast in warm water with 1 teaspoon sugar in large mixing bowl. Blend well with rice. Cover and let rise in warm place overnight. Add eggs, flour, salt, vanilla, nutmeg and sugar. Beat just until smooth. Heat oil in deep fryer to 365.° Drop batter by tablespoon into oil. Fry until golden brown, bouncing each one as it cooks to expand volume. Do not crowd fryer. Maintain constant temperature so that Calas do not become soggy. Drain on paper towels and dust with powdered sugar.

Serve with syrup or honey, if desired. *Rice Calas were the wonderful 'invention' of the frugal housewife to utilize leftover rice. What a delightful way to do so.*

Yield: 2 dozen

Terry L. Thompson (Mrs. Pat)

MIMI'S BAKED PINEAPPLE STUFFING

1/2 cup butter, softened
1 cup sugar
1/8 teaspoon salt
4 eggs
1 (20-oz.) can crushed pineapple,
    drained
5 slices stale white bread,
    trimmed and cubed

In a mixing bowl cream butter and sugar until smooth. Add salt. Add eggs one at a time. Beat well after each addition. Stir in pineapple and bread cubes. Pour into a greased 2-quart casserole dish. Bake, uncovered, in a **preheated 350° oven for 1 hour.** *Excellent served with ham.*

Yield: 6 servings

Kathy Van Wie (Mrs. William)

CARROT DRESSING

4 tablespoons vegetable oil
1 tablespoon all-purpose flour
1 pound ground beef
3/4 cup chopped onion
2 cloves garlic, crushed
1 small bell pepper, chopped
1 pound carrots, grated
1 cup water
1/2 cup Italian seasoned bread
    crumbs
1 tablespoon salt
3/4 teaspoon pepper
1/4 cup bread crumbs
2 tablespoons melted butter

In a large skillet heat oil. Add flour and stir constantly over medium heat to make a nut brown roux. Brown meat in roux and add onions, sauté a few minutes. Add garlic, bell pepper, carrots and water. Simmer 15 minutes. Add bread crumbs, salt and pepper. Place in an 8 x 8-inch baking dish. Top with bread crumbs and melted butter.

Bake uncovered in a **preheated 350° oven 30 minutes.**

Yield: 6 servings

Betty Richard Butcher (Mrs. Thomas, Sr.)

A similar recipe was submitted by
Lillian Montet Dugas

Microwave shortcut: After placing carrot dressing in 8 x 8-inch glass dish, microwave on **HIGH (100%) 7-8 MINUTES,** rotating dish 1 time. *Jean K Durkee*

CRUSTLESS QUICHE

1 cup Half & Half cream
2 tablespoons chopped onion
2 tablespoons chopped green
pepper
3 tablespoons chopped
mushrooms
2 cups grated cheese of choice
5 beaten eggs
Salt and pepper to taste
1 cup cooked and crumbled ham,
bacon, or sausage

Mix cream, onion, pepper, mushrooms, cheese, eggs, salt, pepper and ham. Pour into greased 9-inch pie plate. Bake in **preheated 350° oven 30-35 minutes,** or until brown. May be frozen.

Yield: 6-8 servings

Anita Hardy Atkins (Mrs. Oscar)

CRAB QUICHE

9-inch pastry shell
3 green onion tops and bulbs,
chopped
4 tablespoons butter
10 ounces fresh or frozen
crabmeat
3 tablespoons white wine
3 eggs
1/2 pint whipping cream
1/4 cup grated Gruyère cheese
1 teaspoon salt
1/4 teaspoon red pepper

Partially bake pie shell in **preheated 350° oven 5 minutes.**

In a skillet over medium heat sauté green onions in butter. Add crabmeat and stir 3-4 minutes. Add wine, raise heat and cook until liquid evaporates. Set aside to cool. In a mixing bowl combine eggs, cream, cheese, salt and pepper. Stir in crabmeat mixture. Pour into pastry shell. Place in upper third of oven. Bake in **preheated 375° oven 30 minutes.**

Yield: 4-6 servings

Rosa Belle Stansbury (Mrs. Lyman W.)

OYSTER OMELETTE CHICO

1/4 cup butter
1 small white onion, finely
    chopped
1/4 bell pepper, finely chopped
12 medium size oysters (single
    gulp), drained
1/4 cup chopped mushrooms,
    drained
1 dozen large eggs
1/4 cup Rich's coffee cream
Salt, red and black pepper or
    Creole seasoning
4 tablespoons vegetable oil
2 large omelette skillets

In medium saucepan heat butter. Add onion and bell pepper. Sauté until soft. Drain oysters and mushrooms on paper towels. Add to sautéed vegetables. The oysters will wrinkle their nose at you when done. Mix eggs and cream. Season to taste. Beat to a froth. In each omelette skillet heat 2 tablespoons oil on medium heat. When oil is hot, put 1/2 of the egg mixture in each skillet. Just prior to folding omelette over, spoon oyster and mushroom mixture over one side and fold. Remove with flat spatula. *Created especially for Mr. & Mrs. N. R. Chico.*

Yield: 2 servings

Matthew B. Gordy

COMPANY EGGS

2 tablespoons butter
2 tablespoons flour
1 cup milk
1/4 teaspoon salt
1/4 teaspoon red pepper
1 cup cubed ham
1/4 cup chopped green onions
3 tablespoons butter
12 beaten eggs
1 (8-oz.) can sliced mushrooms,
    drained or 1/2 lb. fresh

Topping:
1/4 cup melted butter
2 cups crushed corn flakes
1/8 teaspoon paprika
1 cup grated cheddar cheese

To make white sauce melt butter in 1-quart saucepan. Stir in flour. Add milk slowly, stirring until mixture thickens. Add salt and red pepper. Set aside. In large skillet sauté ham and onions in butter until onions are tender. Add eggs and stir to form soft curls. When eggs are soft, stir in prepared white sauce and mushrooms. Pour mixture into greased 9 x 13-inch glass baking dish. Combine butter and flakes. Sprinkle over eggs. Top with cheese and paprika. Bake in **preheated 350° oven 20-30 minutes.**

Yield: 6 servings

Betty Baquet Bares (Mrs. Allen)

SHIRRED EGGS WITH CREOLE SAUCE

*Shirred Eggs:
8 ounces smoked ham, chopped finely
1 tablespoon butter
1/2 cup heavy cream
1/2 teaspoon dry mustard
1 teaspoon Worcestershire sauce
4 eggs
Salt and freshly ground pepper
Parsley for garnish

Sauté ham in butter. Whisk together cream, mustard and Worcestershire. Place 2 table-spoons cream mixture in bottom of each 4 individual au gratin dishes. Drop egg into dish. Sprinkle ham over each egg. Salt and pepper to taste. Place 4 au gratin dishes on baking pan. Bake in **preheated 375° oven 10-12 minutes**, or until yolks are set. Spoon Creole Sauce** over each shirred egg and top with freshly torn parsley.

**Creole Sauce:
1/4 cup oil
3 scallions, chopped
1/4 cup chopped celery
1 medium onion, chopped
1/2 bell pepper, chopped
2 cloves garlic, minced
2 large tomatoes, chopped
1/2 cup chicken stock
1/2 cup dry red wine
1/2 bay leaf, crushed finely
1 teaspoon salt
1/4 teaspoon black pepper
1/2 teaspoon thyme
1/2 teaspoon cayenne pepper
2 teaspoons lemon juice

In 12-inch skillet, heat oil. Add scallions, celery, onion, bell pepper and garlic. Add tomatoes and stir to blend. Add chicken stock, wine, bay leaf, salt, pepper, thyme, and cayenne pepper. Blend well and simmer over medium low heat 45 minutes. Just before serving stir in lemon juice and simmer 5 minutes longer.

Yield: Creole Sauce for 4 servings

Terry L. Thompson

Microwave directions for **Creole Sauce: In 8-cup glass measure sauté scallions, celery, onion, bell pepper and garlic in oil on **HIGH (100%) 3 MINUTES.** Add tomatoes, 1/4 cup stock, 1/4 cup red wine and seasonings. Microwave on **HIGH (100%) 12 MINUTES.** Add lemon juice and continue to microwave on **HIGH (100%) 1 MINUTE.** Follow directions above for Shirred Eggs* Microwave each au gratin dish on **HIGH (100%) 60-80 SECONDS.** *Jean K Durkee*

THE BRUNCH BUNCH

1¹/₂ cups shredded cheddar
   cheese
2 tablespoons butter
1¹/₄ cups chopped ham
2 ripe tomatoes, chopped
12 eggs, beaten
1¹/₂ cups Half & Half cream
1 teaspoon dill weed
1 teaspoon onion salt
1/4 teaspoon pepper

Butter a 2-quart round dish. Place cheese on bottom, dot with butter. Layer ham and then tomatoes. Mix eggs, cream, dill, onion salt and pepper. Pour over all layers. Bake in **preheated 325° oven 1 hour 15 minutes.**

Yield: 6 servings

Connie Dutsch Roberts (Mrs. U.D.)

CHILIES SOUFFLÉ

1/2 pound Monterey Jack
   cheese, grated
1/2 pound cheddar cheese,
   grated
3 (4-oz.) cans whole green
   chilies, seeded and chopped
3 eggs, separated
1/4 teaspoon cream of tartar
2 tablespoons all-purpose flour
1 (5.3-oz.) can evaporated milk
1/2 teaspoon salt
1/4 teaspoon black pepper
6 drops TABASCO sauce
4 ounces tomato sauce
4 ounces mild piquante sauce

Toss cheeses and chilies together in 3-quart soufflé or casserole dish with lid. Beat egg whites and cream of tartar until stiff with electric mixer or whisk. In separate bowl, blend egg yolks and flour. Stir in milk, salt, pepper and TABASCO. Fold yolk mixture into egg whites. Pour mixture over cheese and chilies. Cover and bake in **preheated 350° oven 30 minutes.** Spread sauces on top. Bake uncovered **30 minutes more.**

Yield: 4-6 servings

Janet Rauschenberg Begneaud (Mrs. Byron)

the
1940s

V for Victory

V for Vegetables

Patriotism soared in the 1940s! Citizens of Lafayette wanted to help their country. Many young men and women joined the Armed Forces. Those at home helped in many ways. Rationing of food, gas, shoes and tires was foremost in our thoughts. Instead of driving, we walked. Car pools were formed to save gas, or we rode bicycles to work. Because of sugar rationing, "sugar-less dessert" recipes were created. Because canned goods were rationed, everyone planted "Victory Gardens'" of fruits and vegetables.

The nation paid its last respects to Franklin D. Roosevelt in 1945 and Harry Truman became the 33rd President of the United States.

My father, J. A. Anders, was the first county agent in Lafayette Parish during World War I. During World War II he was principal of N. P. Moss School but he gave his time helping others grow Victory Gardens. Even part of the school playground was converted to a large vegetable garden. The home economics department taught canning procedures and the school cafeteria became a canning center for the entire community. Mothers, wives and sweethearts canned goodies, pecans, candy, gumbos to send to loved ones overseas.

The candied yams, developed and produced at Trappey's Lafayette plant were used in field ration kits by the Allied Armed Forces during World War II. About twelve million pounds of sweet potatoes were produced for the military, therefore, the business was expanded considerably.

During World War II area farmers turned for the first time to mechanized farming because of farm labor shortages caused by the military draft. Machines were used in cultivating and harvesting rice, corn, cotton, soybeans and sugar cane. Although area farmers turned to mechanized farming, the home or co-op farmer used horse-driven ploughs during the war years due to gas rationing.

Paul Conrad Richter is an important name in farming and vegetable growing in Lafayette. The Richters, a German immigrant family, arrived in Lafayette before World War I. Older Lafayette residents will remember Mrs. Richter peddling vegetables from her wagon early each morning. She delivered beautiful vegetables, fresh eggs, and milk daily to families all over Lafayette. Now, many know her grandson, David Richter, of the Lafayette Farmers' Market, a third generation vegetable grower in Lafayette.

The Southwest Louisiana Mid-Winter Fair encouraged the development of top quality produce. Local and area farmers competed in growing vegetables, livestock, flowers and citrus fruit. Honors and awards were coveted by all who entered. Miss Myrtice McCutchen, (Mrs. Edmond D'Aquin) was the first Camellia Queen and Miss Bella Nickerson (Mrs. Richard D. Chappuis, Sr.) was the second Camellia Queen.

Broccoli and cauliflower, corn and cabbages, carrots and green peppers, eggplant and sweet potatoes, lettuce and tomatoes, summer squash and zucchini, mirlitons and turnip greens, such a feast for the eyes could easily make us all happy vegetarians, then and now.

Mary Katherine Anders LaFleur (Mrs. Wallace A.)
Lifelong resident of Lafayette
Retired Teacher, Lafayette Parish Schools

Vegetable-Salad

ARTICHOKE STUFFED TOMATOES

8 medium tomatoes, firm, not
    overripe
Salt or seasoning salt
1/2 cup margarine or butter
1 medium onion, chopped
1 tablespoon chopped green
    onion tops
1/2 green bell pepper, chopped
3 ribs celery, chopped
2 pods of garlic, chopped
2 tablespoons chopped parsley
1 teaspoon salt
1/4 teaspoon red pepper
1 cup coarsely chopped &
    drained artichoke hearts
1½ cups toasted bread crumbs,
    divided
1 egg, beaten

Scoop pulp from tomatoes. Season shells with salt or seasoning salt. Turn upside down to drain. Reserve 2½ cups pulp, chop and set aside. Melt butter in large skillet and sauté onion, onion tops, bell pepper, celery, garlic and parsley 5 minutes, stirring constantly until onions are limp. Add 2½ cups reserved tomato pulp, salt and red pepper. Stir over medium heat 10 minutes until mixture thickens. Remove skillet from heat. Add artichokes, 1 cup bread crumbs and egg. Blend but do not mash. Spoon mixture into tomato shells. Sprinkle tops with remaining bread crumbs. Place in a 7 x 11-inch baking pan and bake in **preheated 350° oven 15-20 minutes** or until heated through. (Avoid overcooking, as tomatoes will become mushy.)

Yield: 8 servings

Malise Labbé Foster (Mrs. David S.)

CORN CREOLE

1 small bell pepper, chopped
1 large onion, chopped
1 rib celery, chopped
2 tablespoons bacon drippings
1 pound ground meat
2½ cups whole kernel corn,
    drained
1 egg, beaten
2 cups milk
1/2 cup corn meal
1 teaspoon salt
1 teaspoon pepper
1/2 cup bread crumbs
2 tablespoons butter

In a large skillet or 4-quart pot sauté bell pepper, onion and celery in bacon drippings. Stir in ground meat and cook 2-3 minutes. Add corn, egg and milk. Cook on medium high 5 minutes. Stir in corn meal, salt and pepper. Continue to cook 3 minutes.

Pour into greased 2-quart casserole. Sprinkle bread crumbs on top and dot with butter.

Bake in a **preheated 350° oven 1 hour.** *This recipe is highly nutritious and economical to make and especially so in furnishing a way to use leftover meat. Tuna, crabmeat, shrimp or crawfish may be substituted for meat.*

Yield: 6 servings

Ray B. Theaux (Mrs. Arthur)

BARBECUE BEANS

6-7 slices bacon
1 medium onion, chopped
1/2 bell pepper, chopped
2 (31-oz.) cans pork & beans
1/2 cup catsup
2 tablespoons prepared mustard
1/4 cup brown sugar
1 tablespoon vinegar
1 tablespoon chili powder

Fry bacon in a 5-quart Dutch oven. Remove bacon from pot. Crumble and set aside. Add onion and bell pepper to bacon fat and cook until soft. Add beans, catsup, mustard, brown sugar, vinegar and chili powder. Cook over low heat for 45 minutes.

Yield: 12 servings

Jeanne Lambert Millet (Mrs. Donald)

RANCH BEANS à la DAIGRE

2 pounds ground chuck
1 large onion, finely chopped
2 ribs celery, finely chopped
1 (1-oz.) bottle Mexene chili
    powder
1 teaspoon salt
1/4 teaspoon pepper
1 (3-lb. 5-oz.) can pork & beans
1/2 cup catsup
1/2 cup honey
4 tablespoons brown sugar
1/4 teaspoon garlic powder
4 tablespoons chopped parsley
1/4 cup white wine
1/2 pound Velveeta cheese, cut
    into chunks

Brown ground chuck. Add onions and celery and cook over low heat in 4-quart covered pot until tender. Add chili powder, salt and pepper and cook over low heat for approximately 15 minutes, stirring frequently to prevent sticking. Add remaining ingredients and cook over low heat approximately 1 hour, stirring occasionally.

Yield: 20 servings

John J. Daigre

Microwave reheating: Place 'Ranch Beans' in a 2-quart round glass casserole. Cover and microwave on **HIGH (100%) 3-5 MINUTES** or until heated through. *Jean K Durkee*

THREE BEAN BAKED BEANS

2 (16-oz.) cans pork & beans
2 (16-oz.) cans lima beans
2 (16-oz.) cans kidney beans
1/2 cup butter
2 medium onions, chopped
2 bell peppers, chopped
4 cloves garlic, minced
1 (14-oz.) bottle catsup
2 teaspoons dry mustard
2 teaspoons prepared mustard
2 tablespoons Worcestershire
    sauce
1/4 teaspoon TABASCO sauce
1/2 teaspoon salt
1/4 teaspoon pepper

Drain beans and place in a 4 or 5-quart casserole with cover. Melt butter in large skillet. Add onions, bell peppers and garlic. Sauté until onions are limp, approximately 5 minutes. Add to beans. Stir in catsup, mustard, Worcestershire, TABASCO, salt and pepper. Cover. Bake in **preheated 325° oven 1 hour.**

Yield: 10-12 servings

Susan Alves Bonnette (Mrs. K. Stephen)

MARINATED CARROTS

1 pound carrots, sliced into
    rounds
1/2 bell pepper, sliced into rings
1/2 sweet onion, sliced into rings
1/2 cup vinegar
1 (10¾-oz.) can tomato soup,
    undiluted
1/2 cup sugar
1/4 cup vegetable oil
Dash TABASCO sauce

Cook carrots until just tender.

Drain. Slice pepper and onion.

In a medium saucepan heat vinegar, soup, sugar and oil until just hot. Add TABASCO. Alternate layers of carrots, pepper and onion rings in a 2-quart glass casserole. Pour hot liquid over all and marinate covered, preferably overnight.

Yield: 6-8 servings

Estelle Turner (Mrs. Howard)

NEW YEAR STUFFED CABBAGE

3 pounds ground beef
2 tablespoons vegetable oil
4 medium onions, finely chopped
2 medium bell peppers, finely
    chopped
1 cup finely chopped celery
1 bunch green onions, finely
    chopped
1/2 cup finely chopped parsley
1/2 cup chopped chicken livers
2 teaspoons salt
1 teaspoon pepper
2 pints raw oysters, drained and
    reserve liquid
3 cups cracker crumbs
1 large cabbage or 2 medium-
    size, with leaves separated
    and boiled in lightly salted
    water

In a Dutch oven heat oil and brown ground beef. Drain excess oil as it accumulates. Add onion, bell pepper, celery, green onion and parsley. Cook on medium heat until vegetables are wilted, stirring occasionally. Add chicken livers, salt and pepper. Cover and continue to cook on low heat until livers are cooked. Cut oysters into 2 or 3 pieces and add to meat mixture. Cover and continue stirring and cooking until oysters are tender. Add cracker crumbs and mix well. Mixture should be thick. If more moisture is needed use a small amount of oyster water. Cool meat before stuffing the drained, cool cabbage leaves.

Yield: 14 servings

Evelyn Martin Chiasson (Mrs. Bob)

To assemble stuffed cabbage: Lay 4 of the largest cabbage leaves on a 12-inch serving plate. Spread cabbage with meat dressing. Continue with layers of cabbage and meat graduating to the next size leaves. Rebuild the whole cabbage with meat dressing between each layer of leaves. Press leaves and meat in center and work to outer leaves forming a head of cabbage. Secure with toothpicks then tie with string to hold together. (Can be wrapped in foil at this point and frozen.) Before serving sprinkle top of stuffed cabbage with seasoned bread crumbs. Brown cabbage in **preheated 325° oven 10 minutes.** Cut into slices to serve.

This recipe is still a tradition and has been served in the Chiasson family for over 100 years every New Year's Day.

STUFFED CABBAGE

1 (3-lb.) head of cabbage
1 large onion, chopped
6 tablespoons butter
3 cups saltine cracker crumbs
3 eggs, beaten
2 teaspoons salt
1/2 teaspoon black pepper
1/2 teaspoon white pepper
1/2 yard cheese cloth
1/4 cup butter, browned

Remove large outer leaves of cabbage; rinse well and put aside.

Chop remainder of cabbage and cook in small amount of salted water until tender. Drain well.

Melt butter in skillet. Add onion and sauté over medium heat. (Or: microwave in 4-cup measure on **HIGH (100%) 3 MINUTES**, stirring once.)

Mix cabbage, onion, crumbs, eggs and seasonings well. Place in 18-inch square of cheese cloth in a bowl the size of the cabbage. Place outer leaves inside the cheesecloth, leaving center free to spoon cabbage mixture into. Fold leaves over to form a cabbage and tie cloth securely with kitchen twine. Place bag in boiling water with 1 tablespoon salt. Boil 20 minutes.

Remove and let drain, then untie cloth and transfer to serving dish. Carefully trim any tough stems from outer leaves if necessary. Additional butter which has been browned may be poured over the cabbage. *My parents' family has served this recipe for years.*

Yield: 6-8 servings

Nancy Van Eaton Broussard (Mrs. Arthur)

To reheat in microwave: Place cabbage on glass pie plate. Keep cheese cloth tied. Microwave on **HIGH (100%) 3 MINUTES** to reheat. *Pat C. Andrus*

GREAT OVEN FRIED EGGPLANT

1/2 cup seasoned dry bread
    crumbs
1 teaspoon salt
1/2 teaspoon white pepper
1 small eggplant, approximately
    1¼ lbs.
1 egg, slightly beaten

Mix bread crumbs, salt and pepper in a small bowl. Leaving the skin on, cut eggplant into 1/2-inch slices. Dip slices into beaten egg. Coat with crumbs. Arrange on greased 15½ x 10½ x 1-inch jelly roll pan. Bake in a **preheated 375° oven** uncovered **15 minutes.** Turn slices over and bake **15 minutes longer** or until golden brown.

Yield: 4 servings

Becky Bishop (Mrs. Wiley)

CREOLE EGGPLANT

2 medium eggplants
2 tablespoons vegetable oil
1 onion, finely chopped
1/2 cup finely chopped celery
1 clove garlic, minced
1 cup ground meat
1/2 cup water
1 egg, beaten
1½ teaspoons salt
1/2 teaspoon black pepper
1/2 teaspoon red pepper
1 teaspoon Creole seasoning
2 tablespoons butter
1/2 cup plain bread crumbs
5 green onion tops, finely
    chopped
3 sprigs parsley, finely chopped
Toasted bread crumbs, for
    sprinkling

Peel eggplant. Drop whole eggplant and 2 teaspoons salt into boiling water. Boil until tender. Drain. Split in half and remove larger seeds to prevent bitterness. Mash eggplant with potato masher. Heat oil in large skillet. Add onion, celery and garlic. Sauté 2 minutes. Add meat and brown well on slow heat. Add water, cover and simmer 30 minutes. Add more water if necessary—meat should not be dry. Add mashed eggplant and blend well. Add egg, stirring to prevent curdling. Add salt, black and red pepper, Creole seasoning, butter and bread crumbs. Blend. Remove from heat. Add onion tops and parsley. Place in 1½-quart baking dish. Top with bread crumbs. Bake in **preheated 350° oven 10-15 minutes.** *From the recipe files of Mrs. A. J. Alpha.*

Yield: 6 servings

Hazel Alpha

ONIONS AU GRATIN

4 large yellow onions, sliced
   in rounds
2 tablespoons butter
2 tablespoons flour
1 cup milk
1 teaspoon Worcestershire
   sauce
Dash TABASCO sauce
Salt and white pepper to taste
1 cup grated sharp cheese
Paprika for sprinkling

In a medium saucepan steam onion slices in a small amount of lightly salted water until cooked, but still crisp. Drain well and pour into a 2-quart round glass casserole.

To make a white sauce, melt butter in a small saucepan. Stir in flour to mix. Slowly add milk until blended. Add Worcestershire, TABASCO sauce, salt and pepper. Cook over medium high heat stirring until white sauce thickens. Add white sauce and grated cheese to drained onions. Mix. Sprinkle with paprika. Bake in a preheated 350° oven 25 minutes.

Yield: 4-6 servings

Karen Veillon McGlasson (Mrs. H. Edwin)

Microwave directions: Place onions in a 2-quart covered glass or plastic dish. Do not add water or salt. Microwave on **HIGH (100%) 8 MINUTES** stirring after 4 minutes cooking time. Drain and sprinkle with salt.

To make a white sauce, melt butter in a 4-cup glass measure on **HIGH (100%) 30 SECONDS.** Stir in flour, warm milk, Worcestershire, TABASCO, salt and pepper. Microwave on **HIGH (100%) 2¹/₂-3 MINUTES** or until sauce thickens, stirring at 30 second intervals. Add white sauce and cheese to drained onions. Sprinkle with paprika. Microwave on **HIGH (100%) 6 MINUTES** covered. *Jean K Durkee*

SMOTHERED OKRA

1/4 cup vegetable oil
2 quarts fresh, frozen or canned
   sliced okra
1 medium onion, finely chopped
2 cloves garlic, finely chopped
1/2 bell pepper, finely chopped
1 (28-oz.) can tomatoes, chopped
1 cup hot water
1/2 teaspoon salt
1/2 teaspoon black pepper
1 teaspoon TABASCO sauce

Heat oil in a large, deep skillet or Dutch oven. Add okra, onion, garlic and bell pepper. Cook over medium heat until okra stops stringing, 10 minutes. Add tomatoes, hot water, salt, pepper and TABASCO sauce.

Lower heat and cover pan. Cook 1 hour stirring frequently.

Remove cover and cook down approximately 30 minutes.

Yield: 8-10 servings

Elaine Caldwell Brown (Mrs. Warren L., Jr.)

MAQUECHOU I

4 ears fresh corn
2 tablespoons vegetable oil
1 ripe medium tomato, chopped
1 medium bell pepper, chopped
1 medium onion, chopped
1 teaspoon sugar
1/2 teaspoon salt
1/4 teaspoon white pepper
2 tablespoons butter

Select tender, well-developed ears of corn. Cut lengthwise through less than half of corn kernel. Cut second time to remove rest of grain. Do not cut deeply into corn cob. In a heavy saucepan combine corn, oil, tomato, bell pepper, onion and sugar, Cook over low heat for 20 minutes, stirring constantly. Add salt, pepper and butter. Serve hot. *This is an old Indian-Acadian dish.*

Yield: 4-6 servings

Mrs. Blanche Gauthier

MAQUECHOU STUFFED TOMATOES

4-6 firm tomatoes
4-6 tablespoons butter
Sprigs of parsley

Scoop pulp from tomatoes. Reserve pulp. Turn upside down to drain. Prepare *Maquechou* as shown above using reserved tomato pulp in place of the tomato. Firmly pack each tomato with cooked Maquechou. Refrigerate until ready to use. Place on cookie sheet or Pyrex 7 x 11-inch baking dish. Bake in **preheated 350° oven 5-10 minutes,** or until center is hot and bubbly. Do not overcook. Add a pat of butter on top of each center with a sprig of parsley to serve.

Yield: 4-6 servings

Lucille Roy Procter Copeland (Mrs. Robert)

MAQUECHOU II

15 ears of corn, cleaned
1 large onion, chopped
1/2 bell pepper, chopped
1 large tomato, peeled and
    chopped
1/3 cup vegetable oil
1 tablespoon sugar (optional)
Salt, red and black pepper

Clean corn. Slice each kernel in half. Scrape with knife to remove milk from corn to get the full flavor of the sweet corn. Place corn, onion, bell pepper, tomato, oil, sugar (optional), salt and pepper in large pot. Cook over low heat 45 minutes, stirring occasionally. Add 1/2 cup water if mixture is dry. *Season to taste because French cooks don't measure.*

Yield: 8 servings

Verlie T. Boudreaux (Mrs. Walter, Sr.)

STUFFED MIRLITON

3 medium mirlitons
1 pound sliced cooked ham
1 large onion, quartered
2 cloves garlic
1 bell pepper, quartered
2 ribs celery with leaves
1 tablespoon vegetable oil
1⅓ cups seasoned bread
    crumbs, divided
1/4 cup margarine
1 egg, beaten
1/3 cup grated Parmesan cheese
6 pats of butter

Wash mirlitons. Boil until tender. Cool. Cut into halves, lengthwise. Scoop pulp from shells and set aside. Grind ham, onion, garlic, bell pepper, and celery. In heavy skillet heat oil. Add all ground ingredients. Cook slowly on low heat until thoroughly cooked, about 1½ hours. Add mirliton pulp, 1 cup bread crumbs and margarine. Let cook another 10 minutes. Cool. Add beaten egg and stir well. Fill 6 shells with mixture and place in a 7 x 11-inch baking dish. Sprinkle over each the remaining bread crumbs and Parmesan cheese. Place a pat of butter on each. Bake in **preheated 350° oven 25 minutes.**

Yield: 6 servings

Lucille E. Coumes

Microwave shortcut: Cut 3 mirlitons into halves lengthwise. Remove seed. Place in plastic bag on micro-safe plate. Twist end of bag to close. (Do not use twist ties.) Microwave on **HIGH (100%) 12 MINUTES.** Cool. Scoop pulp from shells and set aside. Follow directions above. *Jean K Durkee*

133

STUFFED SWEET PEPPERS

6 medium bell peppers
3 tablespoons margarine
1/2 pound ground beef, ham,
　or shrimp
1 onion, finely chopped
1/2 cup finely chopped celery
1 clove garlic, minced
1/2 cup water
4 slices toasted bread, wet
　with water
1 beaten egg
2 tablespoons margarine
3 sprigs parsley, minced
5 green onion tops, finely
　chopped
2 teaspoons salt
1/2 teaspoon red pepper
Seasoned bread crumbs for
　sprinkling

Cut peppers in half lengthwise. Remove seeds and membrane. Drop into boiling water. Parboil 5 minutes. Drain and set aside.

Heat margarine in a large skillet. Add meat, onion, celery and garlic. Cook over low heat until meat browns and vegetables are tender. Add water and simmer covered 30 minutes. Add more water, if necessary, to make a moist mixture. Wet toast with water, squeeze and add to beaten egg. Blend well into meat mixture. Add margarine, parsley, onion tops, salt and pepper. Mix thoroughly.

Fill pepper shells with mixture.

Sprinkle bread crumbs on top. Place in a shallow 9 x 13-inch baking pan. Add 1/4-1/2 cup water and bake in a **preheated 350° oven 15-20 minutes,** until peppers are cooked. *This recipe was perfected by my mother, Cecile Doucet Alpha (Mrs. A. J.) who was also Aunt and Godmother of Marie Louise Comeaux Manuel.*

Yield: 6 servings

Hazel Alpha

SWEET POTATO PONE

4 medium sweet potatoes
　or yams
2 eggs well beaten
1 cup milk
1 cup sugar
1/3 cup butter, melted
1/2 teaspoon salt
1/2 teaspoon allspice
1/2 teaspoon nutmeg
1/8 teaspoon cinnamon
Juice of 1/2 orange

Peel and grate raw sweet potatoes. Mix with eggs, milk, sugar, butter, salt, allspice, nutmeg, cinnamon and orange juice in mixing bowl. Pour into buttered 8 x 8-inch dish. Bake in **preheated 350° oven 55-60 minutes** or until knife inserted in center comes out clean.

Yield: 6 servings

Judith Mouton Hebert (Mrs. Henry P., Jr.)

ORANGE SWEET POTATO WHIP

8 medium sweet potatoes
1/2 cup butter, softened
3/4 cup dark brown sugar
3 tablespoons cream
1/3 teaspoon allspice
1/3 teaspoon cloves
1/3 teaspoon cinnamon
1/3 teaspoon ginger
1/4 teaspoon salt
1/2 cup chopped candied
　　orange rind

*Crunch Topping
2 tablespoons butter
2 tablespoons flour
1/2 cup dark brown sugar
1 teaspoon nutmeg
1 cup pecan halves

Boil sweet potatoes in skins, cool and peel. Whip potatoes in electric mixer with butter, brown sugar, cream and spices. Add chopped candied orange rind (see recipe on this page). Place in an 8 x 8-inch Pyrex dish. Mix ingredients for Crunch Topping* with pastry blender until the texture of cornmeal. Spread topping over sweet potato mixture. Place pecans in rows, covering the top. Press into topping slightly. Bake in **preheated 300° oven 1 hour.** If top is not brown, place under broiler 1 minute. *From the Carmelite Nuns of Lafayette.*

Yield: 8 servings

Betty Richard Butcher (Mrs. Thomas, Sr.)

Microwave directions: Follow directions above. Microwave Orange Sweet Potato Whip on **HIGH (100%) 15 MINUTES.** Rotate dish 2 times. *Jean K Durkee*

CANDIED CITRUS RIND

4 medium oranges
6 cups boiling water
1/2 cup sugar
1 cup water

Use vegetable/fruit peeler to pare strips of orange zest. Then cut strips into thinner strips. Drop strips into pot of boiling water. Boil 10 minutes, or until zest becomes transparent. Drain well. Dissolve sugar in 1 cup water in small saucepan. Boil 5 minutes over medium heat. Add zest and remove from heat, allowing zest to soak in syrup 15 minutes. Remove from syrup and dry several hours on a plate.

Yield: 1/2 cup zest

Terry L. Thompson (Mrs. Pat)

Microwave directions: To dry quickly, spread zest on a paper towel lined paper plate. Cover with a paper towel. Microwave on **HIGH (100%) 2 MINUTES 30 SECONDS.** *Jean K Durkee*

POTATOES ROMANOFF

5 cups cooked potatoes, cubed
1 cup dairy sour cream
2 cups creamed cottage cheese
1/4 cup minced green onion tops
1 small clove garlic, crushed
1 1/2 teaspoon salt
1/2 cup grated cheddar cheese
Paprika for sprinkling

Boil potatoes in lightly salted water. Drain and cube. In a 1-quart mixing bowl mix sour cream, cottage cheese, onion tops, garlic and salt; stir into cubed potatoes. Place in a 2-quart greased casserole dish. Top with grated cheese. Sprinkle with paprika. Bake in a **pre-heated 350° oven for 40 minutes.**

Yield: 6-8 servings

Rita Mendoza O'Neal (Mrs. Earl C.)

POTATOES WITH HAM AU GRATIN

4 cups diced potatoes
2 cups chopped green onion
    bulbs and some tops
5 tablespoons butter
5 tablespoons all-purpose flour
2 1/2 cups milk
2 tablespoons Lea & Perrins
    Worcestershire sauce
1/2 teaspoon prepared yellow
    mustard
1 teaspoon salt
1/2 teaspoon pepper
1/4 teaspoon paprika
4 diced pimiento
2 cups grated cheddar cheese
2 cups cubed ham, 1/2-inch cubes
1/2 cup plain bread crumbs
4 tablespoons butter

In a saucepan cook potatoes and onions together in lightly salted water until tender, 12-15 minutes. Drain. To make a white sauce melt butter in a medium saucepan. Add flour stirring until blended. Cook and slowly stir in milk. Add Worcestershire, mustard, salt, pepper, paprika and pimiento. Stir until thick. Place 1/2 of the cooked potatoes and onions in a large buttered 3-quart baking dish. Cover potatoes with 1/2 of the cheese. Spread all the ham on the cheese. Cover with remaining potatoes. Pour white sauce over all. Sprinkle remaining cheese on top. Place bread crumbs on cheese. Dot top with butter. Bake in **preheated 350° oven** until top is melted **10 minutes.**

Yield: 10-12 servings

Rosemary Ham (Mrs. Harold)

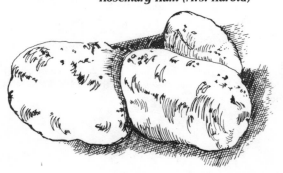

CREOLE SPINACH TIMBALES

15 ounces (1½ packages) fresh
   spinach
2 tablespoons butter
1 tablespoon flour
1/2 cup milk
1/2 cup heavy cream
1 clove garlic, finely minced
3/4 teaspoon salt
1/8 teaspoon cayenne pepper
1/2 teaspoon freshly grated
   nutmeg
1 tablespoon Herbsaint or other
   licorice flavored liqueur
2 eggs

Both creamed spinach and Herb-saint are old South Louisiana standbys. Combining the two makes a very special dish.

Rinse spinach leaves and remove stems. Cook in boiling salted water 3 minutes. Place in colander and run under cold water. To remove all excess water press spinach firmly between 2 dinner plates. Chop spinach finely.

In a sauté pan melt butter and add spinach. Sauté 2 minutes on high heat. Stir in flour. Add milk, cream, garlic, salt, pepper and nutmeg. Add Herbsaint, stir to blend and remove from heat. Butter 4 small custard cups or babba or dariole molds. Lightly beat eggs and mix with warm spinach mixture. Spoon into molds. **Note:** Fold 3 paper towels to fit a 7 x 11-inch glass baking dish to act as a buffer. Place molds in baking dish on top of towels with 1 inch of very warm water and bake in **preheated 375° oven 20-30 minutes** or until set. Unmold and serve.

Yield: 4 servings

Terry L. Thompson (Mrs. Pat)

SPINACH FOR NON-SPINACH LOVERS

1 (10-oz.) package chopped
   spinach, frozen
1/2 cup butter
6 tablespoons flour
1/2 pound Velveeta cheese
6 eggs, slightly beaten
24 ounces cottage cheese
1 teaspoon Lawry's seasoned
   salt
1 teaspoon black pepper

Thaw spinach and drain well. Melt butter and add flour, stirring to blend. Add Velveeta cheese, eggs, cottage cheese, spinach, salt and pepper. Place in well greased 13½x8¾-inch Pyrex dish. Bake in **preheated 350° oven 1 hour.**

Yield: 12 servings

Diana D. Broussard (Mrs. Joseph M.)

137

SQUASH ACADIEN

2 pounds yellow squash, fresh
   or frozen
1/4 cup butter or margarine
5 green onions, bulbs and tops,
   chopped
1/2 cup chopped celery
2 (1-inch) slices French bread
   torn into pieces
1/2 cup milk
2 teaspoons sugar
2 tablespoons butter
Bread crumbs for sprinkling

Boil squash in lightly salted water. Drain. Melt butter in large saucepan, add chopped onion bulbs, celery and 1/2 of onion tops. Sauté until tender. Soak bread in milk, gently squeeze out excess milk. Add bread, squash, sugar and remaining 1/2 of onion tops. Blend well.

Pour into 7 x 11-inch baking dish. Dot top with butter. Sprinkle with bread crumbs. Bake in **preheated 350° oven 15-20 minutes** until crumbs are brown.

Yield: 6 servings

Hazel Alpha

SQUASH DELANEY

2 pounds yellow squash or
   2 (16-oz.) cans
1/2 cup butter or margarine
1 (8-oz.) package Pepperidge
   Farm Herbed Stuffing Mix,
   divided
1 (10¾-oz.) can cream of chicken
   soup, undiluted
1 cup dairy sour cream
1 small onion, chopped
1 carrot, grated
1 (2-oz.) jar pimiento, drained
   and chopped

Boil squash until tender. Drain. Melt butter in a large skillet. Stir in 4 ounces (half of package) of herbed stuffing mix. Add soup, sour cream, onion, carrot and pimiento, stirring to mix. Add drained squash. Place in a 2-quart 7 x 11-inch baking dish or 2 small casserole dishes. Top with remaining stuffing mix. Cover and bake in **preheated 350° oven 45 minutes** or until brown. Freezes well.

Yield: 8-10 servings

Jane Delaney (Mrs. Jerry)

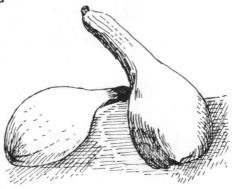

CHEESY SQUASH BAKE

6 whole yellow squash
1/4 cup oil
1/4 cup flour
1 large onion, chopped
1 pound ground beef
1 teaspoon salt
1/2 teaspoon black pepper
1/2 teaspoon garlic powder
1/2 teaspoon red pepper
Seasoned bread crumbs
1/2-1 cup grated cheddar or
    American cheese

Boil 6 or more whole yellow squash in salted water until tender. In large skillet make a brown roux with oil and flour. Add onion to roux. Sauté until tender. Add meat and brown in roux. Season with salt, pepper, garlic powder and red pepper. Drain squash, mash and add to meat mixture. Add enough bread crumbs to thicken. Place mixture in a 7 x 11-inch glass dish. Sprinkle cheese on top. Bake in **preheated 350° oven 30 minutes.** Cheese should be bubbly.

Yield: 6 servings

Pat W. Link (Mrs. Bobby)

Microwave shortcut: After placing mixture in 7 x 11-inch glass dish microwave on **HIGH (100%) 7-8 MINUTES.** *Jean K Durkee*

SQUASH PECAN

2 pounds yellow squash, sliced,
    cooked, drained
1/2 cup butter, melted
2 tablespoons sugar
2 eggs, beaten
1 cup mayonnaise (Hellmann's)
3/4 cup grated mild cheddar
    cheese
Salt and pepper to taste
1 cup chopped pecans
Buttered soda cracker crumbs
    for sprinkling

Cook sliced squash in a 2-quart saucepan in lightly salted water. Drain well. In another pan or 4-cup measure (for microwave) melt butter. Add sugar, eggs, mayonnaise, cheese, salt and pepper. Mix together and add to drained squash. Toss lightly to blend. Place in greased 7 x 11-inch baking dish. Top with nuts and crumbs. **Hint:** To make buttered soda cracker crumbs, place 20 crackers and 1 tablespoon butter in food processor. Process off and on until butter has blended with crumbs. **Bake in a preheated 400° oven 20 minutes.** *People who dislike squash like this!*

Yield: 6-8 servings

Louise Larcade (Mrs. Harold W.)

Microwave directions: Microwave Squash Pecan in a 7 x 11-inch glass dish on **HIGH (100%) 5 MINUTES.** Rotate dish 1 time. *Jean K Durkee*

TURNIP SAUTÉ

3 pounds turnip roots
8 strips lean bacon fried, reserve
   drippings
2 medium onions, chopped
1 large bell pepper, chopped
2 ribs celery, chopped
2 egg yolks, beaten
2 teaspoons salt
1 teaspoon white pepper
1/2 teaspoon black pepper

Peel and cut turnips into chunks. Boil in lightly salted water. Add a pinch of baking soda (this takes bitterness away from turnips).

When cooked, drain and mash thoroughly with potato masher. Fry bacon until crisp, drain on paper towels and crumble. Remove half the drippings. Sauté onion, bell pepper and celery in remaining fat until soft. Add mashed turnips, crumbled bacon, beaten egg yolks, salt, white and black pepper. Stir well. Place in greased 1½-quart casserole. Bake in **preheated 350° oven 10-15 minutes** until heated through.

Yield: 6-8 servings

Karen Veillon McGlasson (Mrs. H. Edwin)

CREAMY ZUCCHINI BAKE

5 or 6 small zucchini
1/4 cup butter
1 large onion, cut into rings
2 cloves garlic, chopped
2 slices Swiss cheese, broken
   in pieces
1/2 cup commercial sour cream
1/4 teaspoon salt
1/4 teaspoon pepper
3 dashes TABASCO sauce
1/4 teaspoon celery salt
1/4 cup bread crumbs
4 ounces mozzarella cheese,
   shredded
Paprika for sprinkling

Cut unpeeled zucchini into 3/4-inch rounds. Simmer 10-15 minutes until tender in a pot of salted boiling water. Drain and set aside. In a large skillet melt butter and sauté onion and garlic until clear and tender. Add drained zucchini. Fold in Swiss cheese on low fire until melted. Add sour cream, salt, pepper, TABASCO sauce and celery salt. Put mixture into a 7 x 11-inch baking dish. Top with bread crumbs, mozzarella cheese and paprika.

Bake in a **preheated 350° oven 10-20 minutes, until bubbly.**

Yield: 8 servings

Ann H. LeJeune (Mrs. Womack)

CHERRY-PINEAPPLE SALAD

1 (3-oz.) box lemon gelatin
1 (3-oz.) box lime gelatin
2 cups boiling water
1 (5.33-oz.) can evaporated milk
1 cup mayonnaise
1 (8-oz.) can pineapple chunks
    with juice
1 (6-oz.) jar maraschino cherries,
    drained and quartered
1 cup shredded sharp cheese

Dissolve gelatin in 2 cups boiling water. Chill until beginning to jell. In a large bowl thoroughly mix evaporated milk and mayonnaise. Add pineapple chunks and juice, cherries and cheese. Combine with chilled gelatin. Place in 8 x 12-inch Pyrex dish. Let set. Serve on lettuce leaves.

Yield: 10-12 servings

Lucille "Sweet" Hernandez (Mrs. Hugh)

SWEET SPRING SALAD

1 (3-oz.) box lemon gelatin
1 (3-oz.) box lime gelatin
1 cup boiling water
1 cup cold water
8 ounces cream cheese,
    softened
1 (8¼-oz.) can crushed
    pineapple
1/2 cup mayonnaise
5.3 ounces evaporated milk
1 cup chopped pecans

Place lemon and lime gelatin in large bowl. Add boiling water, then cold water, stirring to dissolve. Mash cream cheese and add to warm gelatin liquid. Use egg beater to blend well. Add pineapple, mayonnaise, milk and pecans. Pour into gelatin mold. Chill in refrigerator until set. Turn mold onto plate. Garnish with lettuce leaves, strawberries and sprigs of mint.

Yield: 12-14 servings

Olympe Arceneaux Butcher (Mrs. William)

NUTTY CRANBERRY MOLD

1 tablespoon powdered gelatin
1/4 cup cold water
1 (3-oz.) package lemon Jello
3/4 cup hot water
1 cup chopped fresh cranberries
3/4 cup sugar
1 (16-oz.) can crushed pineapple,
    drain and retain 1 cup of juice
1/2 cup toasted chopped pecans
1 cup chopped celery

Dissolve gelatin in cold water.

Dissolve Jello in hot water.

In a mixing bowl add sugar to cranberries. Stir in dissolved gelatin, Jello, 1 cup crushed pineapple, 1 cup juice, toasted pecans and celery. Pour into a 1-quart mold sprayed with vegetable spray. Refrigerate until firm. Serve on lettuce leaves.

Yield: 8 servings

Virgie F. Wallace (Mrs. Wayne)

CRANBERRY-APPLE SALAD

2 (1-lb.) cans whole berry
    cranberry sauce
2 cups boiling water
1 (6-oz.) package strawberry
    gelatin
2 tablespoons lemon juice
1/2 teaspoon salt
1 cup mayonnaise (Hellmann's)
1 large red apple, diced (2 cups)
1 (8-oz.) jar orange marmalade
1/2 cup chopped walnuts

In a saucepan melt cranberry sauce over medium heat. Drain liquid from berries, reserving liquid. In large bowl mix together cranberry liquid, boiling water and gelatin. Stir until gelatin is dissolved. Add lemon juice and salt. Chill until mixture mounds slightly on spoon. Add mayonnaise, beat until smooth. Fold in cranberries, apple, marmalade and nuts. Pour into 2-quart glass mold. Chill overnight.

Yield: 10-12 servings

Neloise M. Groth (Mrs. Walter)

CRANBERRY CARDINAL

2 (3-oz.) boxes raspberry gelatin
1 cup hot water
1 cup cold water
1 (8-oz.) can crushed pineapple
  and liquid
1 (16-oz.) can whole cranberry
  sauce
1/2 cup chopped pecans

Dissolve gelatin in hot water. Add cold water and chill until slightly thickened. Add pineapple, liquid, cranberry sauce and pecans. Stir to distribute fruit and nuts. Pour into oiled individual molds. Chill several hours or overnight. Serve on lettuce leaf with mayonnaise.

Yield: 8 servings

Frances P. Zink (Mrs. William)

CRANBERRY SALAD WITH PORT AND PECANS

1 quart fresh cranberries
2 navel oranges
Zest of 1 orange
1½ cups sugar
1 tablespoon unflavored gelatin
1/4 cup water
6 ounces raspberry Jello
1 cup boiling water
1 cup cold water
3/4 cup port wine
1 cup chopped pecans

Cheese topping:
6 ounces cream cheese,
  softened
6 ounces blue cheese
1/4-1/2 cup heavy cream

Blend cranberries, peeled oranges, zest (rind) of one orange in blender, grinder or food processor with steel blade. Add sugar and refrigerate overnight. Sprinkle gelatin in 1/4 cup water. Set aside and allow to become spongy. Add 1 cup boiling water to raspberry gelatin. Stir to dissolve and add unflavored gelatin. Add cold water, wine, raw cranberry mixture and pecans. Chill until consistency of egg whites. Pour into individual molds or 12 x 16-inch glass dish. Chill 6-8 hours or until firmly set. Beat cream cheese and blue cheese together, adding enough cream to form a fluffy topping. Place a mound of topping on each mold. Serve on lettuce leaves.

Yield: 8-10 servings

Patricia Cashman Andrus (Mrs. Robert)

FROZEN FRUIT CRÈME

2/3 cup evaporated milk
2 tablespoons lemon juice
1 (8-oz.) package cream cheese
1/2 cup sugar
1/3 cup mayonnaise
1/2 cup chopped nuts, walnuts
    or pecans
1 cup fresh strawberries or
    1 (10-oz.) package frozen,
    sliced in half
2 ripe medium bananas, sliced

Chill milk in small mixing bowl in freezer until ice crystals begin to form. When icy, beat milk and lemon juice together until very stiff.

In a larger bowl beat cream cheese until softened. Add sugar and mayonnaise, beating well. Stir in nuts, strawberries and bananas. Add whipped milk to bowl. Fold fruit in roughly. Turn into a 9 x 5 x 2-inch loaf pan lined with foil, or spoon into miniature cupcake pans (liners may be used).

Freeze until firm. Wrap tightly in foil. Store in freezer until ready to use. Slice and serve on lettuce leaf.

Yield: 10 servings

Mrs. C. O. Sinclair

PLANTATION FROZEN FRUIT SALAD

4 egg yolks
4 tablespoons sugar
4 tablespoons vinegar
1 pint whipping cream, whipped
1 (16-oz.) can crushed pineapple,
    drained
1 (16-oz.) can sliced peaches,
    drained
1 (10-oz.) bottle maraschino
    cherries, drained and
    cut in half

Mix yolks, sugar and vinegar in top of double boiler. Cook over hot water until thick. Cool. Whip cream until soft peaks form. Add pineapple, peaches, and cherries (or any kind of fruit you like). Stir in cooled cooked mixture. Pour into a 9 x 13-inch dish. Freeze. Cut into squares and serve on lettuce. *This was our traditional Christmas Day salad at the Hugh C. Wallis home, 'Myrtle Plantation'.*

Yield: 20 servings

Virginia Wallis Hagelin (Mrs. John A.)

FROZEN PINEAPPLE SALAD

1 (8-oz.) can crushed pineapple
  and liquid
8 ounces miniature
  marshmallows
1/2 pint whipping cream,
  whipped
1/4 cup mayonnaise
8 ounces cream cheese,
  softened

*Ogile Salad Dressing:
1 cup whipped cream
1 cup mayonnaise

Heat pineapple and liquid with marshmallows in medium saucepan. Stir until dissolved. Cool. Mix whipped cream, mayonnaise and cream cheese. Add to pineapple/marshmallow mixture. Place in greased mold or 9-inch square pan. Place in freezer 3 hours, or until firm. Serve on lettuce leaves with Ogile Salad Dressing* and buttered crackers.

To make dressing, mix whipped cream and mayonnaise.

Yield: 8-9 servings

Bella Nickerson Chappuis (Mrs. Richard D.)

STRAWBERRY SUPREME

8 ounces cream cheese,
  softened
3/4 cup sugar
10 ounces frozen strawberries
  thawed in their liquid
1 (8-oz.) can crushed pineapple,
  drained
1 cup chopped nuts
3 small or 2 large bananas,
  sliced
1 (12-oz.) carton whipped
  dessert topping
6 whole strawberries for garnish

In a large mixing bowl, cream sugar and cream cheese. In a separate bowl mix together strawberries and strawberry liquid, pineapple, nuts and bananas. Fold into cream cheese mixture. Add whipped dessert topping. Fold until well-blended. Pour into 9 x 13-inch dish (or 2 smaller dishes). Garnish top with whole or sliced strawberries. Freeze. Defrost slightly before serving as salad or dessert.

Yield: 48 servings

Louise Demanade Swan (Mrs. Erick)

FROZEN FRUIT FLUFF

2 (8-oz.) packages cream
cheese, softened
1 (16-oz.) carton whipped
dessert topping
2 (16-oz.) cans fruit cocktail,
drained
1 (16-oz.) bag miniature
marshmallows

Soften cream cheese. In a large mixing bowl beat cream cheese until smooth. Add whipped topping. Stir until blended. Fold in fruit and marshmallows. Line cup-cake baking pan with paper liners and fill with mixture, rounding off tops. Freeze. After frozen place in plastic bags for freezer storage.

Yield: 3 dozen

Catherine Escuriex Mestayer (Mrs. Karl)

SUNSHINE SALAD

1 (3-oz.) box lemon gelatin
3/4 cup hot water
1/2 cup cold water
1 tablespoon vinegar
Pinch salt
1 cup grated carrots
1 (8-oz.) can crushed pineapple
and liquid
1 cup cheddar cheese, cubed
in ¼-inch cubes

Dissolve gelatin in hot water. When dissolved add cold water, vinegar and salt. Chill until slightly thickened. Add carrots, pineapple, liquid and cheese. Stir to distribute evenly and pour into individual oiled molds. Chill overnight. Serve on lettuce leaf with mayonnaise.

Yield: 4 servings

Frances P. Zink (Mrs. William)

PEAR DELIGHT

1 (16-oz.) can pears, drain and reserve juice
1 (3-oz.) package lime Jello
1 teaspoon lemon extract
2 (3-oz.) packages cream cheese, softened
1 (1.4-oz.) package Dream Whip dessert topping, whipped

In a 2-quart saucepan, bring 1 cup pear juice to boil. Add Jello and lemon extract. Stir to dissolve. Add softened cream cheese to hot mixture and blend with egg beater. Chill until slightly jelled. Mash drained pears and add to mixture. Prepare dessert topping and fold into mixture. Pour into an 8 x 12-inch glass dish. Chill until firm.

Yield: 8-10 servings

Loma Knighten

PARTY FRUIT SALAD

2 (11-oz.) cans mandarin oranges, drain and reserve 1 cup juice
1 (20-oz.) can pineapple chunks, drain and reserve 1 cup juice
1 (3$\frac{1}{8}$-oz.) package vanilla pudding (not instant)
3 bananas, sliced

Pour 2 cups of fruit juices in a saucepan. Add package of pudding. Cook and stir over medium heat until mixture comes to a boil. Set aside and cool.

Place drained oranges, pineapple and sliced bananas in serving bowl. Pour cooled sauce over fruit. Chill. Serve as a salad or in compotes as dessert.

Yield: 6 servings

Connie Dutsch Roberts (Mrs. U. D.)

SPINACH SALAD

4 cups chopped fresh spinach
1/2 teaspoon seasoned salt
1 1/2 teaspoons wine vinegar
1/2 teaspoon hot pepper sauce
3/4 cup finely chopped celery
1/4 cup finely chopped bell
   pepper
2 tablespoons finely chopped
   onion
3 hard cooked eggs, diced
1/2 cup diced American cheese
1/2 cup mayonnaise
2 teaspoons creamed
   horseradish

Sprinkle spinach with seasoned salt. Mix vinegar and pepper sauce; toss with spinach. Add celery, bell pepper, onion, eggs and cheese. Mix mayonnaise and horseradish. Toss with spinach mixture. Chill.

Yield: 6-8 servings

Amy Mendoza Montgomery

SALLY'S RICE SALAD

Salad:
2 cups cooked rice
1 cup chopped green onion tops
1 cup chopped dill pickle
1 cup chopped sweet pickle
1 cup chopped celery
1 cup chopped pimiento stuffed
   olives
1 1/2 cups chopped hard cooked
   eggs
1 cup chopped green bell pepper

Dressing:
1 cup salad dressing or
   mayonnaise
4 tablespoons DURKEE'S
   dressing
2 tablespoons prepared mustard
1/8 teaspoon cayenne pepper
1/4 teaspoon salt (if desired)
Olive Oil
Wine vinegar

In a large bowl or container with a fitted cover, combine rice, onion tops, dill and sweet pickles, celery, olives, eggs and bell pepper.

In a small bowl, mix salad dressings, mustard, pepper and salt. Add olive oil slowly to desired smooth consistency. Add a few dashes of wine vinegar for flavor. Stir dressing into salad and mix thoroughly. Cover and refrigerate overnight.

Yield: 8 servings

Sally Ross Moores (Mrs. John D.)

CREAMY AVOCADO MOLD

1 (6-oz.) package lime gelatin
1 cup boiling water
2 tablespoons lemon juice
1 cup mayonnaise
1 (15¼-oz.) can crushed
    pineapple, well drained
1 cup mashed avocado (about
    3 small, soft avocados)
1 cup whipping cream, whipped

In a large bowl mix gelatin, water and lemon juice. Chill until partially congealed. In another bowl mix mayonnaise, pineapple and avocado. Then mix well with the partially congealed gelatin. Fold whipped cream into gelatin mixture. Pour into 2-quart mold, cover and return to refrigerator until set.

Yield: 8-10 servings

Eva Dell Daigre (Mrs. John J.)

SHRIMP REMOULADE

1½ pounds fresh shrimp
1 teaspoon crab boil
Salt and pepper
6 tablespoons olive oil
3 tablespoons vinegar
3 tablespons hot Creole mustard
1 tablespoon paprika
1 teaspoon creamed horseradish
1/2 teaspoon salt
1/4 teaspoon red pepper
3 green onion tops, finely
    chopped
1/2 cup finely chopped celery
    hearts
1/4 cup minced parsley
1/2 head of lettuce

Boil shrimp in shells in seasoned water. Peel and chill.

Mix olive oil, vinegar, mustard, paprika, horseradish, salt, pepper, onion tops, celery and parsley together. Mix with shrimp and chill. Crisp lettuce in iced water. Spin dry. Shred fine. Add half of lettuce to shrimp and sauce. Serve shrimp on remaining shredded lettuce.

Yield: 4-6 servings

Beverly McLean (Mrs. C. M.)

TREEN DRESSING

1/4 cup sugar
1 heaping teaspoon salt
1 heaping tablespoon Creole
    mustard
1/3 cup vinegar
1 cup vegetable oil

In a pint jar add sugar, salt, Creole mustard, vinegar and oil. Cover and shake well. Keeps well in refrigerator for weeks. *This dressing is served in the mansion often.*

Yield: 1 pint

Dodie Treen (Mrs. David C.)

149

FRESH BROCCOLI SALAD

1 large bunch fresh broccoli
4 green onions and tops,
    chopped
2 tomatoes, coarsely chopped
3 tablespoons lemon juice
1/2 cup sour cream
1/2 cup mayonnaise
1/2 teaspoon salt
1/8 teaspoon black pepper
Cherry tomatoes for garnish

Cut fresh uncooked broccoli into bite-sized flowerets. Add green onions and fresh tomatoes. Squeeze fresh lemon juice over vegetables.

Make dressing by mixing sour cream, mayonnaise, salt and pepper together. Mix with vegetables. Garnish with cherry tomatoes. *If tightly covered this salad will keep in the refrigerator for several days, even with the dressing on vegetables.*

Yield: 6-8 servings

Susan Alves Bonnette (Mrs. K. Stephen)

FRENCH BEAN AND BROCCOLI SALAD

2 (10-oz.) packages frozen
    French green beans
1 (10-oz.) package frozen
    chopped broccoli
1/2 teaspoon salt
1 (8¼-oz.) can artichoke hearts,
    drained and quartered
1 package original Ranch style
    buttermilk dressing
1 cup mayonnaise
1 cup milk

Cook vegetables by package directions, drain well. Season with salt. Chill. Prepare salad dressing. Combine vegetables, artichokes and dressing in salad bowl. Toss lightly.

Refrigerate until ready to serve.

Yield: 6 servings

Louise Larcade (Mrs. Harold W.)

Microwave directions: Remove outer waxed wrapper from frozen vegetable packages. Place all 3 packages on a microwave safe plate. Microwave on **HIGH (100%) 21 MINUTES.** Drain vegetables in colander and season with salt. Chill and follow directions above. *Jean K Durkee*

In 1893, the United States Supreme Court declared that the tomato is a vegetable, not a fruit.

CRACKER SALAD

1/2 pound saltine crackers
1 medium onion, chopped fine
1/2 cup chopped sweet pickles
1/4 cup chopped pimiento
    stuffed green olives
2 tablespoons sweet pickle juice
2 tablespoons milk
1 cup mayonnaise
4 hard boiled eggs, diced
Paprika for sprinkling

Crumble crackers in medium mixing bowl. Add onion, pickles and olives. With a fork stir in pickle juice and milk—enough to moisten. Add mayonnaise. Toss with fork and mix well. Add diced eggs. Sprinkle heavily with paprika. *This is a recipe my mother developed during the depression trying to feed a large family inexpensively. Cracker salad is a must at all our family reunions.*

Yield: 6-8 servings

Doris O. Reddell

MOLDED CRAWFISH SALAD

3 tablespoons unflavored gelatin
1/2 cup cold water
2 chicken bouillon cubes
1 small onion, chopped
2 ribs celery with leaves,
    chopped
2 garlic cloves, minced
1 pound peeled crawfish tails
    with fat, chopped
Juice of 1/2 lemon
1/4 cup ketchup
1 teaspoon liquid shrimp and
    crab boil
1 1/2 teaspoon Worcestershire
    sauce
1 cup tomato juice
1 cup mayonnaise
2 1/2 tablespoons creamed
    horseradish
1/2 teaspoon salt
Chopped capers and sliced
    black olives for garnish

In 2-cup measuring cup, sprinkle gelatin over 1/2 cup cold water. Drop in bouillon cubes and let sponge 5 minutes. Melt in microwave on **MEDIUM (50%) 1 1/2 MINUTES.** Stir to dissolve bouillon cubes. In a large bowl mix remaining ingredients together, tossing lightly to blend. Stir in gelatin mixture. Place in a lightly oiled 6-cup mold or 10-12 small decorative molds. Refrigerate at least 4 hours. Unmold and serve on lettuce leaves. Arrange a sprinkling of chopped capers and sliced black olives over top.

Yield: 12 servings

Patricia Cashman Andrus (Mrs. Robert M.)

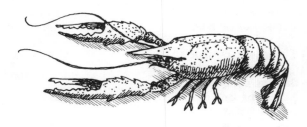

MISS LOU SLAW

1/2 head green cabbage, chopped
2 hard boiled eggs, chopped
1 large tomato, chopped
2 teaspoons chopped green onion tops
1/2 teaspoon sugar
1 teaspoon salt
1/2 teaspoon pepper
1/2 cup mayonnaise

Mix chopped cabbage, eggs, tomato and onion tops. Stir and add sugar, salt and pepper. Blend in mayonnaise. Chill until served.

Yield: 4 servings

Jane F. Seale (Mrs. B. B.)

SAUERKRAUT SALAD

2/3 cup white vinegar
1/2 cup water
1¼ cups sugar
1/2 cup vegetable oil
1 cup finely chopped celery
1 large onion, finely chopped
1 bell pepper, chopped
1 (4-oz.) jar pimiento
1 (16-oz.) can sauerkraut, well-drained

In a 2-quart bowl or dish mix vinegar and water. Add sugar, stir until dissolved. Add oil. Stir well and add celery, onion, bell pepper, pimiento and well-drained sauerkraut. Refrigerate overnight.

Yield: 8 servings

Daisy Hernandez (Mrs. Alex)

GERMAN GARDEN SALAD

4 large tomatoes, unpeeled, cut into bite-size cubes
1 large white onion, sliced into rings and cut in half
1 small bell pepper, cut into 1-inch slivers
3 heaping tablespoons mayonnaise (Hellmann's)
Salt and pepper to taste
6 slices bacon, fried and crumbled
2 teaspoons bacon fat

In medium size salad bowl add tomatoes, onions, bell pepper, mayonnaise (add more if desired), salt and pepper to taste. Toss until all is well coated. Fry bacon in skillet or microwave until very crisp. Crumble into salad. Add bacon fat. Mix well again. Serve at once. *From the recipe files of my great-grandmother.*

Yield: 8-10 servings

Betty Brownsberger Palmintier (Mrs. D. J.)

CHICKEN MOUSSE ALMANDINE

3 cups finely chopped cooked
    chicken
2 (1-oz.) envelopes unflavored
    gelatin
1/2 cup white wine
3 egg yolks
1 cup milk
1 cup chicken broth
1/2 cup finely chopped almonds
1/4 cup mayonnaise
2 tablespoons minced parsley
2 tablespoons chopped green
    olives
1 teaspoon lemon juice
1 teaspoon onion juice
1 teaspoon salt
1 teaspoon celery salt
1/2 teaspoon cayenne pepper
1/8 teaspoon paprika
1/2 cup chilled whipping cream

Cook a 3$^1/_2$ pound chicken. Bone and chop fine. (Microwave directions on page 159.)

Dissolve gelatin in wine. Beat yolks in top of double boiler. Add milk, stirring constantly. Stir in chicken broth. Cook over boiling water until mixture coats silver spoon. Add softened gelatin, mixing well. Chill mixture, stirring occasionally until it begins to gel. Blend almonds and finely chopped chicken into chilled mixture. Fold in mayonnaise. Add parsley, olives, lemon juice, onion juice, salt, celery salt, cayenne and paprika. Beat whipping cream to soft peaks. Fold into mixture. Pour into greased 2-quart mold. Chill in refrigerator 2-3 hours.

Yield: 8-12 servings

"Lil" DesOrmeaux

TABOULI

1 cup cracked wheat
4 cups hot water
1 medium garlic clove, peeled
    and crushed
1/2 cup olive oil
Juice of 4 lemons or 1 cup
1 head chilled lettuce
3 medium tomatoes, squeezed
    and seeded
1 cucumber, peeled
2 bell peppers, seeded
2 bunches green onion tops
    and bulbs
2 bunches ruffled parsley
4 teaspoons salt
2$^1/_2$ teaspoons black pepper
1/2 teaspoon garlic powder
1/4 teaspoon crushed mint
    leaves

In a small mixing bowl soak wheat in 4 cups or more hot water. Crush clove of garlic in a large wooden salad bowl. Add oil and lemon juice to bowl.

Finely chop lettuce, tomatoes, cucumber, peppers, green onion and parsley. After chopping add to salad bowl. Season with salt, black pepper, garlic powder and mint leaves.

Squeeze water from wheat by hand or in a strainer. Add to salad mixture. Toss well. Pour off any excess liquid in salad bowl. Chill until serving time.

Yield: 8-10 servings

Sharon Coury Moss (Mrs. William, Jr.)

CAESAR SALAD DRESSING

1 clove garlic
1 egg
2 tablespoons lemon juice
1/2 teaspoon black pepper
1/2 teaspoon salt
1 (2-oz.) can whole anchovies
    and oil (use only ½ can)
1/8 teaspoon TABASCO sauce
1/8 teaspoon Worcestershire
    sauce
1 cup fine olive oil
Crisp lettuce
2 cups cooked chicken, cut
    into bite-size pieces
4 hard boiled eggs, sliced

Process garlic in food processor with steel blade. Add egg, lemon juice, pepper, salt, anchovies, TABASCO, Worcestershire and olive oil. Process all until well-blended (a few seconds). Chill. Serve over lettuce and chicken. Garnish with sliced hard boiled eggs.

Yield: 10 servings

Lucy Stevens Kellner (Mrs. Herbert E.)

MAYONNAISE à la LASTRAPES

1 egg
1 pint corn oil, divided
1 teaspoon vinegar
2 teaspoons lemon juice
1 teaspoon horseradish mustard
1 teaspoon Dijon or regular
    yellow mustard
3/4 teaspoon salt
1/2 teaspoon red pepper

This recipe has been in the Lastrapes family for years. Each family has taught their children how to prepare mayonnaise. Many of the male cousins make it. We try to never be without it.

Beat egg in food processor for **2 minutes.** Keep processor on constantly while adding the remainder of ingredients, and until mayonnaise is made. Add 3 tablespoons of oil to egg in processor and beat **1 minute.** Add vinegar and lemon juice. Beat **30 seconds.** Add 1 cup oil pouring all at once. Add mustards, salt and pepper. Beat **30 seconds.** Add remaining oil all at once. Beat **30 seconds. Total time: 4½ minutes.**

A mixer or blender may be used. Beating time will be a few minutes longer.

Yield: 1 pint

Alice Lastrapes Carlin (Mrs. Arthur G.)

154

DAD'S SALAD DRESSING

1 small onion, cut up
1 cup mayonnaise
1/3 cup salad oil
1/4 cup catsup
2 tablespoons sugar
2 tablespoons salad vinegar
1 teaspoon prepared mustard
1/2 teaspoon salt
1/2 teaspoon paprika
1/4 teaspoon celery seed
1/8 teaspoon black pepper
4 ounces crumbled blue cheese

Place all ingredients except blue cheese in blender. Blend until smooth. Remove from blender and pour into 1-pint jar. Stir in blue cheese. Cover. Chill. Serve over lettuce or shrimp.

Yield: 1¹/₂ cups

Flora W. Rickey (Mrs. Horace, Sr.)

THOUSAND ISLAND DRESSING

1 egg
1 teaspoon dry mustard
1/2 teaspoon salt
1/4 teaspoon garlic powder
1/8 teaspoon red pepper
3 tablespoons apple cider
    vinegar
1 cup corn oil
3 ounces prepared chili sauce
2 tablespoons finely chopped
    chives
1 tablespoon finely chopped bell
    pepper
2 teaspoons chopped pimiento
1/4 teaspoon salt
1/8 teaspoon paprika
2 hard boiled eggs, finely
    chopped

Blend egg, mustard, salt, garlic powder, red pepper and vinegar in blender a few seconds until well mixed. With blender on, pour oil in a slow steady stream until mayonnaise is thick and creamy. Stir in chili sauce, chives, bell pepper, pimiento, salt, paprika and chopped eggs. Pour into jar and chill. Serve over lettuce leaves.

Yield: 1/2 pint

Jean Kellner Durkee (Mrs. Robert R., Jr.)

the
1950s

uring the decade of the 1950s, Maurice Heymann broke ground for his oil center and Mrs. Roy Blair began serving a *white* gravy in her restaurant in the Gordon Hotel. Both were marks of changing times in Lafayette.

Elsewhere, it was a decade that saw the beginning of the Korean War, Ike's election, the storybook marriage of Prince Ranier and Grace Kelly, the election of Pope John XXIII, statehood for Alaska and Hawaii, the Sputnik-launched beginning of the Space Age.

But in Mrs. Blair's kitchen, the cooks were wondering over what this town would come to, what with these Texans flocking in to find our oil, bringing with them their chicken fried steaks and gravy without a roux.

What it would come to was the launching of Lafayette's own space age, when population began to soar like a rocket, corporate boundaries would begin leapfrogging outward, and the town would truly lay claim to its distinction as the Hub City of Acadiana.

The year 1952 might be marked as the beginning of Lafayette's leap forward. It had been just five years before, in 1947, that Kerr-McGee's "gamble in the Gulf" had paid off with the first offshore oil well out of sight of land. Now oilmen were looking for a central place from which to push farther and farther into Gulf waters. In June, 1952, several of them sat down with Maurice Heymann—already an enormously successful entrepreneur—and began to develop the idea that would still be fueling Lafayette's growth three decades later.

By 1954, Mr. Heymann was promoting his new oil center as the "Million Dollar Mile." By 1955 there were 30 offices there, most of them housing folks who had been somewhere else just a few short years before, most of them talking with a Texas twang or an Oklahoma drawl, rather than in the lyrical language of the Cajun's French. Confirming the Oil Center activity the first biennial Louisiana Gulf Coast Oil Exposition, LAGCOE, the "working man's oil show," was held October, 1955.

In 1950, when we began, there were 33,541 folks living in Lafayette. By 1960, population had jumped by twenty percent, to more than 40,000. In the next decade it would jump by twenty percent again, and also in the decade after that.

As the population grew, other good things began to happen to Lafayette. The television age arrived here in 1953, when the Camelia Broadcasting Co. began sending its signals from KLFY-TV. Oil-inspired business travel brought the need for a new airport terminal. The largest bond issue ever in Lafayette's history until then, paid for a flock of new schools and renovations to old ones. The Lafayette Sanitarium began the growth that would evolve into a new Lafayette General Hospital. Our Lady of Lourdes Hospital, founded in 1949, expanded as the numbers of patients and physicians here grew. Retail trade grew like Topsy and Lafayette served not only its own expanding population but assumed a larger role as the distribution center for all Acadiana. Enrollment at the Southwestern Louisiana Institute had nearly doubled from 2,556 in 1950 to 4,910 in 1960, the year it would become the University of Southwestern Louisiana. Along the way, it had been the first campus in Louisiana and among the first in the south to open its doors, without fanfare or incident, to the black people in the state.

Lafayette had arrived. She was firmly established as the commercial, educational, medical, media, transportation, distribution and oil center for south Louisiana.

And, best yet, it was only the beginning of even greater growth and prosperity to come.

Jim Bradshaw
Freelance writer

Poultry~Meat

COOKED CHICKEN à la MICROWAVE

1 (3-lb.) chicken cut up
3 cups hot water
1/4 cup white wine, optional
1/2 onion, sliced
1 rib celery and leaves, cut
2 bay leaves
1 teaspoon salt
1/2 teaspoon pepper
1/2 teaspoon cayenne pepper

Place chicken, water, wine, onion, celery, bay leaves, salt and pepper in 3-quart casserole. Cover. Microwave on **HIGH (100%) 25 MINUTES.** Remove chicken, reserve stock for future use. Proceed with recipe requiring cooked chicken.

Yield: 2 cups cooked chicken

Tout de Suite à la Microwave II

CHICKEN SPINACH au GRATIN

2 (3-lb.) chickens, cut into pieces
Salt and pepper
1/4 cup butter
1/4 cup flour
1 cup milk
1 cup chicken stock
5 ounces uncooked small egg
    noodles
1 (10-oz.) package frozen
    chopped spinach
1 pint sour cream
1/3 cup lemon juice
1 (8-oz.) can mushroom pieces
    and liquid
1 (8-oz.) can sliced water
    chestnuts, diced
1 (4-oz.) jar chopped pimiento
1/2 cup chopped onion
1/2 cup chopped celery
2 teaspoons seasoned salt
2 teaspoons pepper
1 teaspoon *each* Accènt, paprika,
    salt
1/2 teaspoon cayenne pepper
1¹/₂ cups grated cheddar or
    Monterey Jack cheese

Cook chicken in seasoned water. (See this page for microwave directions.) Bone chicken and cut into large bite-size pieces (4 cups). Save stock for cream sauce. Melt butter in large saucepan. Stir in flour. Add milk and chicken stock. Cook over low heat, stirring until cream sauce thickens. Cook noodles; drain well. Cook spinach; drain well. To cream sauce add sour cream, lemon juice, mushrooms and liquid, water chestnuts, pimientos, spinach, noodles, onion, celery and seasonings. Mix well. Butter 3-quart casserole (9 x 13-inch). Spread layer of cream sauce mixture. Add layer of chicken. Repeat layers and top with cheese. Bake in **preheated 350° oven 25 minutes.**

Yield: 10-12 servings

Jean Hennington (Mrs. Herbert M.)

Microwave shortcut: Remove outer waxed wrapper on spinach carton. Place paper carton of frozen spinach on microwave safe plate. Microwave on **HIGH (100%) 7 MINUTES.** Drain. *Jean K Durkee*

CHICKEN SAUERKRAUT

1 (5-6½ lb.) hen, dressed
Salt, red and black pepper
1 quart sauerkraut, homemade
    preferably
3 ounces raisins
1 recipe of thick cornbread
    or biscuit mix, uncooked

Wash and season hen with salt and pepper inside and out. Rinse sauerkraut to remove vinegar. Add raisins. Stuff hen with sauerkraut/raisin mixture. Lay chicken on side on rack in oven baking pan. Cover with foil. Bake in **preheated 325° oven 2 hours.** Turn to other side and bake 1½ **hours**. Drop thick cornbread mix or biscuit mix in gravy for last 30 minutes. *This early 1900 recipe is from Grandma DeJean who cooked just 'out of her head.' She was a most innovative cook.*

Yield: 6-8 servings

Judith Mouton Hebert (Mrs. Henry P., Jr.)

Microwave shortcut: Prepare hen as above except substitute Micro Shake for salt on outside. Stuff hen and place in Brown-In-Bag. Use rubber band to close bag leaving opening size of quarter. Place on micro-safe plate. Microwave on **MEDIUM (50%) 30 MINUTES.** Turn hen over in bag and microwave on **HIGH (100%) 30 MINUTES**, until tender. Drain hot stock from bag to make drop biscuits in conventional oven. *Jean K Durkee*

DEVILED CHICKEN BREASTS

6 chicken breast halves
Salt and pepper
1 cup water
4 tablespoons margarine,
    softened
1 tablespoon prepared mustard
1 tablespoon vinegar
1¼ teaspoons paprika
1 teaspoon celery seed
1/2 teaspoon salt
1/2 teaspoon lemon juice
1/2 small onion, grated
1/8 teaspoon pepper

Season chicken lightly with salt and pepper. Place chicken in saucepan with 1 cup water. Cover. Steam 20 minutes over medium heat. Reserve stock. In small bowl make paste with margarine, mustard, vinegar, paprika, celery seed, salt, lemon juice, onion and pepper. Place steamed chicken in baking pan and cover with paste. Broil 10 minutes; then pour reserved stock over chicken. Cover with foil and bake in **preheated 350° oven 30-40 minutes.** Remove cover and brown under broiler if necessary.

Yield: 3-4 servings

Jean G. Leland (Mrs. Rodney C.)

Microwave shortcut: To steam chicken, place in 2-quart glass dish with 1 cup water. Cover. Microwave on **HIGH (100%) 5-6 MINUTES**, rearrange chicken at 3 minutes. Reserve stock and continue to follow recipe above. *Jean K Durkee*

CHICKEN CURRY CONTINENTAL

8 chicken pieces
6 cups water, salt and pepper
6 tablespoons butter
1 cup chopped apple
1 cup chopped onion
1 clove garlic, chopped
1/4 cup all-purpose flour
2¹/₂ teaspoons curry powder
1 teaspoon salt
1 teaspoon ginger
1/4 teaspoon pepper
2 teaspoons lime juice
3 cups reserved chicken broth

*Side-dishes:
Raisins   Grated Coconut
Chutney   Chopped Bananas
        Chopped Peanuts
Chopped Green Onion Tops
Sieved Hard Boiled Eggs

In a 4-quart covered pot, place chicken pieces in 6 cups of seasoned water. Simmer until done, approximately 20 minutes. Set aside and reserve stock. Bone cooked chicken and cut into bite-size pieces.

In a large skillet melt butter and add apple, onion and garlic. Sauté until tender. Stir in flour, curry, salt, ginger, pepper and lime juice.

Add 3 cups chicken broth and stir to thicken. Add boned chicken and simmer until gravy is blended. Adjust seasoning. Serve chicken over white rice with Side-dishes* sprinkled on top. Add gravy last over all.

Yield: 6-8 servings

Ann H. LeJeune (Mrs. Womack)

CHICKEN COUNTRY CAPTAIN

3 (2¹/₂-3 lbs.) fryers, cut up
1 cup flour
2 teaspoons salt
1 teaspoon *each* red pepper,
    black pepper and paprika
1 cup vegetable oil
1¹/₂ cups hot water
4 medium onions, chopped
3 bell peppers, chopped
3 cloves garlic, chopped
1/2 cup water
3 (14¹/₂-oz.) cans whole
    tomatoes, blended
1/2 teaspoon thyme
1 teaspoon curry powder
1/2 cup chopped parsley
Salt and pepper to taste
1¹/₂ cups currants
1/2 pound blanched toasted
    almonds

Rinse chicken pieces and pat dry. Place mixture of flour, salt, pepper and paprika in paper bag. Add chicken pieces. Close bag and shake to coat chicken. Heat oil in large skillet. Brown chicken. Transfer to large Dutch oven. Add hot water, cover and steam slowly. Remove 1/2 cup oil from skillet chicken was cooked in. Add onion, bell pepper and garlic. Add 1/2 cup water. Cook 15 minutes. Stir in tomatoes, thyme, curry, parsley, salt and pepper to taste. Cook until smooth. Pour mixture over chicken and simmer 45 minutes. Add currants and almonds. Serve over wild, brown or white steamed rice.

Yield: 12 servings

Hascal Hardy (Mrs. Irby)

161

POULE de la MER

3 pounds (8-10) chicken breasts,
    boned and skinned
Creole seasoning for sprinkling
1/2 cup butter
3/4 cup flour
1/2 pint Half & Half cream
1/2 pint whipping cream
1 (4-oz.) can chopped
    mushrooms, drained
2 cups peeled and coarsely
    chopped raw shrimp
1 teaspoon salt
1 teaspoon celery seed
1/2 teaspoon paprika
1/2 pound Velveeta cheese,
    cubed
1/2 cup sherry
12 ounce box fettuccini
    noodles, cooked

Season chicken breasts with Creole seasoning or salt and pepper. Place in a 9 x 13-inch baking dish. Cover and bake in a **preheated 400° oven 45 minutes**. After cooking, drain and reserve liquid. Cut chicken in large bite-size pieces. Melt butter in large saucepan and blend in flour. Add Half & Half and whipping cream slowly. Stir until mixture thickens. Add mushrooms, shrimp, salt, celery seed and paprika. Cover and cook over medium heat 15 minutes. Add cheese and sherry. Simmer uncovered 10 minutes. Add 2 tablespoons reserved chicken drippings if mixture is too thick. Pour sauce over chicken in 9 x 13-inch baking dish. Cover and bake in **preheated 350° oven 20-30 minutes.** Serve with cooked fettuccini noodles.

Yield: 10-12 servings

John J. Daigre

Microwave directions: Place seasoned chicken (omit salt until after cooking) in 7 x 11-inch glass baking dish. Cover with wax paper. Microwave on **HIGH (100%) 8-9 MINUTES**. Stir or rearrange chicken after 4 minutes cooking time. Drain and reserve liquid. Cut chicken into bite-size pieces. To prepare sauce, melt butter in 8-cup glass measure on **HIGH (100%) 1 MINUTE**. Stir in flour. Slowly add 1/2 pint whipping cream (omit Half & Half). Microwave on **HIGH (100%) 1 MINUTE**, stirring at 30 seconds. Add mushrooms, shrimp, salt, celery seed and paprika. Cover and microwave on **HIGH (100%) 4 MINUTES**. Stir in cheese until melted. Add sherry. Pour sauce over chicken in 7 x 11-inch dish. Add reserved liquid if needed to thin sauce. Cover and microwave on **HIGH (100%) 5 MINUTES** or until shrimp are pink. *Jean K Durkee*

OUT OF SIGHT CHICKEN SPAGHETTI

2 (3-lbs.) chickens, cut into
    pieces
5 quarts water
1¹/₂ pounds spaghetti
1/2 cup margarine
2 small onions, chopped
6 ribs celery, chopped
1 (10-oz.) can Ro-tel tomatoes
    and green chilies & liquid
1 (32-oz.) can whole tomatoes,
    drained and crushed
1 (8-oz.) can sliced mushrooms,
    drained
1 tablespoon salt
1 teaspoon red pepper
3/4 teaspoon garlic powder
1/2 pound grated cheddar
    cheese
1/2 pound grated sharp cheese
Parmesan cheese for sprinkling

In a large pot boil chicken in water seasoned with salt and pepper 1 hour. Cool and remove bones. Reserve stock. Bring stock to rolling boil. Add spaghetti, let it come to boil again and stir to separate. Turn off heat. Cover and let stand 20 minutes. Melt margarine in a small saucepan. Sauté onions and celery. Combine chicken with cooked spaghetti. Add tomatoes, mushrooms, salt, pepper, garlic powder, cheese, sautéed onions and celery. Stir well. Spoon into 2 large greased 7 x 11-inch baking dishes. Sprinkle with Parmesan cheese. Bake in **preheated 375° oven 30 minutes** or until hot and bubbly.

Yield: 12-14 servings

Louise Larcade (Mrs. Harold W.)

Microwave directions: Follow the above recipe. After spooning spaghetti mixture into baking dish cover with wax paper and microwave **each** dish on **HIGH 100% 7-8 MINUTES.** *Jean K Durkee*

CHICKEN ARTICHOKE

1 (3-lb.) chicken, cooked, boned,
    cut into bite-size pieces
1/2 cup margarine
1 large onion, minced
1/4 cup flour
2 cups milk
1/2 to 1 teaspoon salt
1/4 teaspoon black pepper
1/4 teaspoon red pepper
1 cup grated cheddar cheese
2 (8-oz.) cans drained or (1-lb.)
    fresh mushrooms, sliced
2 (8¹/₂-oz.) cans artichoke hearts,
    drained and sliced
Seasoned bread crumbs

Follow directions on page 159 for *Cooked Chicken*. Reserve stock. In a large saucepan sauté onion in margarine until tender. Stir in flour until smooth. Add milk, salt, pepper and cheese. Simmer until thick and smooth. Add chicken, mushrooms, artichokes and reserved chicken stock if needed to thin sauce.

Place mixture in a 9 x 12-inch baking dish. Sprinkle with bread crumbs. Bake in a **preheated 350° oven 30 minutes.**

Yield: 8 servings

Elisabeth Denbo Montgomery (Mrs. Thad)

CHICKEN ARTICHOKE CRÊPES

Basic Crêpes:
1 cup milk
3 eggs
2/3 cup all-purpose flour
4 teaspoons soft butter

2 cups cooked, diced chicken
5 tablespoons butter, divided
1 small onion, chopped
1/4 pound mushrooms, sliced
3 tablespoons all-purpose flour
2/3 cup chicken broth
1/2 cup light cream
1 (8½-oz.) can artichoke hearts,
　　drained and cut into 1/8ths
2 tablespoons chopped parsley
1 teaspoon salt
1/4 teaspoon white pepper
1/2 cup shredded Swiss cheese

Whirl milk, eggs, flour and butter in blender. Let rest at least 1 hour or overnight in refrigerator. Stir batter before using. Pour batter into small greased skillet or crêpe pan. Turn to brown other side. Makes 12 (6-inch) crêpes.

Cook chicken your favorite way or see recipe for Cooked Chicken on page 159.

Melt 2 tablespoons butter in skillet over medium heat. Add onion and mushrooms. Fry lightly. Stir in remaining butter until melted. Add flour, cook until bubbly. Gradually stir in broth and cream, stirring until it boils and thickens. Remove from heat. Add artichokes, chicken, parsley, salt and pepper. Cool. Divide filling among crêpes, spooning down center of each. Fold to enclose. Place in buttered 7 x 11-inch dish. If crêpes are to be frozen, line the dish with foil. When ready to serve, bake covered with foil in **preheated 375° oven 20 minutes**. (35-40 minutes if frozen). Remove covering. Sprinkle 1 tablespoon Swiss cheese over each crêpe. Return to oven until cheese melts.

Yield: 12 crêpes

Elaine W. Malin

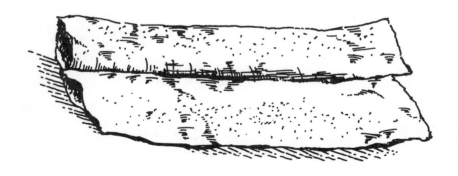

CHICKEN ON PASTA

6 boneless chicken breasts,
   (1½-lbs.)
1/2 cup butter
2 cloves garlic, minced
1 bunch green onion tops and
   bulbs, chopped
1 pound fresh mushrooms,
   sliced
1½ pints heavy cream
4 ounces white wine
1½ teaspoons salt
1/2 teaspoon white pepper
1/4 teaspoon cayenne pepper
8 ounces plain or spinach
   fettuccini

Remove skin from boned chicken and cut into julienne strips. Set aside. Melt butter in a large sauté pan. Add garlic and green onion and sauté until tender. Add chicken and mushrooms and cook until chicken loses its pinkness.

Add cream and wine and reduce by a third. Add salt, white pepper and cayenne pepper. Cook fettuccini in salted water according to package directions. Serve over fettuccini.

Yield: 12 servings

Chef Joseph Gonsoulin
Chez Marcelle

ITALIAN EGGPLANT CHICKEN

3 pounds chicken, cooked
1/2 teaspoon garlic powder
1½ pounds (2 medium)
   eggplant, peeled and sliced
   ¼ inch thick
3 eggs, beaten
2 cups Italian seasoned bread
   crumbs
3/4 cup vegetable oil
Salt and white pepper
2 tablespoons vegetable oil
1/4 cup chopped bell pepper
1 tablespoon chopped onion
1 (16-oz.) can tomato sauce
1/2 cup reserved chicken broth
1 teaspoon basil leaves
1/2 teaspoon oregano
1/2 teaspoon salt
1/2 cup grated Parmesan
   cheese
1 (8-oz.) package mozzarella
   slices, cut into triangles

Cook chicken according to directions on page 159. Reserve broth. Bone chicken and cut into bite-size pieces. Sprinkle with garlic powder. Dip eggplant slices into beaten eggs. Coat with crumbs. In large skillet heat oil. Brown eggplant slices. Drain on paper towels. Sprinkle with salt and pepper.

Heat 2 tablespoons oil in medium skillet. Add bell pepper and onion. Sauté 2 minutes. Add tomato sauce, broth, basil, oregano and salt. Simmer 2 minutes. In buttered 9 x 13-inch baking dish lay 1/3 of the eggplant slices. Spread 1/3 of chicken evenly over eggplant. Spread 1/3 tomato sauce mixture over chicken. Sprinkle with 1/3 Parmesan cheese and top with 1/3 mozzarella triangles. Repeat layers and sprinkle with remaining cheese. Bake in **preheated 350° oven 30-45 minutes.**

Yield: 8 servings

Virginia Gardiner Arceneaux (Mrs. E. G., Jr.)

CHICKEN AND WILD RICE

2 (3-lb.) chickens, cut into pieces
Salt, pepper, garlic powder
1 medium onion, quartered
2 cups raw wild rice, cooked
3/4 cup butter
1 cup chopped onions
1/2 cup flour
2 cups chicken stock
1 (8-oz.) can sliced mushrooms,
    reserve liquid
1 pint whipping cream
1½ teaspoons salt
1/2 teaspoon pepper
1/2 cup slivered almonds,
    optional

In a large Dutch oven cook chicken in 6 cups water seasoned with salt, pepper, garlic powder and onion. Cook covered until tender. Remove chicken from bone and dice. Reserve stock. Cook rice according to package directions.

To make a white sauce melt butter in a 2-quart saucepan. Add onions and sauté until transparent. Add flour, stirring constantly. Add chicken stock, mushroom liquid and cream. Add salt and pepper and cook on medium heat until thickened.

Mix diced chicken, drained mushrooms and cooked rice in a 5-quart or, 2 (2½-quart) casseroles. Stir in white sauce. Sprinkle with almonds. Bake uncovered in **preheated 350° oven 30 minutes**, or until heated through.

Yield: 8-10 servings

Karen Veillon McGlasson (Mrs. H. Edwin, Jr.)

SMOKED TURKEY

1 handful hickory chips
12-17 pound turkey
Salt and pepper
1 bell pepper, quartered
2 medium onions, quartered
1/4 cup margarine
Lawry's seasoned salt
Vegetable oil
1 cup fruit juice

Prepare charcoal smoker for 8-12 hours; electric smoker, 6-8 hours. Soak hickory chips in water. Rinse and dry turkey. Season cavity with salt and pepper. Stuff with bell pepper, onion and margarine. Rub outside with oil and seasoned salt. Add fruit juice to water bath of smoker. Place turkey on rack and smoke 3-4 hours. Wrap turkey tightly in heavy-duty aluminum foil and finish smoking 4 hours or longer. Well done—185° internal thigh temperature. Remove and let stand 20 minutes covered. Turkey will fall off bones. Use bones for soup. Reserve liquid for gravy or gumbo. *Mangons à Lafayette!*

Yield: 10-15 servings

Susan B. Winkler (Mrs. Robert)

CHICKEN à la SAUCE PIQUANTE

1 (3-lb.) chicken, cut up
1/2 cup vegetable oil
1/2 cup all-purpose flour
2 large onions, chopped
1 rib celery, chopped
3 cloves garlic, minced
1 (6-oz.) can tomato paste
1 (14-oz.) can tomatoes,
    chopped with liquid
1 cup warm water
1/2 cup chopped bell pepper
1 tablespoon sugar
1 teaspoon Creole seasoning
Salt, red and black pepper to
    taste
1/2 cup sliced fresh or canned
    mushrooms
1/2 cup sliced ripe olives
1/2 cup chopped green onion
    tops
1/4 cup chopped parsley
Cooked rice for serving

Season chicken with salt, red and black pepper. Set aside.
Heat oil in a large Dutch oven. Add flour and stir constantly to make a roux. When golden brown add seasoned chicken. Coat with roux. Then, add onion, celery, garlic, tomato paste and tomatoes. Stir well. Lower heat and cook 10 minutes, stirring often. Add water, bell pepper, sugar, Creole seasoning, salt, red and black pepper to taste. Cover and cook slowly until chicken is tender, about 1 hour. Add more water if needed. Add mushrooms and olives. Cook 10 minutes. Add onion tops and parsley. Serve with cooked rice or spaghetti and garlic French bread.

Yield: 8 servings

Rubye Valentine Shelton (Mrs. Louis)

TURKEY MORNAY

6 croissant rolls, split
2 cups sliced cooked turkey
1 (16-oz.) can green asparagus
    spears, drained
8 ounces Swiss cheese, sliced
1/4 cup butter
1/4 cup flour
1/2 teaspoon salt
1/2 teaspoon white pepper
1 cup milk
1 cup heavy cream
1 cup grated Parmesan cheese
1/2 cup chopped green onion
    tops

Butter an 8 x 12-inch baking dish. Split rolls and line bottom of dish. Layer turkey slices, asparagus spears and slices of cheese. To make Mornay sauce, melt butter in a 2-quart saucepan. Blend in flour, salt and pepper. Cook over low heat, stirring until smooth and bubbly. Remove from heat. Stir in milk. Bring to boil, boil 1 minute, stirring constantly. Cook until thickened, 10 minutes. Add cream. Heat, stirring constantly. Stir in Parmesan cheese and onion tops. Pour sauce over layers in baking dish. Bake in **preheated 350° oven 30 minutes** or until cheese is melted and sauce is bubbling.

Yield: 8 servings

Mary Albaugh Usner (Mrs. Larry)

167

DAUBE GLACÉ BELLEVUE

1 (5-lb.) thick rump roast
1 tablespoon salt
2 cloves garlic, minced
1/4 teaspoon red pepper
2 tablespoons shortening
1/2 cup chopped onion
1/2 cup chopped celery
6 cups water
2 bay leaves
1½ teaspoons whole allspice
1½ teaspoons whole cloves
5 (1/4-oz.) envelopes unflavored
    gelatin
4 (10-oz.) cans consommé,
    undiluted
3 tablespoons lemon juice
3 tablespoons Worcestershire
    sauce
1/2 teaspoon TABASCO sauce,
    or to taste (season highly)
1/2 cup chopped parsley
1 (2-oz.) jar chopped pimiento
1/2 raw carrot, chopped
Parsley sprigs for garnish

Stuff roast with mixture of salt, garlic and red pepper. Brown roast in shortening. Remove roast from pot. Add onion and celery. Sauté until tender. Drain off all fat. Add water, bay leaves, allspice and cloves. Return meat to pot. Simmer until meat is tender, 2½-3 hours. Slice thinly. Strain liquid, about 3 cups. In a 2-quart bowl dissolve gelatin in strained liquid. Add consommé, mixing well. Season with lemon juice, Worcestershire and TABASCO. In a greased 13 x 9 x 2-inch dish, place parsley, pimiento and carrot. Add enough gelatin/consommé mixture to jell and hold firm. Refrigerate. When firm, add thinly sliced meat on top. Pour remaining gelatin/consommé over all. Refrigerate until firm. Turn out onto a large slicing board or serving platter. Garnish with parsley.

Yield: 12 servings—cut into smaller pieces
        for cocktail party

This is my grandmother, Mrs. Overton Cade's, recipe. Alterations have been made, of course. The jelly used to be made with calves feet and more water was added. Grandfather Cade was prominent in the history of Lafayette Parish as was his father, Robert Cade, who lived in Vermilionville/Lafayette before settling at Bellevue Plantation in 1830.

Tolley C. Davis (Mrs. F. H., Sr.)

FILET BRAISE AUX OIGNONS

3 pounds round steak
2 tablespoons vinegar
1 tablespoon salt
1 teaspoon pepper
1/2 teaspoon cayenne pepper
1 tablespoon flour
3 tablespoons shortening
1/4 cup water
1 large onion, finely sliced
1/2 cup water
3 sprigs parsley

Beat steak well with meat tenderizer. Pour vinegar on both sides. Mix salt, pepper and cayenne; season steak with mixture. Dredge steak with flour. Melt shortening in deep skillet. Brown meat on both sides over hot fire. When brown add 1/4 cup water. Cover and simmer 30 minutes or until tender. Remove steak. Place onion in skillet, brown. Add 1/2 cup water. Return steak to skillet. Cover and cook over low heat 30 minutes. Move steak in pan so it will not stick. Place on serving plate. Garnish with parsley.

Yield: 4-6 servings

Hazel Alpha

VEAL HAMILTON

1½ pounds veal or baby beef cutlet, 1/2 inch thick
1/4 cup flour
1 teaspoon Creole seasoned salt
1/4 cup vegetable oil
2 cloves garlic, minced
1 onion, finely chopped
1/2 cup white wine
1 tablespoon lemon juice
1/4 cup water
1 (8-oz.) can sliced water chestnuts, drained
1 (8-oz.) can sliced mushrooms
1 bay leaf
1 teaspoon salt
1/4 teaspoon pepper
3 whole cloves
1 tablespoon cornstarch
Cooked rice for serving

Rub meat with a mixture of flour and Creole seasoned salt. Heat oil in heavy skillet. Add veal, garlic and onion. Cook until meat is browned. Add wine, lemon juice, water, water chestnuts, mushrooms, bay leaf, salt, pepper and cloves. Cover and simmer gently 45-55 minutes or until tender. Thicken sauce with cornstarch. Serve with cooked rice.

Yield: 6 servings

Mary Elizabeth Hamilton (Mrs. Herbert)

BRAISED BRISKET OF BEEF

4 pound beef brisket
2 cloves of garlic, slivered
Salt and seasoned pepper
1/4-1/2 cup all-purpose flour
2 tablespoons cooking oil
1 cup canned beef broth
1 cup beer or 1 cup red wine
Worcestershire sauce
TABASCO sauce
McCormick Salad Herbs
1 bay leaf
3 or 4 large onions, sliced

Trim excess fat from meat. Make gashes in meat and insert slivers of garlic. Rub meat with salt and seasoned pepper. Dredge meat in flour. **Heat** 2 tablespoons oil in 9 x 12-inch pan in **preheated 450° oven** until very hot.

Then coat all sides of meat in hot oil. Place uncovered in **450-500° oven 30 minutes** or until well-browned. Turn meat once during browning. When browned, remove meat from pan. Pour off excess oil. Add to pan 1 cup beef broth and 1 cup beer or red wine. Liquid should cover about half the thickness of the meat. Season to taste with salt, seasoned pepper, Worcestershire, TABASCO, Salad Herbs and bay leaf. Stir well. Place meat back in pan. Add onion slices over and around meat. Cover pan tightly with foil and bake **325° 1 hour 30 minutes** or until tender. This roast makes its own gravy.

Yield: 6 servings

Peggy French Rogers (Mrs. Frank)

PLUCKETT'S BARBECUE BRISKET

Seasoning mix:
1/2 pound salt
1 ounce garlic powder
1 ounce Accènt
1 ounce black pepper
4 ounces paprika
Red pepper for sprinkling

7-9 pound brisket

Hint: Barbecue 2 briskets at one time and freeze one. There will be plenty (3 cups) of seasoning mix.

Mix salt, garlic powder, Accènt, pepper and paprika in bowl or 1-quart jar.

Take a whole brisket and wash and soak in sink or in a big pan of cold water. Remove from water. Dust brisket with red pepper. Rub whole brisket with Mr. Pluckett's seasoning mix until completely coated. Place on **barbeque pit on slow (low) fire** with fat side up and cook slowly **4 to 6 hours** or done to your satisfaction. Remove from grill, and while still hot wrap in foil, and place immediately in an insulated styrofoam ice chest and seal. This allows seasoning to tenderize the meat. Let brisket cool down 6-8 hours in the sealed chest.

Yield: 25 servings

Matthew B. Gordy

BARBECUED BEEF BRISKET

2 (3-lb.) beef briskets or
    1 (5-6 lb.) brisket
2 teaspoons salt
1/4 teaspoon pepper
1/2 teaspoon garlic powder
1/8 teaspoon paprika
1/4 cup prepared liquid smoke

*Barbecue Sauce:

4 cups water
6 beef bouillon cubes
1/4 cup liquid smoke
1 cup catsup
1/4 cup mustard
3 tablespoons brown sugar
2 tablespoons Worcestershire
    sauce
1 teaspoon garlic powder
1 teaspoon salt
4 dashes TABASCO sauce

Yield: 6 cups

Trim excess fat from brisket and weigh meat to determine cooking time of 30 minutes per pound. Rinse well and pat dry with paper towels. Mix together salt, pepper, garlic powder, paprika and liquid smoke. Rub seasoning into brisket. Cover tightly and refrigerate overnight. Place brisket on a rack uncovered. Bake in **preheated 350° oven 1 hour 15 minutes**. Pour off excess fat. Remove rack setting brisket in pan.

Bring Barbecue Sauce* ingredients to a boil. Pour over meat. Cover and continue baking **350° 1 hour 30 minutes** longer for a 5-6 pound brisket. Baste a time or two, until fork tender. When meat is done, slice thinly. Place in shallow dish and cover with sauce. Freezes very well.

Yield: 12-14 servings

Elsie Parker Henderson (Mrs. W. C.)

Microwave shortcut: Mix barbecue sauce ingredients in an 8-cup glass measuring cup. Microwave on **HIGH (100%) 12 MINUTES**. Stir once or twice. *Jean K Durkee*

RICHARD'S BAR-B-Q SAUCE

1 cup corn oil
1/2 cup lemon juice or cider
    vinegar or a combination
2 tablepsoons sugar
1/2 teaspoon TABASCO sauce
1 teaspoon salt

Combine oil, juice and/or vinegar, sugar, TABASCO and salt in saucepan. Bring to fast boil. Boil 2 minutes. *Great for basting chicken and pork ribs on the barbecue pit.*

Yield: 1½ cups

Yvonne Richard (Mrs. Leopold)

DAUBE

5 pounds rump or round roast
    beef
1 large onion, chopped
3 cloves garlic, chopped
1 tablespoon chopped parsley
1 teaspoon black pepper
1 teaspoon red pepper
2 tablespoons salt
1/4 pound bacon or salt pork, cut
    into pieces
1/3 cup vegetable oil
1/2 cup water
1 (4-oz.) can sliced mushrooms

Remove fat from roast. Mix onion, garlic, parsley together with black and red pepper and salt. Make 10 incisions, 3-4 inches deep, in the roast. Insert pork pieces and half the seasoning mixture. Season the outer surfaces of the daube with the remaining seasonings. (This may be done ahead and placed in refrigerator the night before.)

In a large pot, brown meat thoroughly on all sides in hot oil, completing with incisions at top. Cover.

Place in **preheated 325° oven.** Cook for 2½ **hours** or 30 minutes per pound. Remove roast from pot. Skim grease from drippings. Add 1/2 cup cold water to residue in pot, scraping sides and bottom thoroughly. Add mushrooms to gravy. If gravy is too thin mix 1 teaspoon flour with cold water, add to gravy and allow to boil 2 minutes. *L'appetit des Acadiens*

Yield: 10 servings

Marie Louise Comeaux Manuel (Mrs. John D.)
Retired, Director of School of Home
Economics, University of Southwestern
Louisiana

SWISS STEAK

2 pounds round steak
1 cup all-purpose flour
1 teaspoon salt
1 teaspoon black pepper
3 tablespoons bacon fat
4 cups diced potatoes
2 cups diced carrots
2 cups diced onions
2 cups diced bell pepper
1 teaspoon salt
1 tablespoon sugar
2 tablespoons wine vinegar
1 cup water
1 quart canned tomatoes or
    6 large fresh, chopped

Rub flour, salt and pepper on both sides of steak. Pound with meat tenderizer. Brown both sides of steak in hot bacon fat or oil in heavy roaster or Dutch oven. Place potatoes, carrots, onions, bell pepper, on top of meat. Add any remaining flour to salt, sugar, wine vinegar and water. Mix until smooth. Pour over vegetables. Spread tomatoes on top. Cover. Bake in **preheated 350° oven 2 hours.** Remove cover last 15 minutes to brown slightly.

Yield: 8 servings

Donna Thompson Rylee (Mrs. James E.)

CREOLE GRILLADES AND GRITS

2 pounds round steak, 1/2-inch
    thick
Flour seasoned with salt and
    pepper
4 tablespoons oil
2 onions, chopped
1 bell pepper, chopped
2 ribs celery, chopped
3 cloves garlic, crushed
1 (10-oz.) can Ro-tel tomatoes
    with green chilies, chopped
3 tablespoons tomato paste
1 teaspoon sugar
1 bay leaf
1/4 teaspoon *each* thyme, basil
    and oregano
Salt and pepper to taste
1 tablespoon Worcestershire
    sauce
1 1/2 cups beef broth
1/2 cup dry red wine
2 tablespoons *each* chopped
    parsley and green onion
    tops

Trim and cut steak into serving-size pieces. Sprinkle liberally with seasoned flour. Beat with tenderizing mallet until flour is pounded in and meat is thin. Brown meat in oil in large skillet. Remove from skillet and set aside. Add onion, bell pepper, celery and garlic to skillet. Sauté until wilted. Add tomatoes, tomato paste and sugar. Simmer 4 minutes. Add bay leaf, thyme, basil, oregano, salt and pepper to taste. Add Worcestershire, broth, wine, parsley and onion tops. Bring to boil. Reduce heat, add meat. Cover. Simmer over low heat 30-40 minutes until meat is tender and gravy is thick. Serve over hot Cheese Garlic Grits.*

Yield: 8-10 servings

*Cheese Garlic Grits:
1 1/2 cups quick yellow grits
6 cups water
1 1/2 teaspoons salt
1 (6-oz.) roll garlic cheese, grated
1/2 cup butter
2 tablespoons heavy cream
2 eggs, beaten

Add grits to boiling salted water in large saucepan. Bring back to boil, reduce heat and cook stirring 5 minutes. Add cheese, butter, cream and eggs. Stir until cheese melts. Pour into greased 9 x 13-inch or 3-quart casserole dish. Bake in **preheated 350° oven 30-40 minutes.** Serve with grillades.

Keith E. Courrège

PARTY MEATBALLS

Meatballs:
2 pounds ground beef
1 medium onion, grated
1 medium bell pepper, grated
1 bunch green onion tops,
    finely chopped
1/4 cup finely chopped parsley
2 eggs, beaten
3/4 cup seasoned bread crumbs
1/2 teaspoon salt
1/4 teaspoon pepper
1/4 teaspoon garlic powder

Mix beef, onion, bell pepper, onion tops, parsley, eggs, bread crumbs, salt, pepper and garlic powder in a large bowl. Roll into very small meatballs, approximately 110-130, and place on large cookie sheet. Bake in **preheated 350° oven 25 minutes.** Serve in Sauce* with wooden picks. Meatballs and sauce freeze well.

*Sauce:
2 tablespoons vegetable oil
3 large onions, grated
2 medium bell peppers, finely
    chopped
1 cup finely chopped celery
1/2 cup finely chopped parsley
1 bunch green onion tops,
    finely chopped
24 ounces tomato sauce
1 teaspoon salt
1 teaspoon pepper
1¹/₂ cups catsup
1¹/₂ cups barbecue sauce
1 tablespoon Worcestershire
    sauce
1/4 teaspoon oregano

Heat oil in a large 4-quart pot. Add onion, bell pepper, celery, parsley and onion tops. Cook vegetables until wilted and slightly browned. Add tomato sauce and simmer 1 hour, stirring occasionally. Add salt, pepper, catsup, barbecue sauce, Worcestershire sauce and oregano. Continue to simmer for 20 minutes. Add cooked meatballs and serve with wooden picks.

Yield: 110-130 meatballs

Evelyn Martin Chiasson (Mrs. Bob)

TROY'S B.B.Q. SAUCE

1 1/2 cups margarine
2 medium onions, finely
    chopped
1 1/2 tablespoons ground black
    pepper
1 teaspoon TABASCO sauce
1/4 clove garlic, finely chopped
3 tablespoons soy sauce
2 tablespoons Worcestershire
    sauce
3/4 cup catsup
3/4 cup prepared barbecue
    sauce, plain or hickory
    smoked
1/2 cup molasses or syrup
1 (10-oz.) can of beer

In a 3-quart saucepan melt margarine. Add onions and sauté until clear. Add pepper, TABASCO and garlic while sautéing. Reduce heat and add soy sauce, Worcestershire, catsup and barbecue sauce. Bring back to boil, stirring often to prevent scorching. Add molasses, stir well and remove from heat. Cool slightly. Add up to one can of beer and stir well. *Great sauce for chicken and hamburgers, too.*

Yield: 1 1/2 quarts

Troy Mason

BEEF SPAGHETTI SAUCE

1 pound ground beef chuck
1 medium onion, chopped
1/2 medium bell pepper,
    chopped
Salt and pepper to taste
1 (16-oz.) can stewed tomatoes
1 clove garlic, minced
1/2 teaspoon *each* oregano,
    basil, thyme, salt and black
    pepper
1 (4-oz.) can mushroom pieces,
    undrained
Cooked spaghetti
Parmesan cheese

In large skillet brown ground chuck with onion and bell pepper, adding salt and pepper to taste. In blender pour tomatoes and liquid, garlic, oregano, basil, thyme, salt and pepper. Blend 5 seconds on low speed, just enough to cut up tomatoes. Pour into ground chuck mixture. Stir in mushrooms. Cover. Simmer on low heat for 1 hour 30 minutes. Serve over cooked spaghetti. Top with Parmesan cheese.

Yield: 4 servings

Ann C. Altamirano (Mrs. Mario)

BEEF & BISCUITS

1½ pounds ground beef
1 medium onion, chopped
1/2 cup chopped bell pepper
1 teaspoon salt
2 teaspoons chili powder
1 teaspoon garlic powder
1 (8-oz.) can tomato sauce
1 egg, beaten
1/2 cup sour cream
1½ cups shredded cheddar
　cheese, divided
1 (10-oz.) can refrigerated
　biscuits

Sauté ground beef, onion and bell pepper in a large skillet until tender. Drain. Add salt, chili powder, garlic powder and tomato sauce. Simmer 3 minutes. Combine egg, sour cream and 1 cup shredded cheese. Blend well. Add to meat mixture. Separate biscuits into halves. Line lightly greased 7 x 11-inch baking dish with 10 halves, pressing together with fingers to form crust. Spoon meat mixture over crust. Press remaining biscuit halves with fingers and lay on top of meat mixture. Sprinkle with remaining cheese. Bake in a **preheated 350° oven 20-25 minutes** or until lightly browned.

Yield: 6-8 servings

Ruth Luthi

KETTY'S SPAGHETTI

1 pound lean bacon
1 pound thin spaghetti
3 large eggs, beaten
1/4 teaspoon pepper
1/2 cup bacon fat
1 cup grated Parmesan cheese

Fry bacon and cut into small bits, reserving 1/2 cup fat. Keep fat warm and set aside. Cook spaghetti in salted water. Drain. Add spaghetti to beaten egg and pepper mixture. Toss with 2 forks. Add bacon, bacon fat, cheese and toss again until well mixed. Serve immediately on warmed plates.

Yield: 6-8 servings

Victoria Clausen Ovitz (Mrs. Robert)

Microwave shortcut: Place 8 slices of bacon at a time on microwave safe bacon rack. Cover with wax paper. Microwave on **HIGH (100%) 6 MINUTES** (or 45 seconds per slice of bacon). Repeat until all bacon is cooked.

LASAGNA

1 tablespoon oil
2 pounds ground beef
1/2 bell pepper, chopped
2 medium onions, chopped
1/2 cup chopped celery
2 cloves garlic, minced
1 (6-oz.) can tomato paste
2 (6-oz.) cans water
1 (10-oz.) can Ro-tel tomatoes
    and green chilies, blended
4 teaspoons oregano
2 teaspoons basil
1/2 teaspoon sugar
1/2 teaspoon salt
Pepper to taste
1 (8-oz.) package lasagna
    noodles, cooked and
    drained
2 (8-oz.) cartons sour cream
24 ounces mozzarella cheese

Heat oil in 4½-quart Dutch oven. Brown meat, bell pepper, onion, celery and garlic. Add tomato paste, water, tomatoes, oregano, basil, sugar, salt and pepper. Simmer sauce 2 hours. In a greased 9 x 13-inch baking dish layer as follows: cooked noodles, sour cream, sauce and mozzarella cheese. Repeat to make 2 layers. Bake in **preheated 350° oven 45 minutes.** *This lasagna freezes well.*

Yield: 8 servings

Louise Larriviere Cordell (Mrs. Robert M.)

CREAMY NOODLES ITALIANO

2 cups cooked egg noodles
1½ pounds ground meat
1 (6-oz.) can tomato paste
3/4 cup water
2 teaspoons salt
1 teaspoon pepper
1 teaspoon garlic powder
1 large onion, chopped
1/2 cup chopped bell pepper
3/4 cup milk
1 (8-oz.) package cream cheese,
    cubed
1/2 cup Parmesan cheese

In a large pot cook noodles in lightly salted water according to package directions. Drain and set aside.

Brown meat in a large skillet. Drain. Add tomato paste, water, salt, pepper, garlic powder, onion and bell pepper. Cook over medium heat until vegetables are tender. Heat milk and cubed cream cheese. Add to drained noodles and stir until smooth. Alternate meat and noodle mixture in layers. Spread the first layer of meat in a greased 9½ x 11-inch pan. Sprinkle top with Parmesan cheese. Bake in **preheated 350° oven 20-25 minutes.**

Yield: 6-10 servings

Bea Delarue Riley (Mrs. Robert W.)

Microwave shortcut: Heat milk and cream cheese in the microwave in a 4-cup glass measuring cup on **HIGH (100%) 2 MINUTES.** Stir to blend. *Jean K Durkee*

177

ROTI de PORC PILETTE

1 (5-6 lb.) fresh pork ham or
    pork shoulder roast
2 large cloves garlic, minced
1 tablespoon minced bell pepper
1 teaspoon or 1 dried red pepper
    pod, seeded
2 tablespoons Wishbone Italian
    salad dressing
1 teaspoon salt
1/2 teaspoon black pepper
Rind of 1 orange, grated
3 tablespoons all-purpose flour
3 tablespoons vegetable oil
1 cup beef broth
Juice of 1 orange

*Gravy:
1 large onion, chopped
1/2 bell pepper, chopped
8 ounces fresh mushrooms,
    sliced
1 tablespoon olive oil
Fresh parsley for garnish

Remove excess fat from roast and thick skin if fresh pork ham is used. Wipe roast thoroughly with a damp cloth. In a kitchen cup mix garlic, bell pepper, red pepper, salad dressing, salt and pepper. Using a sharp knife make 6 or 7 deep incisions all around and stuff mixture into the roast. Rub roast all over with remaining mixture and then with grated orange rind. Cover and marinate 6 hours or overnight. Before cooking, sprinkle roast with flour and press as much as possible into roast. Heat oil in 4½-quart Dutch oven. Braise roast on all sides until brown. Remove roast and discard fat. Add beef broth and orange juice to pot, scraping bits and residue. Bring to boil. Add roast back to pot, cover and bake in **preheated 350° oven approximately 3 hours** (175° internal temperature). Add more broth if necessary. Remove from oven to serving platter and let roast rest 20 minutes. To make Gravy,* sauté onions, peppers, mushrooms and oil in saucepan. Simmer 10 minutes. Add remaining liquid, without fat, from roasting pot. Add more beef broth if necessary. Check seasonings of gravy. Slice meat. Garnish with parsley. Serve gravy in sauceboat.

Yield: 6-8 servings

Deanie Chesson (Mrs. Douglas M.)

PORK ROAST WITH GINGER SAUCE

1 (3-4 lb.) pork roast
Salt and pepper

*Ginger Sauce:
1/2 cup chopped onions
1/2 cup chopped celery
1/4 cup chopped bell pepper
2 cloves garlic, minced
1 small fresh ginger root, peeled,
    crushed and minced
2 teaspoons cornstarch
2 tablespoons soy sauce
2 tablespoons vinegar
1 tablespoon brown sugar
2 tablespoons chopped green
    onion tops
2 tablespoons chopped parsley
Cooked rice

Season roast with salt and pepper. Place on rack and bake in **preheated 350° oven** until well done, 45 minutes per pound or internal temperature of 180.° If roast begins to brown too much on outside, cover with a tent of foil. To make Ginger Sauce,* scrape drippings (this can be done last 30 minutes of cooking time) from roasting pan. Place 2 tablespoons fat plus any residue in a saucepan. Stir fry onions, celery, bell pepper, garlic and ginger root in fat. Let stand 5 minutes. Combine cornstarch, soy sauce, vinegar and sugar. Add to vegetables. Simmer 5 minutes. Add small amount of water if sauce is too thick. Add onion tops and parsley. Serve over hot rice with sliced roast.

Yield: 4-6 servings

Eloise Fung

PORK AND ARTICHOKES
Braciola alla Calabresa

3 tablespoons olive oil
4 pork chops
2 slices bacon, cut into small
    pieces
1/4 pound small white boiling
    onions, peeled
1/2 pound fresh mushrooms,
    sliced
1 (8½-oz.) can artichoke hearts,
    quartered, reserve liquid
1 cup white wine
2 tablespoons tomato sauce
1/2 teaspoon salt
1/4 teaspoon pepper

In a large skillet brown pork chops in hot oil. Sprinkle with salt and pepper. Remove and set aside. Add bacon pieces, sautéing until cooked, not crisp. Add onions, mushrooms and artichokes. Cover and cook until onions are fork tender. Add wine, tomato sauce, salt and pepper. Return pork chops to skillet, cover and simmer at least 20 minutes.

Add small amount of artichoke liquid if mixture becomes dry.

Yield: 4 servings

Laura Lane Robertson (Mrs. Tal)

PORK PINWHEEL

1 pound lean ground pork
1/2 cup fine bread crumbs
1 egg, slightly beaten
1 teaspoon salt
1/4 teaspoon pepper
1/2 teaspon Worcestershire
   sauce
1 pound sauerkraut, drained
   and snipped
1/4 cup chopped onion
5 slices bacon

Combine pork, crumbs, eggs, salt, pepper and Worcestershire. Mix thoroughly. On foil pat meat mixture onto a 7 x 10-inch rectangle. Mix sauerkraut and onion. Spread evenly over meat. Starting with narrow side, roll jelly roll fashion. Place loaf in shallow baking dish with seam side down. Arrange bacon slices across top. Bake in **preheated 350° oven 1 hour.**

Yield: 6 servings

Mahdeen Rucker (Mrs. J. Ray)

PORK à l'ORANGE

1 (6-7 lb.) pork loin roast
2 cloves garlic, sliced
2 teaspoons rosemary
1 teaspoon salt
1 teaspoon black pepper
1/4 cup Dijon mustard
1/4 cup orange marmalade
2 tablespoons light brown sugar
1 cup orange juice, divided
2 navel oranges, thinly sliced
   (garnish)
Fresh parsley (garnish)
2-4 tablespoons Grand Marnier
   or other orange-flavored
   liqueur

Cut small slits in the fat of loin and insert slivers of garlic. Rub with mixture of rosemary, salt and pepper. Place meat, fat side up, on a rack in a shallow roasting pan. Roast in a **preheated 350° oven** until done (170° on meat thermometer). Allow 30-35 minutes per pound. Cover roast except for first 30 minutes and last 30 minutes.

Make orange glaze by mixing mustard, marmalade, brown sugar and 4 tablespoons orange juice in a small dish. Mix well.

About 15 minutes before roast is done, brush with orange glaze. Continue roasting 15 minutes. Remove roast to large serving platter. Garnish with orange slices and parsley. Skim fat from roasting pan, add remaining orange juice and Grand Marnier to pan drippings, mixing well. Heat and serve with roast.

Yield: 10 servings

Patricia Cashman Andrus (Mrs. Robert M.)

STACKED ENCHILADAS

2 tablespoons bacon fat
1½ teaspoons red chili pepper
   (Tex Joy)
2 tablespoons flour
1 (8-oz.) can tomato sauce
2 (8-oz.) cans water
1 teaspoon salt
1 pound ground beef, seasoned
   with salt and pepper
1/3 cup finely chopped onion
2 cups grated longhorn cheese
3 cups shredded crisp lettuce
1/2 cup cooking oil
12 corn tortillas

Heat fat in medium saucepan. Stir in red chili pepper and flour. Blend well. Add tomato sauce, water and salt. Stir. Cook until slightly thickened. Cover and set aside, keeping sauce warm. In medium skillet brown ground beef. Cover and set aside, keeping meat warm. Chop onions, grate cheese and shred lettuce. Place in individual bowls for assembly of enchiladas. Heat oil in skillet as large as tortilla is round.

To assemble one Stacked Enchilada: Dip 3 tortillas in oil. Turn over. Take out and dip in sauce. Place first tortilla flat in center of plate. Sprinkle with 1 teaspoon onion. Lay second tortilla on this and sprinkle with 1/2 cup cheese. Lay third tortilla on stack and cover with 1/4 of meat. Repeat assembly for other 3 stacked enchiladas. Surround each enchilada with 3/4 cup crisp lettuce. Pour remaining warm sauce over enchiladas. Serve immediately. *A favorite of my son and daughter-in-law, Dr. & Mrs. Jim D. Cole.*

Yield: 4 servings

Idris Minerva Cole

the
1960s

ello, dere.

"No one has "Hello, dered' me for a long time. Good grief! You look like a ghost!"

*I'm not **a** ghost. I am **the** ghost of the 1960s. Maybe you can help me, dolly. I have this terrific mini-skirt and I was looking for a place to try it on—like a fallout shelter, perhaps?*

"Uh, you might be in for a disappointment. I don't know what happened to fall-out shelters."

Don't worry. I am planning to wear my mini-skirt to Mardi Gras. I'll wear my matching stockings, natch. The Sixties was when Mardi Gras really got rolling in Lafayette.

"Why do you say that? Lafayette had a Mardi Gras way back in the 1890s. Of course, it wasn't until the 1930s that the Southwest Louisiana Mardi Gras Association brought King Gabriel and Queen Evangeline to town. Then the Quota Club's balls in the 1940s were followed by the Order of the Troubadours in the 1950s, just after the Krewe of Gabriel was chartered. The Children's Carnival, Les Brigands de LaFitte, Krewe of Lafayette—they were all going strong before the 1960s."

Yeah, yeah, yeah. But it wasn't until the 1960s that the Municipal Auditorium was opened. All the action moved there, and the girls topped it off with the Krewe of Attakapas. And, we never had to cancel Mardi Gras because of a war, as the 1940s and 1950s did. And, in the Sixties we elected John Kennedy and Lyndon Johnson to the presidency of the United States.

"Don't be so smug. How about the assassinations? And you did have a little thing called Vietnam. It was a rough decade for barbers, too, you know."

Granted. But we were groovy. How about a little thing called 'Fly Me To The Moon'? 'The Eagle Has Landed,' 'Giant step for mankind' and all that jazz. How about another little thing called heart transplants? We even did open heart and vascular surgery here in the Sixties. Another thing, we Sixties are responsible for teaching a lot of people that they could eat meat on Friday. But the best thing they learned was that they could eat fish on the other days of the week.

We're talking about the decade that waved a magic wand and changed S.L.I. to U.S.L.; the decade that brought you The Art Center for Southwestern Louisiana. The Sixties is my name, and Culture is my game.

"Come on! Lafayette was up to here in culture before you showed up. We had the Community Concerts, Little Theater, and The Lafayette Museum in the Forties and Fifties."

***But**, would you believe it took the Sixties to teach people around here how to say 'Lafayette Natural History Museum and Planetarium' all in one breath?*

"Touche! And, would you believe that some people still say 'would you believe'?"

Well, see you later, alligator.

"After while—I mean—it's been nice talking with you."

Eleanor Francisco Straub (Mrs. John)
Freelance writer
Dr. and Mrs. Straub are the parents of nine children.
Of the seven born in the Sixties, three are triplets.

183

Ice Cream ~ Pudding

Pie

HEAVENLY CHOCOLATE ICE CREAM

25 ounces (10-12 bars) Milky
    Way candy, cut into pieces
1 (14-oz.) can sweetened
    condensed milk
1 (5.5-oz.) can chocolate syrup
3 quarts milk (for a creamier ice
    cream replace part of milk
    with 1 pint Half & Half cream)

Microwave shortcut: Place candy and condensed milk in 8-cup glass measure. Microwave on **HIGH (100%) 3 MINUTES.** Stir mixture 1 time during cooking time. Cool and continue to follow recipe. *Anne R. Meleton*

Combine candy and condensed milk in large saucepan. Cook over low heat, stirring constantly, until candy melts. Cool, stirring occasionally. Add 1 quart of milk (or a combination of Half & Half and milk) to the candy mixture. Beat until well-blended. Pour mixture into freezer can of a 4-quart ice cream freezer. Stir in chocolate syrup. Add remaining milk to *fill line* (or within 4 inches from top).

Freeze according to freezer directions. *From one chocolate lover, like myself, to another.*

Yield: 1 gallon

Catherine Escuriex Mestayer (Mrs. Karl)

LEMON ICE CREAM

1 cup fresh lemon juice
1 tablespoon finely grated lemon
    rind
2 teaspoons lemon extract
4 cups sugar
1 quart whipping cream
1 quart Half & Half cream
1 pint milk

In a large container or bowl, mix lemon juice, rind, lemon extract, sugar, cream and milk together. Pour into a 4-quart ice cream container and freeze according to freezer directions.

Yield: 20 servings

Jeanne Bolin (Mrs. John A.)

PEACHES 'N CREAM

10 medium ripe peaches, peeled
    and pitted
2 cups sugar
2 teaspoons lemon juice
1½ quarts milk
1 pint whipping cream

Fill blender 7/8 full with peaches, sugar and lemon juice (process in 2 batches). Pour milk and whipping cream into 1 gallon ice cream freezer container. Add fruit from blender. Stir well to mix. Freeze according to freezer directions. *From the recipe files of Marge Pfeuffer (Mrs. Al).*

Yield: 1 gallon

Carol Pfeuffer Lenard

FROZEN CREAM CHEESE

2 (12-oz.) cartons Creole cottage cheese or small curd cottage cheese
1 cup evaporated milk, undiluted
1 cup sugar
1/2 teaspoon vanilla
1 egg white, stiffly beaten
1 (8-oz.) can crushed pineapple, drained
1 (8-oz.) bottle maraschino cherries, drained and quartered
1/2 cup chopped pecans

Blend cottage cheese in blender until smooth. Pour into mixing bowl. Add milk, sugar and vanilla. Stir until well-blended. Fold in stiffly beaten egg white. Pour mixture into freezer tray. Let remain until half-frozen. Remove from freezer. Place in 1-quart serving bowl. Fold in pineapple, cherries and pecans. Return to freezer until firm. Unmold or spoon to serve. Also, can be frozen in miniature muffin pans.

From the recipe files of my mother, Mrs. Dan Egan.

Yield: 6 servings

"Dukie" Abel (Mrs. Glynn)

CREAM CHEESE ICE CREAM

1 (13-oz.) can evaporated milk, whipped
2 egg yolks
1 cup sugar
2 (8-oz.) packages cream cheese, softened
2 egg whites, beaten

Pour milk into small mixing bowl. Place in freezer and chill until crystals form. Whip until thick.

In a large mixing bowl blend egg yolks and sugar. Add cream cheese, beating until smooth. Fold in beaten egg whites and whipped milk. Pour into large loaf pan. Freeze. Slice to serve.

This was a favorite treat at Great Grandma Scott's every Sunday many years ago. Now it is a specialty at Le Ruth's restaurant of New Orleans.

Yield: 8 servings

Cynthia Scott Habetz (Mrs. Michael A.)

PEACH ICE CREAM

2 (14-oz.) cans sweetened
    condensed milk
4 cups homogenized milk
4 tablespoons lemon juice
1/8 teaspoon almond extract
1 pint mashed sweetened
    peaches, fresh or frozen

Mix condensed milk and homogenized milk together in a 4-quart ice cream freezer container. Add lemon juice, almond extract and peaches. Freeze according to freezer directions. Ice cream will firm in 25-30 minutes.

Yield: 1 gallon

Alice Willy Bower (Mrs. Harold R.)

STRAWBERRY ICE CREAM

3 large eggs
1½ cups sugar
1/2 teaspoon salt
5 cups milk
1 (13-oz.) can evaporated milk
1 (14-oz.) can sweetened
    condensed milk
2 tablespoons vanilla
1 pint mashed sweetened
    strawberries or peeled and
    mashed figs or 6 peaches,
    peeled and mashed

Beat eggs in large mixing bowl. Add sugar and salt, beating until completely blended. Bring 5 cups milk to boil in a large saucepan. Remove from heat. Add hot milk slowly to egg mixture, beating constantly. Add evaporated and condensed milk and vanilla. Add mashed fruit and its juice. Let cool in refrigerator or freezer. Pour into a 4-quart ice cream container. Freeze according to freezer directions. *Peaches or figs may be substituted for strawberries. This old recipe of my mother's was always made for the 4th of July and other occasions, too. It is a favorite of our family.*

Yield: 1 gallon

Rubye Valentine Shelton (Mrs. Louis A.)

Microwave shortcut: Pour 5 cups milk into an 8-cup glass measuring cup. Microwave on **HIGH (100%) 10-12 MINUTES** or until milk comes to a boil. Follow directions above. *Jean K Durkee*

APRICOT SHERBET

2 cups sugar
3/4 cup water
2 egg whites, beaten
1 (15-oz.) can apricots, pureed
with liquid
Juice of 2 lemons
Juice of 1 orange
1 pint whipping cream
1 pint milk

Cook sugar and water in small saucepan to form a thin syrup. Add syrup to beaten egg whites. Fold in pureed apricots. Add lemon juice and orange juice. Stir in cream and milk. Freeze in ice cream freezer or freeze in ice trays.

Yield: 9-10 servings

Alma B. Stuller (Mrs. G. F.)

BANANA PINEAPPLE SHERBET

3¹/₂ cups milk
1 cup sugar
3/4 cup fresh lemon juice
3 ripe bananas, mashed
1 (8-oz.) can crushed pineapple
and liquid

Mix milk and sugar in mixing bowl until sugar dissolves. Add lemon juice, mashed bananas and pineapple. Pour into 9 x 13-inch pan. Place in freezer. When sherbet has hardened on bottom and around edges, beat well with mixer and return to freezer until firm. Serve in sherbet dishes with a thin slice of lemon.

Yield: 6-8 servings

Sue Birdwell Alves

TORTANÉ SQUARES

1¹/₃ cups finely crushed vanilla
wafers
3 tablespoons melted margarine
1 teaspoon almond extract
1/2 gallon vanilla ice cream,
softened.
20 ounces apricot preserves
1/3 cup toasted chopped
almonds

Mix wafer crumbs, margarine and almond extract in small bowl. Layer bottom of 9¹/₂-inch square or 7 x 11-inch dish with crumb mixture, reserving 1/3 cup of mixture for topping. Spread a layer of soft ice cream then a layer of apricot preserves. Alternate layers, ending with ice cream on top. Sprinkle top layer with remaining crumb mixture and toasted chopped almonds. Freeze and cut into squares to serve.

Yield: 16 servings

Hascal Hardy (Mrs. Irby)

FRAN'S PLUM PUDDING

1 cup finely chopped beef suet
    (¼ pound)
1 cup plus 2 tablespoons packed
    brown sugar
1/2 cup milk
2 eggs, well beaten
1 cup currants
1/2 pound candied cherries
1/4 pound candied pineapple
1/4 pound mixed candied citron,
    orange, and lemon peel
1 cup chopped pecans
1¼ cups all-purpose flour
1 teaspoon baking soda
1 teaspoon salt
1 teaspoon cinnamon
1/4 teaspoon mace
1/4 teaspoon nutmeg
1 cup soft bread crumbs
1/2 cup brandy

*Hard Sauce:
1/2 cup butter
Dash of salt
2 cups sifted confectioners
    powdered sugar
Brandy, if desired

Combine suet, brown sugar, milk and eggs. Mix fruits and pecans with 1/4 cup of the flour. Sift remaining flour with soda, salt and spices. Add fruits, crumbs and flour-and-spice mixture to suet mixture. Mix well. Turn into a well greased 2-quart covered pudding mold. Steam 3 hours. (**Steaming directions:** Use steamer or deep covered kettle. If using kettle, place filled and covered mold on trivet or wire rack in kettle. Pour in boiling water to 1/2 depth of mold. Place cover on kettle and steam, replenishing the boiling water when necessary to keep the proper level of 1/2 depth of mold.) Turn out on hot platter, heat brandy in small saucepan, pour over pudding, light brandy and bring pudding to the table flaming. Serve with Hard Sauce.*

Soften butter. Beat in salt and sugar until light and fluffy. Add brandy to taste, beating it in thoroughly.

Yield: 10-12 servings

Frances P. Zink (Mrs. William)

PUMPKIN CUSTARD

3 eggs
2 cups cooked pumpkin
1 1/2 cups evaporated milk, undiluted
1/2 cup sugar
1/4 cup rum
1 teaspoon cinnamon
1/2 teaspoon ginger
1/2 teaspoon salt
1/2 teaspoon vanilla
1/8 teaspoon ground cloves
Whipped cream topping

Mix eggs, pumpkin, milk, sugar, rum, cinnamon, ginger, salt, vanilla and cloves in blender until throughly blended. Pour into 6 or 8 custard cups. Place cups in a pan of hot water about 1 inch deep and bake in **preheated 350° oven 40-50 minutes** or until knife inserted near edge of cup comes out clean. Top with whipped cream before serving.

The day after Halloween is a good time to cook pumpkin for custard, bread or pie. Extra cooked pumpkin freezes well too.

Yield: 6-8 servings

Anne R. Meleton (Mrs. Pierce)

SWEET POTATO PUDDING

3 cups drained and mashed sweet potatoes or 1 (29-oz.) can
1 cup sugar
1/4 cup margarine, softened
2 eggs, slightly beaten
1 cup grated coconut, fresh or frozen
1/2 cup milk
1 teaspoon vanilla extract

*Topping:
1 cup light brown sugar
1 cup chopped pecans
1/2 cup all-purpose flour
1/2 cup margarine, melted
Dash salt

In a mixing bowl, beat together sweet potatoes, sugar, margarine, eggs, coconut, milk and vanilla. Pour into 8 x 8-inch buttered baking dish.

Combine brown sugar, pecans, flour, margarine and salt until well mixed. Spoon Topping* over sweet potato mixture. Bake in **preheated 350° oven 1 hour.**

Yield: 10-12 servings

Dawn Glisson (Mrs. J. P.)

Microwave directions: Follow directions above. Pour mixture into a glass 8 x 8-inch buttered dish. Microwave on **HIGH (100%) 15 MINUTES.** *Jean K Durkee*

CABINET PUDDING

1 (1/4-oz.) package unflavored
    gelatin
1/4 cup water
4 eggs, separated
7 tablespoons sugar
1/2 cup whiskey
20 vanilla wafers, crushed
1 (10-oz.) jar maraschino
    cherries, drained well and
    chopped reserving 8 whole
    cherries for top
1 cup chopped pecans
1 pint whipping cream, whipped,
    divided

Dissolve gelatin in 1/4 cup water. Set aside. Beat egg yolks in the top of a double boiler. Add sugar and then whiskey. Cook over hot water a few minutes until thick. Add dissolved gelatin. Pour mixture into a large mixing bowl. Fold in crushed vanilla wafers, cherries and nuts. Beat egg whites until stiff and fold into mixture. Whip 1 pint cream until peaks form. Fold half of whipped cream into mixture reserving remainder for topping.

Serve chilled pudding in dessert dishes with a cherry on top of whipped cream. *The original ingredient list of this old recipe called for 'two 5¢ boxes of vanilla wafers.'*

Yield: 6-8 servings

Lady W. Hall (Mrs. W. E.)

GRAPE-NUT PUDDING

1/2 cup butter
1 cup sugar
4 eggs
4 tablespoons all-purpose flour
6 tablespoons grape-nuts
1 cup milk
Juice and zest (rind) of 2 lemons
Whipped cream for topping

Cream butter and sugar in mixing bowl. Add eggs and beat well. Add flour, grape-nuts, milk, grated rind and lemon juice. Pour ingredients into a greased 8-inch square or 7 x 9-inch baking dish. Bake in **preheated 350° oven 35 minutes.** Serve warm or cold. For special treat top with whipped cream. *From my father, C. U. Beasley's recipe files.*

Yield: 16 servings

Marjorie Beasley Cloninger (Mrs. Dobin)

191

TOASTED SNOW SQUARES

1 (1/4-oz.) envelope plain gelatin
4 tablespoons cold water
2/3 cup sugar
3/4 cup boiling water
3 egg whites, unbeaten
1/4 teaspoon salt
1 teaspoon vanilla
9 graham crackers crushed or
    3/4 cup crumbs

Sprinkle gelatin over cold water in a small dish. Let soak 5 minutes. Add sugar and hot water. Stir until dissolved. Let cool slightly; then add egg whites, salt and vanilla. Beat on high speed until mixture is light and resembles very thick cream. Turn into a 7 x 12 or 9 x 13-inch oiled or sprayed dish. Cover and chill several hours or overnight. For serving, cut into 12 squares and coat each square in graham cracker crumbs. Place 1 tablespoon of Butter Sauce* in bottom of each dessert dish. Set square on top of sauce and top with 2 tablespoons of Butter Sauce.

*Butter Sauce:
3 egg yolks
2/3 cup sugar
2/3 cup melted butter
2 tablespoons grated lemon
    rind (zest)
4 tablespoons lemon juice
1 cup cream, whipped

With electric mixer beat yolks until thick and lemon colored. While beating gradually add sugar. Add butter, rind (zest) and juice. Blend. Fold in whipped cream.

This can be prepared earlier and blended again before serving.

Yield: 12 servings

Betty Richard Butcher (Mrs. Thomas, Sr.)

CRÈME de CACAO DELIGHT

30 large marshmallows
1 cup brewed coffee
1 teaspoon vanilla
1/2 pint whipping cream,
    whipped
Grated sweet chocolate
Sliced toasted almonds
8 tablespoons Crème de Cacao
    liqueur

In top of double boiler melt marshmallows in coffee over gently boiling water. Add vanilla. Cool. Add whipped cream. Place mixture in 8 serving dishes and refrigerate. 30 minutes before serving sprinkle grated chocolate and toasted almonds on top. Pour 1 tablespoon Crème de Cacao over top of each serving. Refrigerate until served.

Yield: 8 servings

Alice Bower (Mrs. Harold)

BRYAN RICHARD'S BAILEY'S IRISH MOUSSE

7 egg whites
1 quart heavy whipping cream
3/4 cup granulated sugar
3/4 cup Bailey's Irish Cream
    Liqueur
1 ounce Irish whiskey
1/2 teaspoon instant Sanka

Whip egg whites until stiff peaks form; reserve. Whip heavy cream until stiff. Quickly fold in granulated sugar, liqueur, whiskey, Sanka and all of the whipped egg whites.

Serve in pots-de-crème or parfait glasses and garnish with a sprinkle of instant coffee and a lady finger.

Yield: 24 pots-de-crème or 12 parfait glasses

Bryan Richard
Sous Chef Chez Marcelle

COEUR à la CRÈME

1 tablespoon unflavored gelatin
3 tablespoons water
15 ounces Creole Cream cheese
    or large curd cottage cheese
8 ounces cream cheese
8 ounces whipping cream
3 tablespoons confectioners
    powdered sugar
3 tablespoons sweet liqueur,
    Kirsch, Crème de Cacao
    or Amaretto

Sprinkle gelatin over 3 tablespoons water. Dissolve over boiling water. Set aside. Place cottage cheese in food processor with steel blade. Process until smooth. Add cream cheese cut into chunks and continue to process until smooth. Add melted gelatin, whipping cream, sugar and liqueur. Pour into 6-8 traditional coeur à la crème heart shaped molds or 1 (4-cup) large heart mold. Spray molds with Pam for easy removal. *Coeur à la crème is traditionally served surrounded by fresh strawberries. It may be served as an appetizer or a light dessert.*

Yield: 6-8 servings

Felicia Mallet Elsbury (Mrs. Joe W.)

CHOCOLATE DELIGHT

1st layer:
1/2 cup butter, melted
1 cup all-purpose flour
1/2 cup finely chopped pecans

2nd layer:
1 (8-oz.) package cream cheese,
    softened
1 cup powdered sugar
1 (12-oz.) carton refrigerated
    dessert topping, divided

3rd layer:
3 cups milk
2 (5¼-oz.) packages instant
    chocolate pudding

4th layer:
Remainder of dessert topping
1/2 cup coarsely chopped pecans

In a medium bowl mix melted butter, flour and pecans. Press onto a lightly greased 9 x 13-inch pan. Bake in a **preheated 350° oven for 15 minutes.** Cool before adding second layer.

Mix together cream cheese, powdered sugar and 1½ cups dessert topping. Spread over first layer. Refrigerate 1 hour before adding third layer.

Mix milk and pudding together. Spread over second layer.

Cover with remaining dessert topping. Garnish with pecans.

Yield: 16 servings

Kathy Welch Scheumack (Mrs. Jeff)

DATE NUT PUDDING

1½ cups brown sugar
1½ cups hot water
1 tablespoon butter
1 cup chopped dates
1 cup sugar
1 cup chopped pecans
1 cup self-rising flour
1 cup milk

Mix brown sugar, hot water and butter. Spread in buttered 8 x 10-inch baking dish. Mix dates, sugar, pecans, flour and milk. Pour over brown sugar mixture. Bake in **preheated 350° oven 1 hour.**

Yield: 16 servings

Betty Bowen Wiggs (Mrs. Robert A.)

BAKED CUSTARD

5 whole large eggs
3/4 cup sugar
4 cups milk
1/4 teaspoons vanilla

Preheat oven to 350.° Beat eggs and add sugar. Continue to beat until well blended. Add milk and vanilla. Blend well and pour into a 2-quart Pyrex dish. Place dish with custard in a pan of hot water and **bake 350° for 75 minutes** or until kitchen knife inserted comes out clean. Spoon into serving dishes. *My husband's grandmother from New Orleans received this recipe from her mother-in-law whose husband was mayor of the city.*

Yield: 10-12 servings

Laurie Allen Freret (Mrs. Randolph)

CARAMEL CUSTARD

1/2 cup sugar
1 tablespoon water
6 cups milk
9 eggs
3 egg yolks
1¼ cups sugar
1 tablespoon vanilla
1/4 cup bourbon

In a small saucepan over medium heat bring sugar and water to boil. Cook until mixture caramelizes (color is clear medium brown). Quickly pour into 2-quart ring mold and rotate mold to cover as much of bottom and sides as possible. Invert mold on wax paper while preparing custard.

Heat milk in a saucepan or in microwave in 8-cup measure until very hot. In a large mixing bowl beat eggs and egg yolks. Add sugar and beat until very smooth. Continue beating and slowly add hot milk. Add vanilla and bourbon. Strain mixture through sieve into mold.

Place mold in large pan. Add 2 inches boiling water to pan. Bake in **preheated 325° oven 45-50 minutes** or until knife inserted comes out clean.

Chill in refrigerator. When ready to serve, use sharp knife to run around edge. Place large plate on top of mold and invert. Mold should come off easily.

Yield: 10-12 servings

Marilyn A. Tarpy (Mrs. Robert)

PUDDIN'S BREAD PUDDING

1½ pounds French bread or
    stale white bread
1 dozen eggs, beaten
1/2 pound butter, melted
6½ ounces evaporated milk,
    undiluted
2 cups sugar
2 cups homogenized milk
2 tablespoons Mexican vanilla
1¾ cups chopped pecans

Tear bread into pieces. Place in 4-quart mixing bowl. Add beaten eggs, butter, evaporated milk, sugar, milk, vanilla and pecans. Mix well and pour into 9 x 13-inch (2½-quart) baking dish. Bake in **preheated 325° oven 25-30 minutes**. Serve with Whiskey Sauce* on this page.

Yield: 30 servings

Herbert "Puddin" Robin

CUSTARD BREAD PUDDING

3½ cups stale French bread cut
    into cubes and toasted dry
2¼ cups warm milk
4 whole eggs
1/2 cup sugar
1 teaspoon vanilla
3 tablespoons butter or
    margarine
Cinnamon to sprinkle

*Whiskey Sauce:
1 cup butter or margarine,
    softened (2 sticks)
1 cup confectioners powdered
    sugar
1 egg yolk, beaten
4 tablespoons whiskey or sherry

While **preheating oven to 350°** place bread cubes in a 7 x 9-inch glass (oven proof) dish and toast until dry. Remove from oven. Warm milk in a saucepan. In a 2-quart bowl or measuring cup beat eggs. Add sugar, vanilla and warm milk slowly. Mix well. Pour egg mixture over bread cubes. Dot top with butter and sprinkle cinnamon evenly over top. Bake in **350° oven 30-40 minutes** or until knife comes out clean. Let sit 10-15 minutes before serving.

In food processor or electric mixer cream butter. Add powdered sugar and egg yolk. Blend until smooth. Add whiskey a teaspoon at a time, mixing well. Serve bread pudding hot, topped with Whiskey Sauce.*

Yield: 8 servings

Aimeé Billeaud Labbé (Mrs. Donald)

Microwave directions: Place toasted bread cubes in a 2-quart Pyrex ring mold dish. Reduce milk measurement to 2 cups. Place milk in 2-cup Pyrex measure in microwave on **HIGH (100%) 2-3 MINUTES** until heated through. Beat eggs. Add sugar, vanilla and warm milk slowly. Mix well and pour over bread cubes. Dot with butter and sprinkle with cinnamon. Microwave on **HIGH (100%) 7 MINUTES**, rotating dish 2 times. Serve as above with whiskey sauce. *Jean K Durkee*

LOUISIANA BREAD PUDDING

8 slices stale bread, cubed
1/2 cup margarine, cubed
6 eggs
1 cup sugar
3 cups milk
1 teaspoon vanilla
1 cup raisins, or drained
    crushed pineapple

Place cubed bread into a 9 x 13-inch pan or dish. Dot with margarine. Place under broiler just until margarine is melted and bread slightly toasted. Remove from oven. Beat eggs until fluffy. Add sugar, milk and vanilla. Beat until well blended. Pour mixture over bread cubes and stir lightly. Stir in raisins.

Bake in a **preheated 350° oven 45 minutes**. Top will be golden brown.

Yield: 12 servings

Jackie Cockrell (Mrs. Larry)

OLD-FASHION BREAD PUDDING

8 slices dry bread, cubed
3 cups milk, warmed
4 egg yolks, reserve 3 whites
    for meringue
1 egg white
1 (5¹/₃-oz.) can evaporated milk
1 tablespoon vanilla extract
1 cup sugar
1 (8-oz.) can crushed pineapple,
    drained
1/2 cup raisins
1/4 cup butter or margarine,
    melted

*Meringue:
3 egg whites
6 tablespoons sugar
1 teaspoon vanilla

Warm milk in a large saucepan. Add bread cubes and let soak.

In a small bowl beat egg yolks and 1 egg white, gradually adding evaporated milk, vanilla and sugar. Add to bread and milk. Add pineapple, raisins and butter. Pour into a 9 x 13-inch pan or Pyrex dish. Bake in **preheated 350° oven 40-45 minutes**.

Remove from oven. Top pudding with Meringue.* Continue to bake in **350° oven 5-7 minutes** or until meringue is lightly browned. *This recipe was given to me by my mother, Mrs. Delino Babineaux.*

Beat egg whites until fluffy, gradually adding sugar and vanilla. Continue beating until stiff.

Yield: 8 servings

Ira Dell Babineaux Watson (Mrs. Bill)

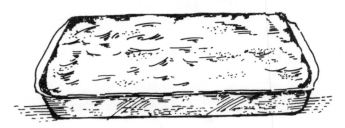

SWEET DOUGH PIES

1/2 cup margarine
1/2 cup shortening
2 1/2 cups granulated sugar
3 eggs
3 tablespoons baking powder
1 teaspoon vanilla
1/2 teaspoon freshly grated
   nutmeg
1 1/2 cups milk
8 cups all-purpose flour

*Filling suggestions:
Fresh fruit, sliced or chopped
Canned fruit, drained
Canned pie filling
Fresh coconut
Canned pumpkin or sweet potato

Cream margarine, shortening, sugar and eggs in mixing bowl with electric beater. Add baking powder, vanilla, nutmeg and milk. Beat 2 minutes. Add flour, 2 cups at a time, using electric beater until thick. Add rest of flour, kneading with hands until well mixed. Refrigerate until chilled. To form bottom of each pie roll half the dough into 40 balls (1 3/4-inch diameter). Roll remaining dough into 40 smaller balls (1 1/4-inch diameter) for top of pies. On a floured surface roll large ball into a 3 x 6-inch rectangle. Place 1 tablespoon filling* on dough. Roll out smaller ball for top. Cut a 'peep hole' in dough with cap from vanilla bottle. Place over filling. Press lightly to seal. Lift with a spatula and place pies close together on a 14 x 17-inch greased cookie sheet. Bake in a **preheated 375° oven 17 minutes** or until golden brown.

This recipe has been handed down by 3 generations of my family. I like to make these pies for my church and for the Lafayette Natural History Museum's annual Native Crafts Festival.

Yield: 40 pies

Bernice Filer Bernard

STRAWBERRY PIE

1 (9-inch) baked, cooled,
   pie crust
1 cup sugar
3 tablespoons corn starch
1 cup water
1/2 teaspoon lemon juice
1 (3-oz.) package strawberry
   Jello
1 pint fresh strawberries
Whipped cream topping

Bake and cool your favorite pie crust. In a medium saucepan stir together sugar, corn starch, water and lemon juice. Cook over medium heat until thick and clear. Add Jello. Remove from heat. Let cool. Slice strawberries into baked pie crust. Pour cooled mixture over strawberries. Refrigerate several hours until chilled. Serve with whipped cream topping.

Yield: 8 servings

Ann C. Altamirano (Mrs. Mario)

198

PIE DAY—HOLY FRIDAY

In the long ago when distances were far and priests came maybe once a month to conduct baptisms and marriages, Good Friday became PIE DAY in the village of Catahoula southeast of Lafayette.

Because everyone was related to everyone else, there was little disagreement, no formality and plenty of fun at all times, it was easy to agree over a disagreement. Yes, it was agreed, the Friday before Easter was a most important day but they weren't too sure whether they should feast or fast, pray or play. So, they did both, to be sure, you know.

First they fasted, not a drop of water, not even coffee. Not a crumb of coush-coush. Not a bite of pain pardue. Nothing, until ten o'clock in the morning.

Starting very early that morning they made sweet dough pies and blackberry pies, pear pies and chocolate pies until the tables, outside, weather permitting, were piled high with pies. At ten o'clock exactly, little children, big children, young mamas and papas, grandparents and friends began to eat and eat and eat. They drank coffee, coffee milk and ice cold lemonade. They would eat slowly, of course, while gossiping with family and friends, because if they stopped eating, they could not start eating again for that would be "eating between meals."

We Cajuns at Catahoula Lake wouldn't dream of breaking a religious rule and rather than take a chance we DO and DON'T. First we *don't* eat pie until ten o'clock then we *do* eat pie without stopping until just before three o'clock when we drop everything and dash off to church to attend the Stations of the Cross Ceremony.

You are invited to join us next Pie Day.
Leona M. Guirard (Tootie)

CHESS PIE

2 unbaked 9-inch pie shells
1 cup butter
1 tablespoon flour
3 cups sugar
2 tablespoons water
2 tablespoons vinegar
6 eggs, beaten
1 tablespoon vanilla

Prepare your favorite pastry for 2 (9-inch) pie shells. In a medium saucepan cook butter, flour, sugar, water and vinegar slowly, until just blended.

In a bowl, beat eggs well. Add cooked mixture to eggs slowly, stirring while pouring. Add vanilla. Pour into prepared pastry. Bake in preheated **425° oven 10 minutes** then **350° 30 minutes.** *From the recipe files of Mrs. J. S. Johnson.*

Yield: 12 servings

Lucille "Sweet" Hernandez (Mrs. Hugh)

PETITE PECAN PIES

Shells:
3 ounces soft cream cheese
1/2 cup soft butter or margarine
1 cup all-purpose flour

Filling:
2 eggs
1 tablespoon soft butter
1 cup brown sugar
2 teaspoons vanilla
1 cup coarsely broken pecans

Mix cream cheese and butter in small bowl or food processor. Add flour. Roll into 2 balls. Refrigerate 30 minutes. Divide dough into 24 small balls and press with thumb and finger tips into 24 mini-muffin pans.

In mixing bowl or food processor beat eggs, butter, sugar, vanilla and pecans. Place 1 teaspoon filling in each shell. Bake in **preheated 350° oven 15 minutes.** Reduce heat to **250° and bake 20 minutes** or until crust is light brown.

Yield: 24 petite pies

Hermine Tate

LOUISIANA PECAN PIE

1 (10-inch) unbaked pastry shell
1 1/4 cup chopped pecans, slightly toasted
3 eggs, slightly beaten
2/3 cup sugar
1 cup dark corn syrup
1/4 cup melted butter
1 teaspoon vanilla extract
1/4 teaspoon almond extract
6-8 whole pecans for top

Prepare your favorite pie crust. Toast pecans in **preheated 375° oven 5 minutes** or on **HIGH (100%) 3 MINUTES** in microwave.

Beat eggs slightly in mixing bowl. Add sugar, corn syrup, butter, toasted pecans, vanilla and almond extract. Pour into unbaked pie shell. Decorate top with whole pecans. Bake in **preheated 350° oven 50-55 minutes** until *set*. May be served with whipped cream or ice cream.

Yield: 10-12 servings

Yvonne A. Champagne (Mrs. George J., Jr.)

CHAMPION PECAN PIE

1 9-inch unbaked pie crust,
    unpricked
4 eggs
1 cup sugar
1 cup light corn syrup
1/4 cup melted butter
1/4 teaspoon salt
1 teaspoon vanilla
1¹/₂ cups small pecans (break
    large ones)

Prepare your favorite pie crust. Do not prick or bake.

Beat eggs with electric beater until smooth. Add sugar, corn syrup, butter, salt and vanilla. Beat to mix. Add pecans and pour into unbaked pie crust. Bake in **preheated 350° oven for 50 minutes** or until inserted knife comes out clean. Cool before serving.

Yield: 8 servings

Marguerite Richard Lyle (Mrs. Michael)

CHOCOLATE PECAN PIE

1 (9-inch) unbaked pie shell
2 (1-oz.) squares unsweetened
    chocolate
3 tablespoons butter or
    margarine
1 cup light corn syrup
3/4 cup sugar
3 eggs
1 teaspoon vanilla
1 cup chopped pecans
Whipped cream for topping,
    optional

Prepare your favorite 9-inch pie crust. Melt chocolate and margarine in double boiler over boiling water. Combine syrup and sugar and boil in saucepan 2 minutes. Add chocolate mixture to syrup mixture. Cool. Pour slowly over slightly beaten eggs, stirring constantly. Add vanilla and pecans. Pour into unbaked pie shell. Bake in **preheated 375° oven 30 minutes.**

Cool, top with whipped cream.

Yield: 8 servings

Dora Becker Durkee (Mrs. Robert, Sr.)

MOM'S CHEESE PIE

Puff pastry:
2 cups all-purpose flour
1/4 teaspoon salt
1/2 cup shortening or margarine
2/3 cup (or less) cold water

Cheese Pie Filling:
1 cup butter
2 cups sugar
6 egg yolks
2 egg whites
2 tablespoons all-purpose flour
1/4 teaspoon cinnamon
1/4 teaspoon nutmeg

Sift flour and salt in mixing bowl. Cut in shortening. Add cold water. Roll out into narrow rectangle. Fold over in thirds. Roll out again, repeat twice. Let rest 10 minutes. Roll out thin. Place in 9-inch pie dish and add filling.

Cream butter and sugar in mixing bowl. Add 6 egg yolks and 2 egg whites. Beat until fluffy. Add flour, cinnamon and nutmeg. Pour into 9-inch pie dish lined with puff pastry. Bake in **preheated 350° oven 1 hour** covered with foil tent to prevent burning. Test by inserting sharp knife in center. Place on rack to cool.

From the recipe files of my mother, Mrs. Hugh C. Wallis.

Yield: 8-10 servings

Virginia Wallis Hagelin (Mrs. John A.)

DOUBLE CRUST LEMON PIE

Lemon pie filling:
2 large lemons
2 cups sugar
4 well beaten eggs
Pastry for top and bottom of
  9-inch dish

Slice lemons as thin as paper, rind and all. Mix with sugar until well mixed. **Let stand 2 hours** or longer, stir occasionally. Prepare pie crusts. After 2 hours, beat eggs well. Add to lemon mixture. Pour into pastry which has been fitted to 9-inch dish. Arrange lemon slices evenly in filling. Cover with top crust. Cut several slits near center to let steam out. Bake in **preheated 450° oven 20 minutes.** Shield edges of pie with foil if too brown. Reduce heat to **375°** and bake **20 minutes** or until silver knife blade inserted near edge comes out clean. Cool on wire rack.

Yield: Filling for 9-inch pie

Betty Hollingsworth (Mrs. William H.)

LEMON CREAM PIE

1 (9-inch) baked pie crust,
  cooled
1/2 cup sugar
6 tablespoons corn starch
1/4 teaspoon salt
1½ cups water
3 egg yolks, beaten
1/2 cup sugar
2 tablespoons margarine
1½ teaspoons grated lemon
  rind (zest)
1/3 cup fresh lemon juice

Prepare and bake your favorite 9-inch pie crust. In a medium saucepan or top of double boiler mix 1/2 cup sugar, corn starch and salt. Gradually add water and mix well. Cook over medium heat, stirring often, until thick and clear. Mix egg yolks with 1/2 cup sugar and add to hot mixture. Cook 1 minute more. Remove from heat. Add margarine and stir until melted. Add rind and juice. Mix well. Place pan over bowl of ice cubes to cool quickly. Stir mixture. Place chilled mixture in baked pie crust. Cover with Whipped Topping* or Meringue Topping.* Chill 2 hours before serving.

*Whipped Topping:
8 ounces whipping cream
1/4 cup sugar
1/4 teaspoon vanilla

Whip cream in a small mixing bowl until thick and stands in peaks. Add sugar and vanilla and mix well. Spread over pie with metal spatula.

*Meringue Topping:
3 egg whites
1/4 teaspoon cream of tartar
6 tablespoons sugar
1 teaspoon vanilla

Beat egg whites with cream of tartar until fluffy. Gradually add sugar and vanilla. Continue beating until stiff peaks form. Spread on pie. Bake in **preheated 350° oven 7 minutes.**

Yield: 8 servings

Ramona Black (Mrs. Jack)

Microwave directions: Place sugar, corn starch and salt in 4-cup glass measure. Reduce water to 1 cup, add and mix well. Microwave on **HIGH (100%) 3 MINUTES,** stirring at 1 minute invervals, until mixture is thick and clear. Mix yolks with sugar, add to hot mixture. Add margarine, zest and juice. Stir well. Chill. Follow directions above. *Jean K Durkee*

PIE CRUST

2 cups all-purpose flour
1 teaspoon salt
1/2 cup Crisco oil
1/4 cup milk

Sift flour and add salt. Stir in oil and milk. Divide dough into 2 balls. Roll crust between 2 sheets of wax paper. Remove top wax paper and transfer crust to pie plate. Chill crusts while preparing filling.

Yield: Double crust for 9-inch dish

Jane Delaney (Mrs. Jerry)

MINCEMEAT PIE FILLING

1 pound lean beef, ground
2 cups water
5 cups shredded apples,* firmly
    packed
3/4 cup *each* diced candied
    lemon peel and orange peel
1/4 cup candied citron
1 pound dried currants
1 pound seedless raisins
1 large orange, juice and grated
    rind
1 lemon, juice and grated rind
1/2 pound finely ground
    beef suet
1¹/₂ pounds dark brown sugar
1¹/₂ teaspoons *each* cinnamon,
    allspice, cloves, coriander,
    mace
1 teaspoon salt
1 teaspoon nutmeg
1 cup brandy or bourbon
1 cup rum or sherry

Simmer beef with water 20 minutes in 5-quart stock pot. Add remaining ingredients, except liquors. Let come to a hard boil. Simmer 5 minutes, stirring. Cool and add liquors. Store in refrigerator 3 weeks before using. Will keep in refrigerator 2 months. Can be frozen. Serve in dessert dishes or as filling for pies and tarts.

*Firm cooking pears may be used in place of apples.

Yield: 4 quarts

Frances P. Zink (Mrs. William)

COCONUT CREAM PIE

1 (9-inch) baked pie shell
1³/₄ cups low fat milk, divided
1/2 cup sugar
1/2 teaspoon salt
3¹/₂ tablespoons flour
2 tablespoons cornstarch
1 egg plus 2 egg yolks, beaten
    (reserve whites)
1/2 teaspoon vanilla extract
1/2 teaspoon almond extract
1/4 cup sugar
3/4 cup grated coconut, frozen
    or canned
Whipped cream for topping

Prepare and bake your favorite pastry. In saucepan scald half the milk. Add sugar and salt. Bring to boil. Mix flour, cornstarch, beaten egg and yolks with remaining milk, vanilla and almond extracts. Beat until smooth. Pour into top of double boiler. Add scalded milk. Cook over hot water until custard is very thick. Cool. Beat 2 egg whites until stiff, adding 1/4 cup sugar. Fold egg whites and grated coconut into custard. Spread in baked pie shell. Chill. Serve with whipped cream.

Yield: 8 servings

Blair Bowden Cabes (Mrs. Robert)

OLIVE'S EGGNOG PIE

1 (9-inch) baked pie shell
1 tablespoon gelatin
3 tablespoons cold water
1 cup milk, scalded
1/2 cup sugar
2 tablespoons cornstarch
1/4 teaspoon salt
3 egg yolks, well beaten
1 1/2 teaspoons vanilla
1/4 teaspoon almond extract
1 cup whipping cream, whipped
1/2 cup almonds, chopped and
    toasted
1 (6-oz. jar) maraschino cherries,
    drained and cut into pieces,
    reserve some to decorate
    top
Nutmeg for sprinkling

Soften gelatin in water. Scald milk in large, heavy saucepan. Mix sugar, cornstarch and salt together. Add to milk. Stirring often, cook until thick and smooth. Continue cooking and stirring over medium heat, 10 minutes longer. Stir a small amount of cooked mixture into egg yolks before adding egg yolks to cooked mixture. Cook 3 minutes more. Add gelatin, vanilla and almond extract. Cool. Whip cream. Fold cream, toasted almonds and cherries into cooled mixture. Pour into baked pie shell. Decorate top with reserved cherry pieces and sprinkle with nutmeg. Chill several hours or overnight. *From the recipe files of my mother, Mrs. George J. Melchior, Jr.*

Yield: 8 servings

L. C. Melchior

FLAKY PIE CRUST

1 cup all-purpose flour
1/2 teaspoon salt
1/3 cup shortening
2-4 tablespoons cold water

Sift flour and salt in bowl. Cut in shortening with pastry cutter or 2 knives until particles are the size of small peas. Sprinkle water over mixture. Toss lightly until dough is moist enough to stick together. Roll out between 2 sheets of wax paper. Place in 9-inch pie plate. Bake in **preheated 425° oven 12-15 minutes.** *My mother, Marge Cora Pfeuffer, used this never fail recipe for all her crusts.*

Yield: 1 (9-inch) crust

Carol Pfeuffer Lenard

KAHLÚA TORTE

2 cups chocolate cookie crumbs
1/2 cup butter, melted
1 (7-oz.) jar marshmallow creme
1/4 cup Kahlúa
2 (8-oz.) cartons whipping cream,
    whipped
Toasted sliced almonds for
    garnish

Butter a 9-inch spring form pan. In a small bowl combine crumbs and butter. Line bottom and sides with crumb mixture. Chill.

Combine marshmallow creme and Kahlúa in a mixing bowl until well blended. Whip cream and fold into marshmallow mixture. Pour into prepared pan. Freeze. Toasted sliced almonds may be added before serving. Keep frozen until serving time. *My favorite party dessert.*

Yield: 8 servings

Elizabeth Carter Montgomery (Mrs. Denbo)

FRUIT TORTE

2 tablespoons sugar
1 cup all-purpose flour
1/2 cup + 1 tablespoons butter,
    melted
1/2 cup chopped pecans

Filling:
8 ounces cream cheese,
    softened
9 ounces whipped dessert
    topping
1 cup sifted confectioners
    powdered sugar
1 (20-oz.) can fruit pie filling,
    any flavor you desire
9 ounces whipped dessert
    topping for top
Sliced fresh fruit
1/4 cup chopped pecans

In a small bowl mix sugar, flour, butter and pecans. Spread on a buttered 12-inch Pyrex plate or metal pan. Bake in **preheated 350° oven 20 minutes** until light brown. Cool crust.

Mix cream cheese, dessert topping and powdered sugar together. Spread filling on cooled crust. Add canned pie filling (strawberry, lemon, blueberry, etc.) on top of cream cheese mixture. Top with more whipped dessert topping. Garnish with fresh sliced fruit and pecans. Chill.

Yield: 8-10 servings

Betty LeBlanc Ellison (Mrs. Guy, Jr.)

BLACKBERRY DUMPLINGS

1 cup all-purpose flour
1 teaspoon baking powder
1/2 teaspoon salt
1/3 cup shortening
1/4 cup milk
1 teaspoon nutmeg
1 quart blackberries or
    dewberries
2 cups sugar

Mix flour, baking powder and salt. Cut in shortening with pastry blender. Add milk to form a soft dough. Roll dough on floured board to 1/4-inch thickness. Cut in 1-inch squares. Bake on cookie sheet until brown and crisp in **preheated 450° oven 7 minutes.** Place squares in a 1½ or 2-quart bowl. Sprinkle generously with nutmeg. In a 2-quart saucepan boil blackberries with water to cover. Add sugar. Cook over medium heat until the consistency of preserves, 1 hour 20 minutes. Pour over dumplings while at boiling temperature. Cover. While steaming press dumplings down into the juice a couple of times. Serve cool. Spoon Vanilla Sauce* on top.

*Vanilla Sauce:
4 eggs
1 cup sugar
2 tablespoons flour
4 cups boiling milk
2 teaspoons vanilla

Beat eggs, sugar, flour with beater. Add slowly to hot milk in 2-quart saucepan. Remove from heat. Add vanilla. Beat until creamy, 1 minute.

Yield: 8 servings

Maude "Muffet" Villien (Mrs. Fred)

FRENCH CHOCOLATE PIE

4 egg whites
1/4 teaspoon cream of tartar
1 cup sugar, divided
1/2 teaspoon vanilla
1/4 cup cocoa
1/2 cup chopped pecans

Beat egg whites until frothy. Add cream of tartar and whip until stiff. Slowly add 1/2 cup sugar and vanilla to egg white mixture. Mix together cocoa, pecans and remaining sugar. Fold into egg white mixture. Spread in a 9-inch pie plate. Bake in **preheated 300° oven 35 minutes** until crust cracks slightly. Cool meringue crust.

Filling:
1 cup whipping cream, whipped
1/2 teaspoon cocoa
1/2 teaspoon powdered instant
    coffee
1 tablespoon sugar

Whip cream until soft peaks form. Add cocoa, powdered instant coffee and sugar. Pour into cooled meringue crust. Chill in refrigerator overnight or 6-8 hours.

Yield: 6-8 servings

Margret D. McCoy (Mrs. Medford A.)

the
1970s

he 1970s were exciting years for Lafayette—years of growth, expansion and productivity. The boom which began with the development of Heymann Oil Center in the 1950s reached its peak in the 70s. The small river town of a century earlier became a metropolis with an ever-changing skyline as multistory office complexes, banks, shopping centers and townhouses mushroomed in all directions.

The emergence of the oil-rich nations abroad left a dent in the economic growth during the mid-70s, but the real pinch of inflation and a growing recession would not be felt until the end of the decade.

Watergate was on our minds and our television sets during the 70s. After Nixon's resignation, the nation watched Ford become our 38th President in 1974 and Carter's inauguration in 1977. And, with a 25-3 record for the New York Yankees, pitcher Ron Guidry received the 1978 Cy Young Award in the American League.

The petroleum industry remained a backbone for Lafayette's economy. Major companies continued to expand their operations in the hub city, moving personnel into the area and constructing larger and larger facilities on the outskirts of town.

Economic growth brought new banks to town and older banks expanded. Guaranty Bank & Trust added 9 floors to complete their 12-story building in 1978 and the First National Bank expanded into a 16-story building in 1975 with the City Club of Lafayette opening in 1979 at the top of FNB Towers, giving diners their first panoramic view of Lafayette.

For the Lafayette Parish Public Library, the 70s were years of "hope, worry and growth," according to Lucille Arceneaux, director emeritus. The library moved from its 20 year old building to a new three-story structure with 64,000 square feet. Finances often proved a problem, but by the end of the decade innovative children's programs, more young adults and adult services, improved reference services and improved interlibrary loan and delivery were realized. The library could look forward to computerization and improved branch libraries.

Lafayette General and Our Lady of Lourdes hospitals both expanded and work began on the University Medical Center. Single-family residences began to take a back seat to townhouses and a joint program sponsored by the Louisiana Department of Education and the Council for the Development of French in Louisiana brought French teachers to teach in elementary schools. The Acadian Village, a major tourist attraction, opened its gates July 4, 1976 and the 125-store Acadiana Mall opened in 1979.

Lafayette is known worldwide for its excellent cuisine, and restaurants sprang up throughout the area, continuing the tradition of "food capital" of southwest Louisiana. Along with this came the Bayou Food Festival, now a part of Festivals Acadiens, an annual celebration of the Cajun way of life. Each year restaurateurs and caterers prepare mouth-watering Cajun delicacies to the delight of thousands for this fall festival. Featured also by the Lafayette Natural History Museum during the Festivals Acadiens is the Lousiana Native Crafts Festival. Here Chitimacha and Koasati Indians demonstrate their basket weaving. Acadian spinning, weaving, quilting and cooking are also demonstrated. A typical menu is Cafe au Lait, Couche-Couche, Shrimp Jambalaya, Benne Pralines and Oreilles de Cochon.

By the end of the decade, Lafayette was still enjoying the fruits of prosperity, despite the growing clouds of recession. As 1979 drew to a close, Lafayette was tightening her belt against hard economic times, but the 70s had been good, prosperous years.

Eleanor Mitchell Yount (Mrs. Ray J.)
Freelance writer
Lafayette Centennial Commission Member

Cookies

Candy

Cake

GRANDMA'S TEACAKES

1 cup butter
2 cups sugar
1/2 teaspoon salt
2 teaspoons baking powder
1/4 teaspoon cinnamon
4 cups all-purpose flour, divided
3 eggs
1 teaspoon vanilla

Cream butter and sugar in mixing bowl until light and fluffy. Sift salt, baking powder, cinnamon and 3 cups of the flour. Add eggs and vanilla to creamed mixture one at a time, beating after each addition. Gradually add flour. Mix well. If dough is too soft add some of the reserved flour. Use remaining flour for flouring board. Roll out to 1/4-inch thickness. Cut into desired shapes with cookie cutter. Bake in **preheated 375° oven 12-15 minutes.** *Our old 'Mammy' used to make these cookies for my mother's family and for us as children every Mardi Gras.*

Yield: 5 dozen

Rhoda Bess Goodson

LES OREILLES DE COCHON

2 cups all-purpose flour
1/2 teaspoon baking powder
1/2 teaspoon salt
1/4 cup butter
2 eggs
1 tablespoon vinegar

Syrup:
1 1/2 cups cane syrup
1/2 cup sugar
1/8 teaspoon salt
1 cup finely chopped pecans

Mix flour, baking powder, salt, butter, eggs and vinegar in food processor to form dough. Roll small pieces of dough separately, paper thin, into 4-inch squares. Make slits in dough with knife. Fry in deep hot fat. Drain on paper towels.

Mix cane syrup with sugar and salt in 2-quart saucepan. Bring to boil. Boil 5 minutes. Add pecans. To serve, pour 1 tablespoon cooled syrup over each "Pig Ear."

Yield: 40 "pig ears"

Maude "Muffet" Villien (Mrs. Fred)

Microwave shortcut: Mix syrup, sugar and salt in 8-cup glass measure. Microwave on **HIGH (100%) 4 MINUTES** or until mixture boils. Continue to cook on **HIGH (100%) 1 MINUTE.** Add pecans. *Jean K Durkee*

CREAM CHEESE COOKIES

3 ounces cream cheese,
   softened
1/2 cup butter, softened
1 cup all-purpose flour
1/2 cup chopped pecans
36 pecan halves

Mix cream cheese and butter together. Add flour, a little at a time. Fold in pecans. Roll into small balls. Place on ungreased cookie sheet. Press top of ball with fork. Place pecan half on top. Bake in **preheated 375° oven 10-12 minutes.**

Yield: 3 dozen

Cindy Crain

FIG PINWHEEL COOKIES

2 pounds fig preserves (about
   2 pints)
1½ cups chopped pecans
1/4 cup water (omit water if figs
   are packed in syrup)
1 cup margarine
2 cups firmly packed brown
   sugar
3 eggs
5 cups all-purpose flour
1 teaspoon soda
1/2 teaspoon salt
1/2 teaspoon cinnamon

Mix fig preserves, pecans and water in medium saucepan. Bring to boil, reduce heat to medium, stirring frequently. Cook until mixture forms a thick paste, about 30 minutes. Set aside to cool before using in dough as filling.

In large mixing bowl, cream margarine and sugar. Add eggs and mix well. Mix dry ingredients together. Add to creamed mixture and blend well. Divide dough into 3 equal pieces. On floured wax paper, roll each piece out to 1/4-inch thickness. Spread with cooled filling and roll up like a jelly roll. Wrap in wax paper and chill overnight before cutting into 1/4-inch slices. (Dough freezes well.) Place on greased cookie sheet. Bake in **preheated 350° oven 16-20 minutes,** or until brown. *My grandmother, Louise Adams Beck's recipe.*

Yield: 6 dozen

Kathryn A. Beck

ANGEL KISSES

4 egg whites
1⅓ cups sugar
1/8 teaspoon salt
2 cups chopped pecans
2 cups (16-oz.) chocolate chips

Preheat oven to 350° Beat egg whites until thick and foamy. Gradually add sugar and beat until stiff. Fold in salt, pecans and chocolate chips. Drop by teaspoonfuls onto foil lined cookie sheets. Place in oven, close door and turn oven off. Leave in oven overnight. Remove next day and store in cookie tins.

Yield: 5 dozen

Catherine Escuriex Mestayer (Mrs. Karl)

BLONDE BROWNIES

3/4 cup margarine or butter
2 cups light brown sugar, firmly
    packed
2 eggs
2 teaspoons vanilla
2 cups self-rising flour, sift
    before measuring
1 cup semi-sweet chocolate
    chips
1 cup chopped pecans

In a mixing bowl, cream butter until soft. Gradually add brown sugar, beating until light and fluffy. Add eggs one at a time, beating well after each addition. Add vanilla. Gradually add flour. Beat until smooth. Stir in chocolate chips and pecans. Spread in greased 9 x 13-inch pan. Bake in **preheated 350° oven 25 minutes.**

Yield: 48-60 squares

Wanda Ham

CABINET COOKIES

1/2 cup butter
1/2 cup crunchy peanut butter
3/4 cup white granulated sugar
3/4 cup brown sugar, packed
1 teaspoon vanilla
2 eggs
1 teaspoon salt
1 teaspoon baking soda
2 cups whole wheat flour

In a large mixing bowl or food processor, cream butter, peanut butter and sugars. Add vanilla, eggs, salt, baking soda and flour. Blend well. Drop by teaspoonfuls on a greased cookie sheet. Bake in **preheated 375° oven for 10-13 minutes** or until bottoms are lightly browned.

Yield: 8 dozen

Pat Mason (Mrs. Troy)

CHEESECAKE BARS

Crust:
1/3 cup butter, softened
1/3 cup firmly packed light
 brown sugar
1 cup all-purpose flour

Filling:
8 ounces cream cheese,
 softened
1/4 cup sugar
1 egg
1 tablespoon lemon juice
1/4 cup chopped glazed red
 cherries
1/4 cup chopped glazed green
 cherries

In 1½-quart mixer bowl, combine butter, brown sugar and flour. Beat at low speed until well-mixed. Reserve 1/2 cup mixture for topping. Press remaining crumb mixture into ungreased 8-inch square baking dish. Bake in **preheated 350° oven 10-12 minutes**, or until lightly browned. In same bowl, mix cream cheese and sugar. Add egg and lemon juice. Beat at medium speed until smooth. Stir in cherries. Spread filling over crust. Sprinkle with reserved crumb mixture. Continue baking in **350° oven 18-20 minutes** or until filling is set. When cool, cut into 36 bars. Cover and refrigerate.

Yield: 36 bars

Rosa Belle H. Stansbury (Mrs. Lyman W.)

COCONUT MACAROONS

6 tablespoons all-purpose flour
1½ cups sugar
1 teaspoon salt
4 cups Angel Flake coconut
6 egg whites, unbeaten
2 teaspoons vanilla

In a mixing bowl, combine flour, sugar and salt. Add coconut, unbeaten egg whites and vanilla. Blend well. Drop by teaspoonfuls onto a well greased and floured cookie sheet. Bake in **preheated 325° oven 15 minutes** or until slightly browned around edges.

Yield: 2½ dozen

Mary Margaret McGlasson

CARAMEL DIAMONDS

Crust:
3/4 cup butter, softened
1/3 cup sugar
1 teaspoon vanilla extract
2 cups all-purpose flour

Topping:
28 Kraft's caramel candy cubes
1/4 cup water
1/4 cup butter, softened
1/4 cup sugar
2 eggs, beaten
1/2 teaspoon vanilla
1/4 teaspoon salt
2 cups finely chopped pecans

With electric mixer or food processor (steel blade), cream butter and sugar until pale yellow and fluffy. Add vanilla and flour. Mix well. Press dough into a 15½ x 10½-inch jelly roll pan. Bake in **preheated 350° oven for 10 minutes.**

Melt caramels in water over low heat, stirring occasionally until smooth. With electric mixer or food processor (steel blade) cream butter and sugar. Add eggs, vanilla and salt. Add melted caramels. Mix well. Remove beaters or blade and stir in pecans. Spread mixture evenly over baked crust. Return to **350° oven.** Bake for **20 minutes.** Cool completely and cut into 2-inch diamonds.

Yield: 5 to 6 dozen

Mary Margaret McGlasson

Microwave shortcut: To melt caramel candies, place 28 candies and 1/4 cup water in a 4-cup glass measure. Microwave on **HIGH (100%) 2 MINUTES**, stir at one minute. Continue recipe directions above. *Jean K Durkee*

CHEWY PRALINE SQUARES

1 cup margarine
16 ounces dark brown sugar, packed
2 eggs, well beaten
1 teaspoon vanilla
1/4 teaspoon salt
1½ cups all-purpose flour
1 cup chopped pecans

In a double boiler, melt margarine and sugar until smooth. Let cool to room temperature for 15 minutes. Grease and flour a 9 x 12-inch baking dish or pan. To sugar and butter add eggs, vanilla, salt, flour and nuts. Pour mixture into pan and spread evenly. Bake in **preheated 350° oven exactly 30 minutes.** Cut into 24 squares when first removed from oven. Let cool and remove from pan.

Yield: 24 servings

Sarah B. Chalin

Microwave shortcut: Place margarine and brown sugar in an 8-cup glass measuring cup. Microwave on **HIGH (100%) 4 MINUTES**, stirring at 2 minute intervals. Let cool 15 minutes and continue recipe directions above. *Jean K Durkee*

CHOCOLATE FUDGE COOKIES

12 ounces semi-sweet chocolate
   chips
1/4 cup margarine
1 (14-oz.) can sweetened
   condensed milk
1 cup all-purpose flour
1 teaspoon vanilla
1 cup chopped pecans

Melt chocolate and margarine in 2-quart saucepan. Add condensed milk. Blend in flour, vanilla and pecans. Drop on greased cookie sheet. Bake in **preheated 350° oven 6-9 minutes.** Remove while cookies look underbaked. Do not overbake.

Yield: 6 dozen

Jill Verspoor Durkee (Mrs. Robert, III)

Microwave shortcut: Melt chocolate and margarine in 8-cup glass measure on **HIGH (100%) 1 MINUTE 30 SECONDS.** Continue to follow recipe above. *Jean K Durkee*

PECAN DREAMS

1 cup butter or margarine
4 tablespoons sugar
2 teaspoons vanilla
2 cups all-purpose flour
2 cups finely chopped pecans
Confectioners powdered sugar,
   for rolling

Cream butter and sugar in mixing bowl. Add vanilla, flour and pecans. Blend well. Roll dough into little balls. Place on ungreased cookie sheet. Bake in **preheated 300° oven 25-30 minutes.**

Cookies should be slightly brown. Remove from oven and roll in powdered sugar while still hot. Let cool and roll again in powdered sugar. *This is an old family recipe. Children love them.*

Yield: 2-3 dozen

Rosa Belle Stansbury (Mrs. Lyman W.)

PECAN WAFERS

1/3 cup sugar
1/4 cup butter
1 egg, lightly beaten
1/4 cup flour
1/2 cup finely chopped pecans
36 pecan halves

In a bowl, cream together sugar and butter until the mixture is light. Add egg and beat well. Sift in flour and fold in chopped pecans.

Heat a buttered baking sheet in a **preheated 350° oven for 1 minute.** Remove from oven. With a teaspoon drop batter in mounds 2 inches apart onto baking sheet.

Spread batter into rounds with back of spoon. Set a pecan half in the center of each round. Bake wafers in **350° oven 8 to 10 minutes,** or until they are golden. Transfer wafers to a rack to cool.

Yield: 36 cookies

Maude M. Escudier (Mrs. Kermit, Sr.)

TANTE MAI'S NOUGATS

3 egg whites, medium size eggs
1/4 teaspoon cream of tartar
1 cup sugar
1 teaspoon vanilla extract
1/2 teaspoon almond extract
2 cups ground pecans

In a 2-quart bowl, beat egg whites and cream of tartar on high speed of electric mixer until whites begin to stand in peaks. Add sugar a little at a time. Continue beating until whites are stiff. Fold in vanilla and almond extract. Then fold in ground pecans.

Form balls the size of walnuts by wetting hands and roll as you would meat balls. Place on oiled cookie sheet. Bake in a **preheated 325° oven 10 minutes** or until cookies are slightly brown. Let nougats stand a few minutes to cool. Remove with spatula. *These freeze well.*

Yield: 2 dozen cookies

Mrs. George N. Baquet

217

VERLIE'S FUDGE BROWNIES

1 cup margarine (Fleischman's)
2 cups sugar
4 eggs
2 teaspoons vanilla
2 cups all-purpose flour
8 tablespoons cocoa
1 cup chopped pecans

Icing:
1/2 cup margarine
1 (1-lb.) box confectioners
  powdered sugar, sifted
6 tablespoons cocoa
1 teaspoon vanilla
Milk or hot water

Cream margarine and sugar in a large mixing bowl. Add eggs and vanilla. Mix in flour, cocoa and pecans. Pour onto a greased and floured 11 x 16 x 1-inch deep cookie sheet or jelly roll pan. Bake in **preheated 350° oven for 20 minutes**. Ice while cake is hot and cut into squares. Leave in pan until cool.

Blend margarine, sugar, cocoa and vanilla in mixing bowl. Add milk or hot water until icing is of smooth consistency for spreading on hot cake.

Yield: 60 servings

Verlie House (Mrs. Dick)

ZUCHER PLÄTZKEN
Sugar Cookies

1 cup butter
2 cups sugar
2 eggs
1 teaspoon vanilla
1 teaspoon baking powder
4 cups all-purpose flour
Sugar for sprinkling

In a large mixer bowl, cream butter and sugar until light and fluffy. Add eggs and vanilla, beat until well-blended. Stir in baking powder and flour a little at a time. Roll dough about 1/8-inch thick on floured board. Sprinkle with sugar. Cut with cookie cutter.

Bake in **preheated 375° oven** for **about 15 minutes**. Remove from cookie sheet and cool on wire rack about 15 minutes.

Yield: 3 dozen cookies

This recipe comes from my grandmother, Josephine Gossen Leonards, who came to this country around 1880 from Gangelt, Germany.

She baked these cookies very often for her 54 grandchildren who gathered together each Sunday afternoon at her home in Roberts Cove, LA (German Cove) near Rayne, LA. Today many of her 54 grandchildren are baking these same cookies for their grandchildren.

Theresa Zaunbrecher Broussard

ORANGE ICED SUGAR COOKIES

4 cups all-purpose flour
1 teaspoon baking powder
1/2 teaspoon baking soda
1/2 teaspoon salt
1/2 teaspoon nutmeg
1 cup soft butter or margarine
1½ cups sugar
1 egg
1/2 cup dairy sour cream
1 teaspoon vanilla extract

Icing:
3 tablespoons butter, melted
1/4 cup orange juice
1 cup confectioners powdered
    sugar

Sift flour, baking powder, soda, salt and nutmeg. Set aside. Cream butter and sugar. Add egg, beating until light and fluffy. At low speed mix in sour cream and vanilla until smooth. Gradually add flour mixture, beating until well-mixed. Form dough into ball. Wrap in wax paper. Refrigerate several hours. Divide dough into 4 parts. On well-floured surface roll dough, one part at a time, 1/4-inch thick. Cut with floured cookie cutter. Place 2 inches apart on lightly greased cookie sheet. Bake in **preheated 375° oven 10-12 minutes** or until golden brown.

Combine butter, orange juice and powdered sugar in a 2-cup measure. Spread over cooled cookies. *From my grandmother, Mrs. Tina G. Trent.*

Yield: 6 dozen

Linda Demanade Frayard (Mrs. Rick)

WHISKEY BALLS

12 ounces vanilla wafers,
    fine crumbs
2 cups ground pecans
1 cup Angel Flake coconut
12 ounces semi-sweet chocolate
    chips
1/2 (14-oz.) can sweetened
    condensed milk
1/2 cup whiskey
Confectioners powdered sugar
    for rolling

Crumble wafers very fine in blender or food processor. In a large bowl combine crumbs, ground pecans and coconut. Set aside. In a saucepan over low heat melt chocolate chips and 1/2 can condensed milk. Add to crumb mixture. Add whiskey and stir well. Roll by hand into 48 balls. Roll each ball in powdered sugar.

Yield: 4 dozen

Bonnie Buratt

BERNICE'S BENNÉ PRALINES

1¹/₂ cups benné seeds (sesame
    seeds)
1 cup granulated sugar
2 cups packed light brown sugar
1 cup evaporated milk
1 teaspoon vanilla
1 tablespoon butter or margarine

Toast benné seeds in heavy skillet or pot, black iron if possible, just until seeds start to pop and sizzle. Stir constantly and remove from pot immediately after toasting.

Mix sugars and milk in a large, heavy Dutch oven. Cook on medium heat stirring constantly until soft ball forms in cold water or 238° registers on candy thermometer, about 8 minutes. Add benné seeds, vanilla and butter. Beat only to combine mixture well. Before mixture thickens quickly drop by tablespoonfuls onto a sheet of foil or wax paper laid over newspaper to prevent sticking. The mixture should spread easily but requires fast work. When cool enough to lift from paper or foil, turn over to finish cooling.

Yield: 45 (2¹/₂-inch) pralines

Bernice Filer Bernard

CHOCOLATE PRALINES

1¹/₂ cups light brown sugar
1 cup granulated sugar
1 cup evaporated milk
1 teaspoon vanilla extract
1 tablespoon butter
3 cups pecan halves
2 tablespoons Hershey's
    squeeze liquid chocolate
1/8 teaspoon salt
1 tablespoon butter

Combine sugars, milk, vanilla, butter, pecan halves, chocolate and salt in a large pot. Bring to a boil. Continue to cook until soft ball stage (238°). Add 1 tablespoon butter. Place a wet towel in bottom of sink. Place pot on towel and beat with a wooden spoon until creamy. Drop by large tablespoons onto foil.

Yield: 2 dozen large pieces

Evelyn McPherson

LOUISIANA PECAN PRALINES

2 cups sugar
1 cup milk (4% butter cream)
2 tablespoons butter
2 tablespoons light corn syrup
1/2 teaspoon salt
1/4 teaspoon baking soda
1½ cups pecan halves
1 teaspoon vanilla

Combine sugar, milk, butter, corn syrup, salt and soda in heavy 3-quart saucepan. Bring to boil. Add pecans. Cook to 238° or soft ball stage over medium heat. Add vanilla and beat until creamy. Drop quickly onto wax paper or foil. *This old Louisiana favorite praline recipe was given to me by Juanelle Caldwell years ago.*

Yield: 2 dozen

Helen L. Todd (Mrs. George)

ALMOND PECAN PRALINES

1 cup granulated sugar
2 cups light brown sugar
1 cup evaporated milk
2¼ cups chopped pecans
1/2 teaspoon almond extract
1 teaspoon cream of tartar
1 tablespoon margarine

Combine white and brown sugar and milk in a heavy Dutch oven pot. Bring to boil on high heat. Reduce heat to medium. Stir constantly until a drop of the mixture will make a soft ball in water (238° on candy thermometer). Remove from heat and add pecans, almond extract, cream of tartar and margarine.

Beat until thick enough to drop on foil or wax paper. (Hint: place newspaper under wax paper so pralines will not stick to wax paper or wax paper stick to counter top.)

Yield: 2 dozen

Bernice Filer Bernard

BOURBON PRALINES

2 cups roasted pecans
2 cups granulated sugar
2¹/₂ cups evaporated milk
    (1 large and 1 small can)
1 teaspoon vanilla
1 ounce (2 tablespoons) bourbon
1/4 cup margarine

On a metal pan in a **375° oven** roast pecans for 20 minutes; **or** on a glass plate in the microwave on **HIGH (100%) 7 MINUTES**. Stir nuts twice during cooking time. Mix sugar and milk together in a large pot until sugar dissolves. Bring to a boil and cook until firm ball stage (260°).

Add roasted pecans, vanilla, bourbon and margarine. Stir until thick. Drop by tablespoonfuls onto aluminum foil.

Yield: 3 dozen

Grace Jenkins Boudreaux (Mrs. Wallace)

GRANDMOTHER'S DIVINITY

1¹/₂ cups sugar
1/3 cup water
1 tablespoon corn syrup
1 large egg white
1 cup chopped pecans
1/2 teaspoon vanilla

Combine sugar, water and corn syrup in a large 4-quart pot. Bring to boil, then lower heat to medium. Cook until soft ball stage 238.° Remove from heat. Beat egg white stiff. Slowly add syrup to egg white while beating constantly with electric beater. Beat until light and fluffy. Add pecans and vanilla. Beat until stiff. Spread into buttered 6 x 10 or 8 x 8-inch pan. Let set before cutting into squares. *Grandmother would let us help prepare her recipe at Christmas time.*

Yield: 36 pieces

Susan Alves Bonnette

DATE NUT LOAF

1 pound miniature white
    marshmallows
1 pound chopped dates
1/2 pint whipping cream
5 cups chopped pecans
1 pound crushed graham
    crackers

Mix marshmallows, dates and whipping cream in Dutch oven. Cook over low heat until all ingredients are melted. Stir constantly to avoid scorching. Remove from heat. Stir in pecans and graham cracker crumbs. (Save enough crumbs to roll each loaf in.) Mix completely. Divide in 8 equal loaves and roll in graham cracker crumbs. Wrap individually in wax paper. Loaves freeze well. Slice to serve.

Yield: 15 slices per loaf

Robyn Cash Melville (Mrs. Micheal)

RUSSIAN TAFFY

3 cups sugar
1½ cups milk
1 cup sweetened condensed
    milk
1 (8-oz.) package dates,
    finely chopped
1 cup chopped pecans

Mix sugar, milk and condensed milk in a 3 or 4-quart saucepan. Cook over medium heat, stirring occasionally until mixture reaches 238° or soft ball stage.

Remove from heat and add dates and then pecans. Beat 2-3 minutes. Immediately pour into 7 x 11-inch greased pan or dish. Cut into pieces when cool. *Evangeline Creole Recipes 1938 Ed Bulliard, Founder, Evangeline Pepper & Food Products.*

Yield: 24 pieces

Belle Bienvenu

CARAMEL CHEWS

36 vanilla caramels
3 tablespoons evaporated milk
1 cup corn flakes
1 cup rice krispies
1 cup flaked coconut
1 cup chopped pecans

Place caramels and milk in top of double boiler over simmering water. Heat until caramels melt. In a mixing bowl toss together cereals, coconut and pecans. Pour caramel mixture over this and mix thoroughly with a buttered spoon. Grease fingers and roll about 1-2 teaspoonfuls into balls. Wrap in plastic wrap and chill.

Yield: 2 dozen

Dolores Johnson Champagne (Mrs. George, III)

Microwave shortcut: Place caramels and milk in 8-cup glass measuring cup. Microwave on **HIGH (100%) 2 MINUTES** until caramels melt. *Jean K Durkee*

JUDY'S CHRISTMAS FUDGE

3 cups sugar
1 envelope unflavored gelatin
1 cup whole milk
1/2 cup light corn syrup
3 (1-oz.) squares unsweetened
    chocolate
1¼ cups butter
2 teaspoons vanilla
1 cup chopped pecans

Butter an 8 x 8 x 2-inch pan. Mix sugar with dry gelatin in a 3½-quart heavy saucepan. Add milk, corn syrup, chocolate and butter. Cook over medium heat, stirring frequently, to 238° on candy thermometer, or until soft ball forms in cold water (usually about 20-25 minutes after mixture begins to boil).

Remove from heat. Pour into large mixing bowl. Stir in vanilla and cool 25 minutes. Beat with wooden spoon until candy thickens (this is an important step). Stir in pecans. Spread in pan. Cool and cut into squares.

Yield: 2½ pounds

Judith Ann Montgomery Skelton (Mrs. Roland)

PERFECT FUDGE

4¹/₂ cups sugar
1 (13-oz.) can evaporated milk
1/2 teaspoon salt
1/2 cup butter or margarine
1 (12-oz.) package semi-sweet
    chocolate chips
12 ounces Baker's sweet
    German chocolate, broken
    into bits
1 (7-oz.) jar marshmallow creme
3 cups chopped pecans
1 teaspoon vanilla

In a large 4-quart pot combine sugar, milk, salt and butter. Bring to boil. Cook 5 minutes, stirring constantly. Add chocolate, marshmallow creme, pecans and vanilla. Stir until chocolate is melted and ingredients are well blended. Pour into 2 buttered 8 x 12-inch baking dishes. Makes about 4 pounds of perfect fudge. *This recipe was given to me by Corita Melchior (Mrs. Tom) Arceneaux.*

Yield: 4 pounds

Alma Bowen Stuller (Mrs. Gilbert)

PINEAPPLE FUDGE

2 cups sugar
1 cup evaporated milk or cream
1/2 cup butter or margarine
1 cup drained crushed pineapple
1 teaspoon vanilla

Combine sugar, milk or cream, and butter or margarine in 3-quart saucepan. Bring to a full rolling boil and boil for one minute. Add pineapple and cook to soft ball stage (238° by candy thermometer or small drop of mixture in cold water forms a soft ball), stirring often. Add vanilla and beat until thick. Turn into a buttered 8 x 8-inch dish or pan. Cool and cut into squares.

Yield: 1¹/₂ pounds

Ramona L. Black (Mrs. Jack)

FIVE MINUTE FUDGE

2/3 cup evaporated milk,
    undiluted
1²/₃ cups sugar
1/2 teaspoon salt
1¹/₂ cups miniature
    marshmallows
1¹/₂ cups semi-sweet real
    chocolate chips
1 teaspoon vanilla
Pecan or walnut halves, optional

Mix milk, sugar and salt in saucepan over medium heat. Bring to boil. Cook 5 minutes, stirring constantly. Remove from heat. Add marshmallows, chocolate chips and vanilla. Stir vigorously for 1 minute or until marshmallows melt. Pour into buttered 8-inch square dish. Garnish with nuts, if desired. Cool, cut into squares.

Yield: 2 pounds

Kathryn A. Beck

ROCKY ROAD SQUARES

12 ounces semi-sweet chocolate
    chips
14 ounces sweetened
    condensed milk
2 tablespoons margarine
2 cups dry roasted peanuts
10¹/₂ ounces miniature white
    marshmallows

In medium saucepan over low heat, melt chocolate with condensed milk and margarine. Remove from heat. In large bowl, combine peanuts and marshmallows. Fold in chocolate mixture. Spread in wax paper-lined 13 x 9-inch pan. Chill 2 hours or until firm. Remove from pan. Peel off wax paper. Cut into squares.

Yield: 30 squares

Jackie D. Cockrell (Mrs. Larry)

MICROWAVE PEANUT BUTTER CANDY

12 ounces semi-sweet chocolate
   chips
12 ounces butterscotch chips
1 cup smooth peanut butter
1 cup graham cracker crumbs
2 cups chopped pecans
1 cup pecan halves
36 (2½-inch) foil or paper
   cupcake baking cups

Place chips and peanut butter into an 8-cup glass measure. Microwave on **MEDIUM HIGH (70%) 5 MINUTES**. Stir until smooth. Add crumbs and chopped pecans, mix well.

Drop by tablespoonfuls into cupcake liners. Decorate each top with 2 or 3 pecan halves. Refrigerate 30 minutes to harden.

Yield: 36 pieces

JoAnn Pugh (Mrs. Nick, III)

BERNICE'S PEANUT BRITTLE

1½ cups white sugar
1/2 cup light corn syrup
1/4 cup water
1 teaspoon vanilla
2 cups shelled raw peanuts
1 teaspoon baking soda
1 teaspoon paraffin

Combine sugar, corn syrup, water, and vanilla in a heavy Dutch oven. Bring to boil and continue to boil 3 minutes. Stir in raw peanuts. Boil 10 minutes or until liquid and peanuts turn light tan (300° hard crack). Stir in soda and paraffin. Spread mixture on a greased cookie sheet. Cool slightly and cut into squares. Remove squares and turn over onto wax paper to cool.

Yield: 36 pieces

Bernice Filer Bernard

GLAZED APPLE CAKE

1¼ cups vegetable oil
2 cups sugar
2 well beaten eggs
2 teaspoons vanilla
1 teaspoon salt
2 tablespoons lemon juice
3 cups all-purpose flour
1¼ teaspoons baking soda
1 cup chopped pecans
3 cups chopped, unpeeled
    fresh apples

*Glaze:
1 cup light brown sugar
1/2 cup butter
1/4 cup milk
1 teaspoon vanilla

Grease and flour a tube pan or Bundt pan. In a large bowl, mix oil, sugar, eggs, vanilla, salt and lemon juice. Mix well.

Add flour, soda, pecans and apples. Pour mixture into prepared pan. Bake in a **preheated 325° oven 1 hour 20 minutes to 1 hour 30 minutes**, or when a cake tester comes out clean. When done, remove from oven and leave in pan. Prepare Glaze* and pour over hot cake while in pan. Cool in pan before removing. *This cake is delicious hot or cold or 3 days old—if it will last that long!*

Mix and cook glaze ingredients for 2 minutes 30 seconds. Use an ice pick to puncture cake. Pour glaze over hot cake. Cool in pan.

Yield: 12 servings

Anita Hardy Atkins (Mrs. Oscar)

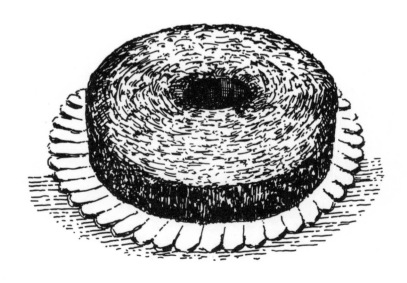

FRESH APPLE CAKE

3 eggs
2 cups sugar
1 1/2 cups vegetable oil
3 cups all-purpose flour
1 teaspoon baking soda
1 teaspoon baking powder
1 teaspoon salt
1 teaspoon cinnamon
1 teaspoon nutmeg
1 cup chopped pecans
3 cups unpeeled chopped
    apples (3 medium)
1 cup chopped dates

In a mixer bowl, beat eggs, sugar and oil on high speed. Add flour, soda, baking powder, salt, cinnamon and nutmeg. Blend well.

Add pecans, apples and dates. Stir well to blend.

Pour mixture into a greased and floured tube pan. Bake in a **preheated 325° oven for 1 hour 15 minutes to 1 hour 30 minutes** or until cake tester is clean. Let stand 15 minutes before removing from pan. *This is my mother's recipe. We make this instead of fruit cake as it is not so sweet and heavy. This cake is better if made several days ahead.*

Yield: 12 servings

Elizabeth Carter Montgomery (Mrs. Denbo)

APPLE WALNUT CAKE

3 eggs
2 cups sugar
1 1/2 cups vegetable oil
3 cups all-purpose flour, sifted
1 teaspoon baking soda
1/4 teaspoon salt
3 cups pared, chopped apples
1 cup chopped walnuts
2 teaspoons vanilla

*Topping:
1 cup light brown sugar, packed
1/4 cup milk
1/2 cup margarine

Grease and flour 10-inch tube pan. In large mixing bowl beat eggs. Add sugar and oil. Beat 3 minutes on high. Mix flour, soda and salt. Add slowly to large mixing bowl. Batter will be stiff. Fold in apples, nuts and vanilla. Pour into prepared pan. Bake in **preheated 350° oven 1 hour 15 minutes**. Remove from oven. Pour Topping* over cake in pan.

Combine sugar, milk and margarine in saucepan. Bring to boil. Let boil 3 minutes. Pour over hot cake and let cool. Invert on a plate. Turn over on another plate so top will be up.

Yield: 16 slices

Neloise M. Groth (Mrs. Walter)

CHRISTMAS PECAN CAKE

3 cups sifted flour, divided
3 teaspoons baking powder
1/2 teaspoon salt
1 teaspoon vanilla
1¹/₃ cups milk
1 cup butter
2 cups sugar
8 egg yolks, beaten
1 cup chopped pecans

Sift 2³/₄ cups flour, baking powder and salt together. Combine vanilla and milk. In a mixing bowl cream butter and sugar well. Slowly add eggs to mixture. Continue beating while adding milk and dry ingredients alternately to creamed mixture. Beat well. Add the pecans to remaining 1/4 cup flour and beat into the batter. Pour into 10-inch greased and floured tube pan. Bake in a **preheated 350° oven 1¹/₄ hours.** This cake keeps very well. *From the recipe files of Mrs. Harold Demanade, Sr. Her friends always looked forward to getting one of her 'nut cakes' at Christmas.*

Yield: 16 servings

Billie Ruth Demanade (Mrs. Felix)

HOLIDAY FRUIT CAKE

1 pound butter
2 cups sugar
6 eggs
2¹/₂ cups all-purpose flour
1 cup sliced glazed cherries
1 cup coarsely chopped candied
    pineapple
2 cups chopped pecans
3 ounces frozen orange juice
    concentrate, thawed

Cream butter and sugar in mixing bowl. Add eggs, one at a time, beating well after each addition. Dredge fruit in 1/2 cup flour, and add remaining flour to creamed mixture. Fold in fruit, nuts and orange juice concentrate. Pour into medium tube pan lined with wax paper on the bottom. Bake in **preheated 275° oven 3 hours.** When cool, wrap in wax paper or plastic wrap and foil.

Yield: 16 servings

Beulah Hebert Stansbury

CARROT SPICE CAKE

3 cups all-purpose flour
2 teaspoons baking soda
1/2 teaspoon salt
2 teaspoons cinnamon
1¹/₂ cups vegetable oil
2 cups sugar
2 cups grated carrots
1 (8-oz.) can crushed pineapple
1/2 cup chopped nuts
2 teaspoons vanilla
3 eggs

Cream cheese frosting:
1/4 cup margarine
16 ounces confectioners
    powdered sugar
8 ounces cream cheese
1/2 teaspoon lemon extract
1 teaspoon vanilla
1/2 cup chopped nuts, optional

Sift together flour, soda, salt and cinnamon. In a large mixing bowl mix oil and sugar. Add half of dry ingredients. Mix well and beat in carrots, pineapple and nuts. Add vanilla and remaining dry ingredients. Add eggs, one at a time. Beat well after each addition. Pour into greased 8 x 12 x 2-inch pan or 2 (9-inch) layer pans. Bake in **preheated 350° oven 45-50 minutes.**

Melt margarine and blend with sugar, cream cheese, lemon and vanilla. Spread over cooled cake. Optional: 1/2 cup chopped nuts sprinkled on top. *From the recipe files of Helen Nichols, former director of U.S.L. Home Management House.*

Yield: 24 servings

Dr. Louise E. Gauthier (Mrs. Robert J.)

SWEETENED CONDENSED MILK

3 tablespoons melted butter
    or margarine
1/3 cup boiling water
2/3 cup sugar
1 cup instant nonfat dry milk
    solids

Combine melted butter, boiling water, sugar and dry milk in electric blender. Process until very smooth. Store in refrigerator.

Yield: 1¹/₄ cups

Vonita Davis Dardeau (Mrs. Luther)

Microwave directions: Combine butter and water in a 2-cup glass measuring cup. Microwave on **HIGH (100%) 1-2 MINUTES** until water boils and butter melts. Stir in sugar and dry milk. Pour mixture into electric blender. Process until smooth.
Jean K Durkee

ORANGE FRUIT CAKE

1 cup butter
2 cups sugar
4 eggs
1/2 cup buttermilk
3¼ cups all-purpose flour
1/4 cup flour for dredging
1 teaspoon baking soda
2 tablespoons orange zest
    (grated rind)
1 cup chopped pecans
1 (8-oz.) package dates, cut into
    small pieces

*Orange Sauce
2 cups confectioners powdered
    sugar (sift if lumpy)
1 cup orange juice
2 tablespoons grated orange
    peel

In a large mixing bowl, cream butter and sugar until light and fluffy. Add eggs beating well after each addition. Add buttermilk. Mix 3¼ cups flour, soda and orange zest. Add to mixture. Dredge nuts and dates in 1/4 cup flour. Stir nuts, dates and remaining flour into mixture and mix well. Pour into a greased and floured tube pan. Bake in **preheated 325° oven 1 hour 15 minutes** or until cake tester comes out clean. Prepare Orange Sauce* during baking time. **Hint:** To help cut dates, dip shears in flour. This keeps dates from sticking together.

In a small bowl or 4-cup measure, mix powdered sugar, orange juice and peel. The sauce mixture will be thin. As soon as cake is removed from oven, pour half of the sauce over cake in the pan. Punch holes in cake with ice pick or fork. Let soak then turn cake out on plate. Slowly pour remaining sauce over cake. *This was one of John's mother's favorite holiday cakes.*

Yield: 16-20 servings

Beulah D. Stephan (Mrs. John E.)

OLD-FASHION SYRUP CAKE

1 cup sugar
1 cup vegetable oil
2 eggs
1 cup cane syrup
2½ cups self-rising flour
1 cup boiling water with
1 teaspoon baking soda added
Whipped cream topping,
    optional

In a large mixing bowl, blend sugar and oil, beat in eggs. Add cane syrup, blend well. Alternate adding flour and water with soda. Bake in a well-greased and floured 9 x 13-inch pan in **preheated 350° oven 35 minutes** or until done. Cut into squares to serve. Top with whipped cream. *Delicious with a cold glass of milk, or a hot cup of French-dripped coffee.*

Yield: 16 servings

Mrs. Donna Schexneider

WINE CAKE

1 cup butter
2 cups sugar
4 eggs
3 cups all-purpose flour,
    reserve 1/2 cup
1 teaspon baking soda
1 teaspoon cinnamon
1 teaspoon ginger
1 cup red wine
3 cups chopped pecans
1 (8-oz.) jar whole maraschino
    cherries, drained & halved
12 ounces raisins

Cream butter and sugar in large mixing bowl until light and fluffy. Add eggs, one at a time, beating well after each addition. Reserving 1/2 cup flour, sift flour, soda, cinnamon and ginger. Add flour and wine alternately to sugar mixture. Mix pecans, cherries and raisins with remaining 1/2 cup flour and add to batter. Pour into greased and floured 10-inch tube pan (bottom lined with wax paper). Bake in **preheated 300° oven 1½ hours**. Let cool in pan 10 minutes.

Yield: 10-12 servings

Pearl Webb Bush (Mrs. Herbert, Jr.)

BETTY'S MINIATURE CHEESECAKES

Cake:
3 (8-oz.) packages cream cheese
5 eggs
1 cup sugar
1½ teaspoons vanilla

Topping:
1 pint sour cream
1/4 cup sugar
1/4 teaspoon vanilla
3 or 4 drops food coloring

Cream softened cheese, add eggs, one at a time, beating after each. Add sugar, beat. Add vanilla, beat. Carefully fill miniature liners in miniature muffin tins to 1/8 inch from top, using scant measuring tablespoon per cup. Bake in **preheated 300° oven 20-25 minutes**. Remove from oven and cool on racks for 5 minutes. Mix sour cream, sugar, vanilla and food coloring in a 2-quart bowl until glossy. Top cakes with one scant teaspoon of topping per cake and bake at same temperature for another 5 minutes. Cool in pans and either refrigerate or freeze on cookie sheets. Store frozen in bags or containers until time to serve. Thaw three minutes before serving; serve cold.

Yield: 10 dozen candy liner size or
      6½-7 dozen miniature liner size

Mary Julia Hooton (Mrs. Claude A.)

CHOCOLATE CHEESECAKE

Crust:
1¹/₂ cups graham cracker crumbs
2 tablespoons sugar
2 tablespoons unsweetened
    cocoa
1/4 cup butter, melted

Filling:
3 extra large eggs
1 cup sugar
24 ounces cream cheese,
    softened
6 ounces semi-sweet chocolate
    squares
3/4 cup butter
1 cup sour cream
2 teaspoons vanilla
3/4 cup coarsely chopped
    pecans, optional
Whipped cream for topping

Mix crumbs, sugar and cocoa in a small bowl. Stir in butter, mixing well. Press crumbs evenly onto sides and bottom of 10-inch spring form pan.

Beat eggs until light and fluffy. Add sugar and beat until thick. In mixer bowl, beat cream cheese until smooth. Gradualy add sugar/egg mixture beating on low speed. Place chocolate, butter, sour cream and vanilla in top of double boiler. Melt over simmering water. Stir, then fold into cream cheese mixture. Add pecans. Pour into prepared crust. Bake in **preheated 350° oven 1 hour 15 minutes.** Cool to room temperature. Chill overnight. Remove from pan and top with whipped cream if desired.

Yield: 12 servings

Karen Veillon McGlasson (Mrs. H. Edwin)

TWO-TONE CHEESECAKE

1¹/₂ cups vanilla wafer crumbs
1/2 cup melted butter
8 ounces cream cheese,
    softened
Juice of 1/2 lemon
1/4 cup sugar
1 large egg
1/2 pint commercial sour cream
1/4 cup sugar
1/2 teaspoon vanilla

Mix crumbs and butter and press in spring paṇ or 8-inch square pan. To prepare filling, thoroughly cream cheese and lemon juice. Mix in sugar and egg. Spread over crust. Bake in **preheated 350° oven 10 minutes.** Let stand exactly 15 minutes while preparing topping. Mix sour cream, sugar and vanilla together. Spoon over top of filling. Return to **350° oven and bake 15 minutes.** Cool to room temperature and then chill.

Yield: 8 servings

Lynn Freeman McIntire (Mrs. Jim)

PUMPKIN CHEESECAKE

Crust:
2¹/₂ cups crushed graham
    crackers
1 cup sugar
1/2 cup butter, melted

Filling:
5 (8-oz.) packages cream cheese
1 cup sugar
4 large eggs
3 egg yolks, stirred
3 tablespoons all-purpose flour
2 teaspoons cinnamon
1 teaspoon cloves
1 teaspoon ginger
1 cup heavy cream
1 tablespoon vanilla
1 (16-oz.) can solid pack
    pumpkin

Topping:
4 tablespoons butter, melted
3/4 cup light brown sugar
1 cup chopped pecans
1/2 cup sliced almonds
5 large pecan halves

Mix crumbs and sugar together in bowl. Add melted butter and mix well. Pat mixture onto sides and bottom of 10-inch spring form pan. Place pan on cookie sheet. Bake in **preheated 350° oven 8 minutes**. Cool.

In mixing bowl, beat cream cheese, sugar, eggs and yolks until well-blended. In a separate bowl, mix flour, cinnamon, cloves and ginger. Add to creamed mixture. Blend well. Add cream and vanilla. Finally, add mashed pumpkin. Beat until all ingredients are thoroughly mixed. Spread mixture into prepared crust. Place pan on cookie sheet. Bake in **preheated 425° oven 15 minutes**. Reduce temperature to **275°** and **bake 1 hour.**

Add sugar and chopped nuts to melted butter and stir until thoroughly mixed. Sprinkle topping around top edge of cake. Bake in **preheated 325° oven 15 minutes**. Turn oven off. Leave cake in oven until oven cools. Chill cake 4 hours in refrigerator. Cover center of cake with almonds and large pecan halves on top of almonds.

Yield: 20 servings

Laila Michelle Asmar

PUMPKIN PIE CAKE

3 eggs, beaten
13 ounces evaporated milk
1/2 teaspoon salt
2 (16-oz.) cans solid pack
    pumpkin
1 cup sugar
4 teaspoons pumpkin pie spice
1 (18.5-oz.) box plain yellow
    cake mix
1/2 cup chopped walnuts
3/4 cup margarine, melted

In a large bowl mix eggs, milk, salt, pumpkin, sugar and spice. Pour into a 9 x 13-inch greased and floured pan. Sprinkle yellow cake mix over mixture then chopped nuts. Drizzle margarine over entire top.

Bake in **preheated 350° oven 1 hour** or until inserted cake tester comes out clean. *This cake with a crunchy top is served right from the pan.*

Yield: 16 servings

Lucy Stevens Kellner (Mrs. Herbert E.)

PUMPKIN SURPRISE

Crust:
1 cup all-purpose flour
1/4 cup brown sugar, packed
5$\frac{1}{2}$ tablespoons butter
1/2 cup walnuts, finely chopped

Filling:
3 ounces cream cheese,
    softened
1 egg
1 (16-oz.) can pumpkin
1 (14-oz.) can sweetened
    condensed milk
1 teaspoon cinnamon
1/4 teaspoon *each:* ginger,
    cloves, nutmeg, allspice
1/2 teaspoon salt
1 cup hot water
Whipped cream for topping

Stir flour and brown sugar together. Cut in the butter and blend until crumbly. Add walnuts. Press down mixture onto bottom of 9 x 9-inch pan in an even layer. Bake in **preheated 350° oven for 20 minutes**.

In a mixing bowl, blend softened cream cheese very well with egg until smooth. Add rest of the ingredients. Pour into the baked crust. Bake in **preheated 350° oven for 50 minutes** or until pumpkin mixture is set and not liquid. Cool before cutting into small squares. This can be served warm or even ice cold from the refrigerator. Top with whipped cream or serve with ice cream.

Yield: 8 servings

Elaine Fritton (Mrs. Anthony E.)

ITALIANO CREAM CAKE

1/2 cup margarine
1/2 cup shortening
2 cups sugar
5 eggs, separated
2 cups cake flour
1 teaspoon baking soda
1 cup buttermilk
1 (3½-oz.) can grated coconut
1 cup chopped pecans
1 teaspoon vanilla

Frosting:

1 (8-oz.) package cream cheese,
    softened
1/4 cup margarine, softened
16 ounces confectioners
    powdered sugar
1 teaspoon vanilla
Chopped pecans for sprinkling

In a large mixing bowl, cream margarine, shortening and sugar until light and fluffy. Separate eggs. Beat whites until stiff and set aside. Add yolks to creamed mixture, mix well. Add flour, soda, buttermilk, coconut, pecans and vanilla. Beat well to blend. Fold egg whites into mixture. Pour into 2 (9-inch) greased and floured cake pans. Bake in **preheated 350° oven 35-40 minutes** or until inserted cake tester comes out clean. Cool 10 minutes in pans. After removing from pans let cake cool completely, then frost.

Cream margarine with cream cheese. Add powdered sugar and vanilla. Beat until completely mixed. Spread on cool cake layers. Stack layers and sprinkle top with pecans.

Yield: 16 servings

Rosa Belle Stansbury (Mrs. Lyman W.)

SOUR CREAM CAKE

1 cup margarine
3 cups sugar
6 large eggs
3 cups sifted all-purpose flour
1/2 teaspoon baking soda
1 cup sour cream
1 teaspoon vanilla
1 teaspoon butter flavoring
1 tablespoon almond extract
1/8 teaspoon nutmeg
1 cup finely chopped nuts,
    optional

Melt margarine with sugar and mix well. Add eggs, one at a time. Beat well after each addition. Sift flour (a must for this cake) and then measure 3 cups. Add soda and sift 3 times. Add to sugar/egg mixture alternately with sour cream, beating at medium speed. Add vanilla, butter flavoring, almond extract, nutmeg and nuts. Coat nuts in flour before adding to batter. Mix well. Pour into greased tube pan. Bake in **preheated 315° oven 1 hour 20 minutes**. Cool 10 minutes before turning out. *From the recipe files of my grandmother, Mrs. C. G. (Louise) Simon.*

Yield: 16 servings

Deborah Ritchey Mahony (Mrs. Robert)

Microwave shortcut: Melt margarine in a 4-cup Pyrex measuring cup on **HIGH (100%) 1-2 MINUTES**. Stir in sugar. Transfer to mixing bowl to complete recipe.
Jean K Durkee

TANTE LULU'S WHITE CAKE

3 cups cake flour
3 teaspoons baking powder
1/2 teaspoon salt
3/4 cup butter
2 cups sugar
1 teaspoon vanilla
1 cup milk
7 egg whites

Fluffy frosting:
2 egg whites, unbeaten
1½ cups sugar
5 tablespoons water
1½ teaspoons light corn syrup
1 teaspoon vanilla
1/2 cup grated coconut

Sift flour once, measure, add baking powder and salt. Sift together 3 times. Cream butter thoroughly in large mixing bowl. Add sugar gradually. Cream until light and fluffy. Add flour, vanilla and milk alternately, a small amount at a time. Beat egg whites until stiff. Fold gently into mixture until completely blended. Pour into 2 well-greased and floured 9-inch layer cake pans. Bake in **preheated 350° oven 30-35 minutes** (or 35-40 minutes for oblong cake). Cool on racks 5 minutes before removing from pans. Spread cooled layers with frosting.

Combine egg whites, sugar, water and corn syrup in top of double boiler, beating with rotary egg beater until thoroughly mixed. Place over rapidly boiling water, beating constantly. Cook 7 minutes or until frosting will stand in peaks. Remove from boiling water. Add vanilla and beat until thick enough to spread. Sprinkle top with coconut. *From the recipe files of Mrs. Lulu Gauthier Levert.*

Yield: 16 servings

Blanche Gauthier

MAMA CAZE'S FUDGE CAKE

3/4 cup + 2 tablespoons butter
4 (1-oz.) squares unsweetened
    chocolate
2 cups sugar
1 teaspoon vanilla
4 eggs
2 cups coarsely chopped
    pecans
1 cup all-purpose flour

Line two 8-inch round cake pans with brown paper. Grease pans.

Melt butter and chocolate in double boiler. Cool. In a small bowl, mix sugar, vanilla and eggs. Blend well and add to chocolate mixture. Dredge pecans in flour. Stir pecans and flour into mixture.

Pour into prepared cake pans. Place a pan of water on lowest shelf of oven. Bake in **preheated 350° oven 40 to 50 minutes** or until cake tester (toothpick) comes out clean. Let cake cool before removing from pan.

Icing:
1 (16-oz.) box confectioners
    powdered sugar
2 tablespoons cocoa
1/4 cup butter, softened
1 teaspoon vanilla
2 tablespoons evaporated milk
1 cup coarsely chopped pecans

Mix one box of powdered sugar, cocoa, butter and vanilla with electric beater. Add milk, a little at a time, mixing until thick. Add pecans and spread on cooled cake. Place in refrigerator 24 hours or longer before cutting.

Yield: 20 servings

Marie Louise LaCaze

CREAM OF COCONUT CAKE

1 (18.5-oz.) Duncan Hines white
    cake mix
1 (15.5-oz.) can Cream of Coconut
    (Piña Colada syrup)
1 (14-oz.) can sweetened
    condensed milk
1 (8-oz.) carton whipped
    dessert topping
1 cup grated coconut

Make cake according to package directions. Pour into a 9 x 13-inch baking pan or dish. Bake in **preheated 350° oven 25-30 minutes.** While hot, punch holes with ice pick. Pour 1/2 can Cream of coconut (Piña Colada syrup) over cake. Let soak in well and leave overnight. Next day, pour 1/2 can condensed milk over cake and spread evenly. Spread top with whipped dessert topping and cover with grated coconut. Refrigerate overnight. The remaining 1/2 can cream of coconut and condensed milk may be used for a second cake!

Yield: 20 servings

Elisabeth Denbo Montgomery (Mrs. C. Thad)

RED VELVET CAKE

1/2 cup margarine
1 1/2 cups sugar
2 eggs
1 ounce red food color
1 ounce water
1 teaspoon vanilla
4 tablespoons dry cocoa
2 1/2 cups all-purpose flour
1/2 teaspoon salt
1 1/2 teaspoons baking powder
1 cup buttermilk
1 teaspoon baking soda
1 teaspoon vinegar

*Cream Cheese Frosting:
8 ounces cream cheese
1/2 cup margarine
16 ounces confectioners
    powdered sugar
1 teaspoon vanilla
1 cup chopped pecans

Beat margarine, sugar and eggs in large mixing bowl. Add food color, water and vanilla. Mix well. Sift cocoa, flour, salt and baking powder. Add to red mixture alternately with buttermilk. Mix well after each addition. Mix soda and vinegar together. Add last to cake batter. Mix well. Pour into 3 (9-inch) greased and floured cake pans. Bake in **preheated 350° oven 20 minutes** until done. Cool completely. Frost with **Cream Cheese Frosting.***

Cream cheese and margarine until fluffy. Gradually add powdered sugar and vanilla. Mix well. Fold in pecans. Frost layers, top and sides of cake.

Yield: 16 servings

Jackie D. Cockrell (Mrs. Larry)

HOT FUDGE COCOA CAKE

2/3 cup butter, softened
1 2/3 cups sugar
3 eggs
2 cups self-rising flour
2/3 cup cocoa
1 1/3 cups milk

Hot Fudge Sauce:
1 cup sugar
1/3 cup cocoa
2 tablespoons all-purpose flour
1/4 teaspoon salt
1 tablespoon butter
1 cup boiling water
1 teaspoon vanilla

In mixing bowl, cream butter, sugar and eggs until fluffy. Beat on high speed 3 minutes, reduce to low speed. Combine flour and cocoa, add alternately with milk to creamed mixture. Pour into buttered Bundt pan. Bake in **preheated 350° oven 45 minutes**. Cool 10 minutes.

To prepare sauce, combine sugar, cocoa, flour, salt and butter. Blend well. Gradually add water, cook over medium heat, stirring constantly until smooth and thick. Bring mixture to boil, boil 2 minutes. Stir in vanilla. Serve hot over cake. Store in refrigerator. Reheat as needed.

Yield: 10-12 slices cake, 1 1/4 cups sauce

Wilma Kirkland Piccione (Mrs. Joseph J.)

AUNT SALLIE'S DEVIL'S FOOD CAKE

2¹/₂ (1-oz.) squares unsweetened
    chocolate
1¹/₂ cups milk, warmed
2/3 cup sugar
1 cup butter or margarine
1¹/₂ cups sugar
3 eggs, beaten
3 cups all-purpose flour
2/3 cup milk
1/4 teaspoon salt
1¹/₂ teaspoons vanilla
1 teaspoon soda
3 tablespoons boiling water

Melt chocolate. Add milk and 2/3 cup sugar. Boil together until slightly thickened. Cool. Cream butter and 1¹/₂ cups sugar in mixing bowl. Add beaten eggs. Add flour and 2/3 cup milk alternately. Add chocolate mixture, salt, vanilla and soda dissolved in water. Pour into 3 greased and floured 9-inch cake pans. Bake in **preheated 350° oven 30 minutes**. Cool and frost each layer, top and sides with **Fluffy Cocoa Frosting.**

Yield: 12-16 servings

Hazel M. Decker

Microwave shortcut: Place chocolate and cold milk in a 4-cup Pyrex measuring cup. Microwave on **HIGH (100%) 4 MINUTES**, stirring at 2 minutes. Stir well at 4 minutes to blend. Follow recipe above. *Jean K Durkee*

FLUFFY COCOA FROSTING

3/4 cup cocoa
4 cups confectioners powdered
    sugar
1/2 cup butter or margarine,
    softened
1 teaspoon vanilla
1/2 cup evaporated milk

Mix cocoa and powdered sugar together. In a large mixing bowl cream butter and add part of cocoa/sugar mixture. Blend in vanilla and half of milk. Add remaining cocoa/sugar and blend well. Add remaining milk and beat to desired spreading consistency. Add more milk, if needed.

Yield: frosting for 3 (9-inch) layers

Ann C. Altamirano (Mrs. Mario)

NANNIE'S BEST GINGERBREAD

1/2 cup butter
1/2 cup sugar
1 beaten egg
2¹/₂ cups all-purpose flour
1¹/₂ teaspoons baking soda
1 teaspoon cinnamon
1 teaspoon ginger
1/2 teaspoon cloves
1/2 teaspoon salt
1 cup molasses
1 cup hot water

Cream butter and sugar in mixing bowl. Add beaten egg. Sift flour, soda, cinnamon, ginger, cloves and salt together 3 times. Mix molasses and water together. Add alternately with dry ingredients to creamed mixture. Beat well after each addition. Pour into well-greased and floured 9 x 9 x 2-inch pan. Bake in **preheated 350° oven 45 minutes**. Serve hot with **Lemon Sauce**.

Yield: 16 servings

Betty Hollingsworth (Mrs. W. H.)

LEMON SAUCE

1/2 cup butter
1 cup sugar
1/4 cup water
1 egg, well beaten
3 tablespoons lemon juice
Grated rind of one lemon

In a saucepan, combine butter, sugar, water, beaten egg, juice and lemon rind. Cook over medium heat stirring constantly, just until mixture comes to boil. Serve warm over any kind of pound cake.

Yield: 1¹/₃ cups

Karen Veillon McGlasson (Mrs. H. Edwin)

FRENCH RIBBON LOAF

1 cup all-purpose flour
3/4 cup sugar
1 1/2 teaspoons baking powder
1/2 teaspoon salt
1/4 cup vegetable oil
3 unbeaten egg yolks
3 ounces cold water
1 1/2 tablespoons grated orange
  rind
4 egg whites (about 1/2 cup),
  stiffly beaten
1/4 teaspoon cream of tartar

Filling:

1/2 cup butter
2/3 cup confectioners
  powdered sugar
2 egg yolks
2 1/2 squares unsweetened
  chocolate, melted
1 teaspoon vanilla
2 egg whites, stiffly beaten
1/2 cup finely chopped pecans

Sift together flour, sugar, baking powder and salt. Make a well in flour mixture and add oil, yolks, water and rind. Beat with a spoon or 3 minutes with mixer until smooth. In large bowl beat egg whites and cream of tartar until **very** stiff, do not underbeat. Pour yolk mixture over whites, gently fold until just blended. Pour into greased 5 x 10 x 3-inch loaf pan. Bake in **preheated 325° oven 50-55 minutes**. Turn pan upside down on rack or let hang between 2 other pans. Remove from pan when cool. Split lengthwise to make 4 layers.

To make filling: Cream butter and confectioners sugar until light and fluffy. Add egg yolks, one at a time, beating after each addition. Beat in melted chocolate and vanilla. Fold in egg whites. Frost each layer, placing one on top of the other. Frost sides and top. Sprinkle top with finely chopped pecans. Chill overnight.

Yield: 10 servings

Beulah Hebert Stansbury

JOAN'S POUND CAKE

1 cup butter
2 cups sugar
2 1/4 cups sifted all-purpose flour
1/4 teaspoon baking powder
1/8 teaspoon salt
5 eggs
3 tablespoons water
1 teaspoon vanilla

Cream butter and add sugar. Mix well. Stir together flour, baking powder and salt. Add dry ingredients to creamed mixture alternating with eggs and water. Add vanilla. Pour into buttered tube pan. Bake in **preheated 325° oven 1 hour 15 minutes**.

Yield: 16 servings

Joan Menefee Hensarling (Mrs. Larry)

GERMAN CHOCOLATE POUND CAKE

2 cups sugar
1 cup shortening
4 eggs
2 teaspoons vanilla
1 cup buttermilk
3 cups all-purpose flour
1/2 teaspoon soda
1 teaspoon salt
1 (4-oz.) package German
    Sweet Chocolate
Whipping cream for topping

Cream sugar and shortening, and add eggs, vanilla and buttermilk. Sift together flour, soda salt, and add to creamed mixture. Mix well. Add German chocolate that has been softened in warm oven or in double boiler or microwave oven. Blend together well. Bake in 9-inch stem pan that has been well-greased and dusted with flour. Bake in a **preheated 300° oven 1½-2 hours**. Remove cake from pan while still hot and place under a tight-fitting cake cover. Leave covered until cold. Serve with whipped cream.

Yield: 12 servings

Linda Bender (Mrs. Glen F.)

CHOCOLATE POUND CAKE

1½ cups margarine
3 cups sugar
5 eggs
3 cups flour
6 tablespoons cocoa
1/2 teaspoon salt
1/2 teaspoon baking powder
1 cup milk
2 teaspoons vanilla

Icing for top of cake:
1 ounce square semi-sweet
    baking chocolate
1/4 cup margarine (1/2 stick)
1 cup sugar
1/3 cup milk

With an electric beater, cream margarine thoroughly. Add sugar gradually until mixture is light and fluffy. Add eggs, one at a time, and beat well. In another bowl sift flour, cocoa, salt and baking powder. Add flour mixture to butter mixture alternating with milk (start and end with flour). Add vanilla. Pour into a greased tube or stem cake pan. Bake in **preheated 325° oven 1½ hours.**

Melt chocolate and margarine in a small saucepan. Add sugar and milk. Boil 1 minute. Remove from heat and beat until stiff. Spread on top of cake. Recipe may be doubled to ice sides of cake.

Yield: 20 servings

Corinne Gauthier (Mrs. Fritz L.)

WHOLE WHEAT POUND CAKE

1 cup butter, softened
2 cups sugar
5 eggs, divided
2 cups whole wheat flour
   (Gold Medal)
2 teaspoons vanilla
1/2 teaspoon salt

In large mixing bowl cream butter. Add sugar and 1 egg. Beat until light and fluffy. Add whole wheat flour, 1/2 cup at a time and 4 eggs, 1 at a time, beating well after each addition. Add vanilla and salt and mix until smooth. Pour into a greased and floured Bundt or tube pan. Bake in **preheated 350° oven 1 hour.**

Yield: 16 slices

Inolia Senegal

PECAN BOURBON POUND CAKE

1 pound butter
3 cups sugar
8 eggs, separated
3 cups all-purpose flour
2 teaspoons vanilla extract
2 teaspoons almond extract
1 teaspoon butter flavoring
4 tablespoons bourbon
2 cups chopped pecans, divided

Prepare a tube pan (angel food cake pan) or 2 (5 x 9-inch) loaf pans. Do not use a Bundt pan. Grease bottom of pan well. Cut wax paper to fit bottom. Grease wax paper. In a large mixing bowl, cream butter and sugar together until fluffy. Add egg yolks and beat well. Mix in flour, vanilla, almond, butter flavoring and bourbon. Beat egg whites until stiff. Fold into batter. Stir in 1 cup pecans. Sprinkle bottom of pan with 1/2 cup pecans. Add batter and sprinkle with remaining 1/2 cup pecans on top. Bake in **preheated 325° oven 1½ to 2 hours** until brown and cake tester comes out clean. To prevent top of cake from cracking open, cover with foil the last 30 minutes of cooking.

Yield: 20 servings

Eva Dell Daigre (Mrs. John J.)

GRANNY MCDOWELL'S SHORTBREAD

1 cup butter
1/2 cup sugar
2¹/₂ cups all-purpose flour
1/8 teaspoon salt

Cream butter and sugar in mixing bowl until fluffy. Add flour and salt. Mix together until moist. Place in metal or glass 8 x 8-inch square pan. Press gently with fork at edges. Bake in **preheated 350° oven 35 minutes** or until lightly toasted. Cool 15 minutes before cutting into squares. *This recipe has been in my family over 80 years.*

Yield: 25 squares

Cloeann McDowell Clement (Mrs. John P., III)

GRANNY'S FIG CAKE

1 cup sugar
3 eggs
2 cups all-purpose flour
1 teaspoon baking soda
1 teaspoon salt
1 teaspoon cinnamon
1/2 teaspoon nutmeg
1 cup milk
1 teaspoon vinegar
1 cup oil
1 cup preserved whole figs
1/2 cup chopped pecans

In large mixing bowl, beat sugar and eggs well. Mix flour, soda, salt, cinnamon and nutmeg. Add to sugar/egg mixture, alternating with milk and vinegar mixture. Mix 2 minutes. Add oil and figs. Beat 4 minutes until figs are crushed. Fold in pecans. Pour into Bundt pan. Bake in **preheated 300° oven 1 hour 20 minutes**. Serve with Amaretto Whip.*

*Amaretto Whip:
12 ounces whipped dessert
    topping
1/4 cup Amaretto liqueur

Mix whipped topping and Amaretto. Refrigerate until serving time.

Yield: 12-15 servings

Betty Baquet Bares (Mrs. Allen)

Did you find 'dere a
mistake or two
Did we misspell gaspergou
or roux?

You'll never know the hours it took
To make this kind of cooking book.

Just look over the missed accents
And think of all the compliments

When you cook these recipes
For family, friends
and company.

Voilà Tout!

the
1980s

s Jimmy Carter's Democratic presidency passed to Republican President Ronald Reagan in the 1980s, Lafayette, Louisiana was having its own quiet revolution. It was subtle change—perhaps started with a modest *boeuf bourgignon* without the kidneys, followed by tacos, and then some half-raw vegetables stir-fried in a wok. Before the poor husband knew it, he was into cosmopolitan cuisine, but perhaps he started the whole thing himself.

An affluent mobile society with roots in Texas, Oklahoma, the North, the East, fell upon the Cajun delights as manna from heaven. Not only was Acadian food being served in restaurants, but a growing number of restaurants opened, catering to everyone's special *"envie."* Leebob Cox, establishing his LaFonda in 1957, began serving Mexican food, Texas-Mexican style, to Louisiana/Texans. Now the choice of cuisine is endless: French, Italian, Greek, Lebanese, Chinese, Japanese, along with specialties in seafood, crawfish and barbecue—served in luxury or fast food drive-ins. Then with the proliferation of countless "How To" cookbooks in gorgeous color, featuring great recipes from everywhere, television chefs, local and international cooking schools, and travel, everyone was into COOKING! Gourmet and gourmand were no longer synonymous.

Skinny was in, fat was out. Lard and saturated fats were taboo, and a variety of vegetable oils guaranteed a long and happy life. Vegetarians and health freaks countered benignly against haute cuisine, but their cause is in the throes of lingering demise.

New and old utensils were invented and reinvented. The old iron pots found their way back to the stove. Frying pans no longer needed grease; some were electric self-contained units that fried, cooked and baked. There were woks, paella pans and crockpots. The avant garde traded their knives and whisks for a Cuisinart. Blenders and food processors were on every kitchen counter. Pressure cookers became popular for a time, but the microwave shoved them aside as recipes were modified to fit the cooking into minutes and seconds.

Food marketing became more than seasonal or preserving for the winter months. Food is dried, dehydrated, concentrated, powdered, flaked, freeze-dried, all for longer shelf life in the super markets and instant meals for the consumer.

From the open fires of the Indians we have come full circle, the hearth, wood stove, kerosene stove, natural gas and electric stoves and microwave ovens, for tried and true home cooking did not die and the smell of weekend barbecues still pervades every neighborhood.

Jake Valentine
A cosmopolitan cook

Old Remedies

Microwave Memos

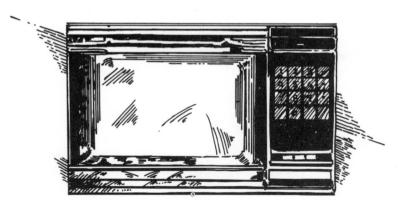

COUGH MIXTURE

Two quarts of rain water, one pound of raisins, five cents worth of licorice, a fourth of a pound of rock candy. Boil this to one quart and strain it. Take two tablespoons three times daily; adding a little vinegar.

FOR HOARSENESS

Beat the whites of two eggs with two spoons of white sugar, a little nutmeg and a cup of warm water; mix well and drink often.

FOR CANKER SORE MOUTH

Burn a corn cob and apply the ashes two or three times a day.

FOR WORMS FOR LITTLE CHILDREN

Stew pumpkin seeds, make a strong liquid, and give a tablespoonful once a day.

SALVE FOR BURNS

Two ounces of Burgundy pitch, a half ounce of beeswax and two tablespoons of lard. Melt all together, spread on a cloth and apply to the burn; do not take it off till the burn is well.

HEALING LOTION

One ounce glycerine, one ounce rosewater, ten drops carbolic acid. Excellent for chapped hands.

CURE FOR POISONING BY POISON IVY

Fill a bottle with soft water and add as much powdered borax as it will dissolve. Bathe parts affected often with the solution and it will afford relief. Cases have been entirely cured by the use of this simple remedy.

TO MAKE THE SKIN SMOOTH

Make a tea of red clover blossoms and wash the face with it two or three times a day.

ORRIS ROOT

Nibble orris root when going to singing school.

Medicinal Recipes, Hints For The Laundry and **Miscellaneous Receipts** *gives us a glimpse of the past, when ideas for homemade medicines, soup, spot removers, insecticides and glue were shared among families and friends.*

Paul Fournet of Lafayette, Louisiana found these "Old-Time" remedies in his mother's 1876 cookbook. His mother, Ann Aurore Labbe Fournet (Mrs. J. J. Fournet), and her mother, Marie Elise Mouton Labbe (Mrs. August V. Labbe) often used this cookbook entitled simply. "76" A Cook Book, entered according to an Act of Congress in the year 1876, in the Office of the Librarian of Congress at Washington.

The Lafayette Centennial Cookbook committee deeply appreciates and thanks the Fournet family for sharing with us this over 100 year old cookbook.

HINTS FOR THE LAUNDRY

Wash day was an all day chore in olden days. Now, in the 1980s, with a quick spray of prewash, a measure of biodegradeable soap and the touch of a button, our perma-press clothes are clean. Remember clotheslines?

COMPOUND FOR WASHING FLUID

One pound of unslacked lime and three pounds of sal-soda. Boil in six quarts of rain water, pour the whole in a tub, add fourteen quarts of water, stir thoroughly and allow it to settle; then bottle. For washing, use one teacup for the first boiler, for each succeeding boiler a half teacup.

TO REMOVE INK STAINS

Apply lemon juice and salt and lay the article in the sun.

TO REMOVE STAINS

Boiling water will remove tea stains and many fruit stains; pour the water through the stain and thus prevent it from spreading over the fabric. Soaking in milk before washing will remove ink stains.

TO REMOVE STARCH OR RUST FROM FLAT-IRONS

Have a piece of yellow beeswax tied in a coarse cloth. When the iron is almost hot enough to use, but not quite, rub it quickly with the beeswax, and then with a clean, coarse cloth. This will remove it entirely.

HARD SOAP

Pour four gallons of boiling water over six pounds of washing soda and three pounds of unslacked lime; stir the mixture well and let it settle until perfectly clear, then drain off the water, add six pounds of grease and boil for two hours, stirring most of the time. If it should be too thick, pour more water over the lime and add it to the boiling mixture; it is well to add a handful of soap. Perfume as you please.

TO TAKE GREASE OUT OF SILKS

Take a lump of magnesia and rub it (wet) over the spot, let it dry; then brush the powder off, and the spot will disappear. Or take a visiting or other card, separate it, rub the spot with the soft internal part, and it will disappear without removing the gloss from the silk.

TO CLEAN CARPETS

Salt, sprinkled upon the carpet before sweeping, will make it look bright and clean. This will also prevent moths. To remove oil from carpets, cover the spot with a paste made by mixing common starch with cold water, let it remain two or three days, then brush off and the oil will have disappeared.

DEATH TO INSECTS

Two pounds of alum dissolved in three or four quarts of boiling water and applied to all cracks and crevices, will keep out ants, roaches, spiders, bedbugs, etc., etc.

MISCELLANEOUS RECEIPTS

GET RID OF MOSQUITOES, RATS AND ROACHES

If mosquitoes or other bloodsuckers infest our sleeping-rooms at night, and we uncork a bottle of the oil of pennyroyal, these animals will leave in great haste, nor will they return so long as the air in the room is loaded with the fumes of that aromatic herb. If rats enter the cellar, a little powdered potash, thrown in their holes, or mixed with meal and scattered in their runways, never fails to drive them away. Cayenne pepper will keep the buttery and storeroom free from ants and cockroaches. If a mouse makes an entrance into any part of your dwellings, saturate a rag with cayenne, in solution, and stuff it into the hole.

HOW TO DESTROY RATS

If a live rat be caught and smeared over with tar or train oil, and afterwards allowed to escape in the holes of other rats, he will cause all soon to take their departure.

Take a pan, about twelve inches deep, and half fill it with water; then sprinkle some bran on the water and set the pan in a place where the rats most frequent. In the morning you will find several rats in the pan.

WAYS TO EXPEL WEEVILS

A muslin bag filled with either whole or pounded cloves, and placed on the pantry shelf will successfully keep the cereals, grains, and flour free of troublesome little weevils.

AMMONIA FOR PLANTS

The effect of ammonia on vegetation is beneficial. If you desire roses, fuschias, geraniums, etc., to become more flourishing, try it upon them by adding five or six drops to every pint of water you give them, but do not repeat the dose oftener than once in five or six days, lest you stimulate them too highly.

CLEANSING VARNISHED PAINT

In cleansing paint which has been varnished there is nothing better than weak tea. All the tea leaves from several drawings should be saved and boiled over early in the morning of the paint cleansing day; if boiled in an old tin pail or pan, the tea can be easily strained off for use. Wet a flannel in it and wipe the oak grained paint and you will be surprised at its brightness. No soap is needed and no milk. The tea is the most capital detergent ever invented. Wipe the paint with a soft cloth; you will find that very little elbow grease is needful. White varnished paint is cleansed as rapidly as the grained.

TO MEND CHINA

Take a very thick solution of gum arabic in water, and stir in plaster of Paris until the mixture becomes of the proper consistency. Apply it with a brush to the fractured edges of the china, and stick them together. In three days the article cannot be broken in the same place. The whiteness of the cement renders it doubly valuable.

TO PURIFY CISTERN WATER

A small sack of charcoal dropped into the cistern every spring, will purify it, and keep the water sweet and clean.

What can we expect in future microwave ovens? As we go to press, Amana intro-duces a 1984 model with 1000 watts power. For the future, control panels will con-tain a microphone and speaker which will assist the cook by listening, talking, and being activated by human voice. An improved door design for the microwave may be one where the door could disappear into the top portion of the unit, operating similarly to an automatic garage door, or as technology advances, the door may slide up similar to the way a rolltop desk opens. The microwave oven door could easily accommodate a flat screen television within its framework. Can you imagine having an appliance that not only cooks but also receives cable, satellite and network broadcasts? Then you can talk to your microwave while your husband watches football games!

1. To melt one stick (1/2 cup) butter or margarine, microwave in a glass measuring cup or dish on **HIGH (100%) 1 MINUTE**. To soften butter, microwave on **HIGH (100%) 10 SECONDS**.

2. To soften 8 ounces cream cheese, microwave on **HIGH (100%) 20 SECONDS**.

3. To thaw a 4½ ounce carton of whipped topping, microwave on **DEFROST (20%) 1 MINUTE**. Stir to blend. Do not overthaw.

4. To soften a 1 pound box of hardened brown sugar, place box of sugar along with 1 cup hot water in microwave. Microwave on **HIGH (100%) 1 MINUTE**.

5. To dissolve gelatin, place liquid and gelatin in a measuring cup. Microwave on **HIGH (100%) 2 MINUTES** per cup of liquid. There will be less stirring to dis-solve gelatin.

6. To scald 1 cup milk, microwave on **HIGH (100%) 2 MINUTES**, stirring at 1 minute.

7. To make dry bread crumbs, cut 6 slices bread into 1/2-inch cubes. Place on paper towels in a 3-quart casserole. Microwave on **HIGH (100%) 6-7 MINUTES** or until dry, stirring after 3 minutes. Crush in food processor.

8. Nuts will be easier to shell if you place 2 cups nuts in a 1-quart casserole with 1 cup of water. Microwave on **HIGH (100%) 4-5 MINUTES**. Drain. The nuts will slip out whole after cracking the shell.

9. To drain fat from ground meat while it is cooking, place 1 pound meat in a plastic colander on a pie plate or set inside a casserole dish. Cover with wax paper. Microwave on **HIGH (100%) 5-6 MINUTES**. Stir meat one time.

10. When thawing ground meat, microwave on **DEFROST (20%) 3 MINUTES**. Re-move outside portions that have defrosted. Continue defrosting meat, taking off thawed portions at short intervals.

11. Shape meatloaf into a ring to eliminate undercooked center. A glass set in the center of dish will help mold the shape.

12. When preparing chicken in a dish, place meaty pieces towards outer edges and boney pieces in center of dish for more even cooking.

13. To enhance the appearance and give a crusty coating to cakes, sprinkle a layer of finely chopped nuts or cookie crumbs evenly onto the bottom and sides of round cake dish or Bundt dish. Pour in batter and microwave as recipe directs. This also makes cake easier to remove from dish.

14. Do not salt foods on the surface as it causes dehydration and toughens the food, especially meat, fish, poultry and vegetables. Surface salt after you remove food from microwave, unless recipe calls for using salt in a mixture or liquid.

15. To roast pecans, microwave on a 12-inch glass plate on **HIGH (100%) 3-4 MINUTES** per cup.

16. Freeze leftover cooked rice in a plastic bag for future reheating. Measure rice and mark bag before freezing. Thaw and reheat in one step. Place slightly opened bag on a plate and microwave on **HIGH (100%) 1-2 MINUTES** per cup rice.

17. To microwave a frozen pie shell, remove while frozen from foil pan. Place in a glass or ceramic pie plate. When pliable, press to fit dish and flute edges. Microwave on **HIGH (100%) 5-6 MINUTES**, rotating dish at 2 minute intervals.

18. To make a disposable bacon rack, fold a sturdy paper plate in half and wedge it inside a 5 x 7-inch glass loaf dish. Drape the bacon over the paper plate, cover with wax paper and microwave on **HIGH (100%) 1 MINUTE** per slice of bacon. If microwaving more than 4 slices, reduce time to 45 seconds per slice. All the grease drains into the dish. Remove bacon and throw away the paper plate.

19. To test a dish for safe microwave cooking, place the empty dish to be tested in the microwave. Place a 2-cup glass measuring cup filled with one cup of water in or beside the dish. Microwave on **HIGH (100%) 2 MINUTES**. If dish remains cool it is considered microwave safe.

20. To clean inside of microwave oven, place 1 cup of water, with a squeeze of lemon juice or a teaspoon of vanilla or almond extract, in microwave on **HIGH (100%) 2 MINUTES**. Use a dry cloth to wipe inside of oven clean. Gives kitchen a nice aroma, too!

21. Dampen 4 or 6 finger tip towels in water with a sprinkle of Dr. Tichenor's Antiseptic, for a minty aroma. Roll and place in a glass dish or basket. Microwave on **HIGH (100%) 1 MINUTE**. Great to pass to guests after eating crab, shrimp or crawfish.

22. Make your own Bundt pan when baking large cakes. After pouring batter into a large round baking dish, press a juice glass, right side up, into the center. This prevents an uncooked center and insures uniform baking throughout.

23. To help the bottom of the cake cook evenly, place cake on top of an inverted saucer or on a roasting rack.

24. Use a paper egg carton to hold miniature paper liners for tiny cheesecakes and pies while microwaving.

25. For stamp collectors, place a few drops of water on stamp to be removed from envelope. Heat in microwave on **HIGH (100%) 20 SECONDS** and stamp will come right off.

These microwave memos are a collection of helpful hints I have given at cooking schools. Jean K Durkee

INDEX